Waste in Ecological Economics

CURRENT ISSUES IN ECOLOGICAL ECONOMICS

Series Editors: Sylvie Faucheux, *Professor of Economic Science* and Martin O'Connor, *Associate Professor of Economic Science, C3ED, Université de Versailles–Saint Quentin en Yvelines, France,* John Proops, *Professor of Ecological Economics, School of Politics, International Relations and the Environment, Keele University, UK* and Jan van der Straaten, *Retired Senior Lecturer, Department of Leisure Studies, Tilburg University, The Netherlands*

The field of ecological economics has emerged as a result of the need for all social sciences to be brought together in new ways, to respond to global environmental problems. This major new series aims to present and define the state-of-the-art in this young and yet fast-developing discipline.

This series cuts through the vast literature on the subject to present the key tenets and principal problems, techniques and solutions in ecological economics. It is the essential starting point for any practical or theoretical analysis of economy-environment interactions and will provide the basis for future developments within the discipline.

Titles in the series include:

Greening the Accounts
Edited by Sandrine Simon and John Proops

Nature and Agriculture in the European Union
New Perspectives on Policies that Shape the European Countryside
Edited by Floor Brouwer and Jan van der Straaten

Waste in Ecological Economics
Edited by Katy Bisson and John Proops

Waste in Ecological Economics

Edited by

Katy Bisson

Principal Research Analyst in Staffordshire Police Authority, UK

and

John Proops

Professor of Ecological Economics in the School of Politics, International Relations and the Environment, Keele University, UK

CURRENT ISSUES IN ECOLOGICAL ECONOMICS

Edward Elgar
Cheltenham, UK • Northampton, MA, USA

Published by
Edward Elgar Publishing Limited
Glensanda House
Montpellier Parade
Cheltenham
Glos GL50 1UA
UK

Edward Elgar Publishing, Inc.
136 West Street
Suite 202
Northampton
Massachusetts 01060
USA

A catalogue record for this book
is available from the British Library

Library of Congress Cataloguing in Publication Data
Waste in ecological economics / edited by Katy Bisson, John Proops.
    p. cm. — (Current issues in ecological economics)
Includes index.
1. Waste (Economics) 2. Refuse and refuse disposal—Economic aspects.
I. Bisson, Katy, 1973- II. Proops, John L. R., 1947- III. Series.

HC79.W3 W37 2002
363.72'8—dc21   2002072186

ISBN 1 84064 648 9
Printed and bound in Great Britain by MPG Books Ltd, Bodmin, Cornwall

Contents

List of Figures   vi
List of Tables   vii
List of Contributors   viii
Preface   ix

1.   An Introduction to Waste   1
     Katy Bisson and John Proops

PART I PHYSICAL AND HISTORICAL PERSPECTIVES

2.   Thermodynamics of Waste Generation   13
     Stefan Baumgärtner
3.   History of Waste   38
     Verena Winiwarter

PART 2 WASTE POLICY

4.   Attitudes to Waste   57
     Katy Bisson
5.   Economics of Waste   73
     Jane Powell, Kerry Turner, Michael Peters and Barbara Strobl
6.   Waste Law   101
     David Wilkinson

PART 3 SPECIFIC WASTE ISSUES

7.   Municipal Waste   117
     Eduardo Barata
8.   Toxic Waste   146
     Francis O. Adeola
9.   Nuclear Waste   178
     John Proops

Index   197

Figures

2.1   The thermodynamic structure of industrial production   23
5.1   Environmental policy framework   82
5.2   Schematic representation of project strategy   84
5.3   Summary of economic valuation of waste management   91
scenarios for Norfolk, UK
5.4   Strategic decision support process: an integrated assessment   97
approach

Tables

2.1   Exergy values and molecular weights of the different chemicals   26
       involved in the reduction of iron ore to pure iron
5.1   Results of lifecycle assessment inventory analysis for Norfolk   89
       County, UK
5.2   Economic valuation of Norfolk lifecycle assessment   90
8.1   Department of Transportation hazardous materials classification   154
       system
8.2   Sources and types of toxic waste by industry or generators   155
8.3   Metal ore and metal waste production in the US, 1960-1990   156
8.4   Top 20 hazardous substances and substances most frequently   157
       found in completed exposure pathways
8.5   Toxic synthetic organic compounds commonly present in   165
       chemical wastes and their health effects
8.6   Selected Federal Statutes regulating hazardous and toxic   170
       substances in the US, 1965-2001
A8.1   Industrial toxic chemical releases by States in the USA, 1999   177

Contributors

Francis O. Adeola, Environmental Social Science Research Institute, University of New Orleans, USA

Eduardo Barata, School of Politics International Relations and the Environment, Keele University, UK

Stefan Baumgärtner, Alfred Weber Institute, University of Heidelberg, Germany

Katy Bisson, Staffordshire Police Authority, UK

Michael Peters, Centre for Social and Economic Research on the Global Environment, University of East Anglia, UK

Jane Powell, Centre for Social and Economic Research on the Global Environment, University of East Anglia, UK

John Proops, School of Politics International Relations and the Environment, Keele University, UK

Barbara Strobl, Centre for Social and Economic Research on the Global Environment, University of East Anglia, UK

Kerry Turner, Centre for Social and Economic Research on the Global Environment, University of East Anglia, UK

David Wilkinson, School of Politics International Relations and the Environment, Keele University, UK

Verena Winiwarter, Institute for Anthropology, University of Vienna, Austria

Preface

This volume is a further contribution to the Current Issues in Ecological Economics series, which aims to provide comprehensive and authoritative overviews of a range of areas of interest in ecological economics. We believe waste to be an issue of enormous importance in modern societies, and one that a series in ecological economics must address.

However, any book with a title as broad as this runs the risk of disappointing its readership. In particular, risks of an edited volume include inconsistency of approach by the contributing authors and, in particular inconsistency of 'world view'. We hope and believe that this text has achieved consistency of both approach and world view, as the editors were able to select authors they knew to be both expert and sympathetic to the ecological economics approach. Also, this book was generated *ab initio*, without the existence of prior papers or conference contributions. Instead, we were privileged to be able to set the scene not only for the whole book, but also for each individual chapter. When the chapters were commissioned from the authors, it was on the basis of quite detailed suggestions on approach, to give the book, we hope, a feeling of being a multi-authored single text, rather than a collection of interesting but disparate papers.

Because of this rather didactic, but we hope not too oppressive editorial stance, the experience of the editors has been very positive. As the contributions arrived we were delighted to find that our hopes of consistency combined with coverage and intellectual breadth, were more than met. The editorial process of reading and re-reading the texts has convinced us that we have been very fortunate in our collaborators, who have produced chapters that are scholarly, dense in information and interpretation, but still accessible to non-specialists. We offer our thanks to all of the contributors, and hope that they too will feel this is a with which book to be more than satisfied.

Katy Bisson and John Proops

1. An Introduction to Waste

Katy Bisson and John Proops

1.1 OVERVIEW

Waste is a quintessentially ecological economic issue. The generation of waste is rooted in the very laws of nature, as argued by Stefan Baumgärtner in Chapter 2. However, as Verena Winiwarter shows us in Chapter 3, waste is also a social construct, and what we understand to be waste has evolved with human societies. Therefore, a crucial issue in modern waste management is the understanding of attitudes to waste, as explored by Katy Bisson in Chapter 4. Thus an encompassing understanding of waste requires that one bring to bear a range of natural science and social science disciplinary approaches, including economics (Jane Powell et al. in Chapter 5) and law (David Wilkinson in Chapter 6). In other words, waste is a prime candidate for analysis within the 'multidiscipline' of ecological economics.

However, if one checks through the ecological economics literature over, say, the past ten years, one finds rather little on waste *qua* waste. Of course, one finds a large amount published on such waste-related pollution issues as global warming (from waste carbon dioxide emissions), and on the wider issues of air and water pollution (largely deriving from the dumping of unvalued wastes into the environment). But on issues such as toxic waste (Francis Adeola in Chapter 9), nuclear waste (John Proops in Chapter 9), or even the everyday municipal waste (Eduaro Barata in Chapter 7), we find almost nothing in the ecological economics literature. Of course, in the specialist journals that deal with the engineering and the social management of these forms of waste, we do find a considerable literature. However, almost always these publications take a uni-disciplinary approach and, tacitly at least, seem to assume that while dealing with 'wastes' is a problem, the concept of 'Waste' is not. Or perhaps more fairly to this literature, the concept of 'Waste' is simply not addressed.

Thus we feel there is a huge gap in two literatures. In ecological economics, there has, as yet, been no sustained analysis of waste as a general (almost universal) issue for humans as producers and consumers, whose activities impact on nature. In the technical waste literature, we feel the conceptualisation of 'Waste' is very incomplete; waste has yet to be situated in the wider framework of interdisciplinary understanding. In summary, we feel there is a need to bring together the conceptual tools of ecological economics with the technical understanding found in the waste literature. In this volume we offer a brief and, we recognise, partial attempt to fill this gap.

1.2 WHAT IS THIS THING CALLED 'WASTE'?

Part of the problem of waste lies in saying precisely what it is. As noted by David Wilkinson in Chapter 6, the legal definitions of waste that have evolved over the past century are largely unsatisfactory, both for legal practice and for service as a the basis of wider understandings. So what do we mean by 'Waste'? One approach is to look to a combination of thermodynamics (see Chapter 2) and economics (see Chapter 5). Beginning with thermodynamic analysis, this suggests several physical consequences of production.

1.2.1 Thermodynamics and Waste

First, most goods that we find useful have relatively low specific entropy (i.e. low entropy per unit of mass). We can tell this because they 'wear-out' with use, becoming more and more 'mixed-up' with the environment. (Did you ever wonder what happened to the soles of your shoes or the tyres on your car? Just where does that matter go?)

Second, in industrial societies, much of what we produce is derived from raw materials that have rather high specific entropy; an archetype here is iron ore. We value the iron from this ore, and to extract it we use large quantities of (very low specific entropy) fuels. The Second Law of Thermodynamics tells us that the entropy coming out of such production processes must be greater than the entropy going in. In other words, if the desired output is low specific entropy iron, there must also be, in some form, an output with high specific entropy. If the iron gets low entropy from the fuel, what happens to the high entropy from the ore (plus the extra entropy produced by the smelting process itself)? The answer is that this high entropy comes out in several forms: as solid slag (containing the silicaceous material from the ore); as carbon dioxide (from the combustion of the carbon-based fuel); and as vast quantities of waste heat. Thus, 'all production is joint production' (Faber et al., 1998). With any desired, low specific entropy product, there must come high specific entropy joint products.

So do we have a comprehensive, thermodynamic theory of waste? Is it just high specific entropy joint products? Well, no. The problem is rather more complicated, for several reasons. First, some high specific entropy materials are valued. For example, bricks and concrete are, thermodynamically, of very high specific entropy, but these are still valued commodities. Indeed, it is their high specific entropy that, for the purposes of construction, makes them valuable. Their high specific entropy means that they do not tend to decompose (unlike wood) or burn (unlike plastic); this, combined with their high structural strength, means that as building materials they are long lasting and fire-resistant. So high specific entropy has attributes that, for some social purposes, are highly valued.

The second problem with an overly simple thermodynamic interpretation is that some wastes have rather low specific entropies. Faeces are a good example. They are clearly relatively low specific entropy, as they decompose; indeed, for some species (e.g. dung beetles and a vast range of bacteria and other 'primitive' creatures) faeces are a principal food source. More evidence of the relatively low specific entropy of faeces is that when dried, they serve as a common fuel in some parts of the world. (Of course, we recognise that faeces have higher specific entropy than the food from which they were derived, but the thermodynamic inefficiency of most animals' digestive tracts means that this 'higher' entropy joint product still has relatively low specific entropy.)

So while many wastes have high specific entropy, some do not. It seems that while thermodynamics does give us insights into the production of wastes, it gives us neither a necessary nor a sufficient condition for a material to be classified as waste.

However, we feel the general notion that wastes are undesired joint products seems robust. Indeed, we have been unable to think of any wastes (as distinct from pollutants) that do *not* satisfy this requirement.

1.2.2 Economics and Waste

Let us now turn to economics to see if it offers alternative insights. Here, rather surprisingly, we believe that very simple microeconomic principles, as taught in any introductory economics course, take one quite a long way in understanding. The fundamental principles needed for this discussion (all very contestable, and contested, in ecological economics) are as follows:

- Humans need and desire consumption.
- Humans seek to minimise their personal costs of consumption.
- Humans are more concerned with their own benefits than those of others.

These properties are those of the archetypal *homo oeconomicus*, or what Sagoff called the human as 'consumer' (Sagoff, 1988). While they do not reflect the best aspects of human nature, they do perhaps reflect aspects that we can recognise in ourselves. What follows from these assumptions for an understanding of waste?

First, let us suppose that, from the above discussion, wastes are undesired joint products of the manufacturing process, and that manufacturing is directed to satisfying consumption. So production has two aspects: the social one, of satisfying the first above assumed principle; and a physical aspect, of generating undesired joint products.

Turning now to the second assumed principle, of seeking consumption at minimum cost, how do we deal with the undesired joint products? As they are undesired, no narrowly rational individual would want to pay for them. As a consequence, they could be 'left where they fell'. If this is an inconvenient location, then they could be left where they are less troublesome, but which still has low costs.

What are the consequences of this 'discard into nature' principle for these undesired joint products? This very much depends on the precise nature and location of the undesired joint product. A common joint product of manufacturing is water vapour. We know of no study of the social or environmental impacts of these emissions, but one cannot imagine them as being anything more than trivial.

As noted above, another very common joint product is waste heat. When this is discarded in small quantities into an area of low population density (e.g. a car driving down a remote country road), the effect is negligible, probably even unmeasurable. When it is discarded at high levels in densely populated areas, the effect can be considerable (e.g. modern Western cities always have higher ambient temperatures than neighbouring countryside). Indeed, this effect may be socially beneficial, such as by reducing heating costs. Conversely, waste heat from power stations may be dumped into neighbouring water bodies, with severe impacts on aquatic ecosystems.

More commonly, we are aware of the damaging effects of some wastes when dumped into nature (e.g. smoke, carbon dioxide, etc.). If these materials cause damage, what would be the response of our 'selfish' individuals. From the third behavioural principle above, the response would largely be inaction, as while the damaging effect on nature or society as a whole may be considerable, the direct effect on any individual will be rather small. Therefore our 'consumer' would not act like Sagoff's 'citizen', and be concerned for wider social benefits. In particular, any effort spent to mitigate damage from wastes by any individual would benefit others also. Here, of course, the analysis of waste merges into the analysis of pollution as a 'public bad', with its corresponding issues of 'free-riding' and the determination of the 'optimal' level of pollution, regulation, Pigovian taxes, tradeable pollution permits, etc.

1.2.3 A First Definition of Waste

At this stage, a word of caution is needed. It is not the case that all waste causes pollution, nor is it the case that all pollution is caused by waste. Counter examples are easy to come by. We have already seen that water vapour and heat are ubiquitous forms of waste, but often (perhaps usually) they do not cause the external disbenefits that constitute a public bad, and so they do not qualify as pollution. On the other hand, there are some materials that cause pollution, which would not qualify as wastes; oils spills are a clear example. The essence of waste is that, economically, it is undesired, so it has no economic value.

We can now combine these two aspect of waste, the physical and economic, to offer a first definition of waste:

> Waste is something which is produced as an undesired joint product; as such, it has no economic value. If this waste is disposed of into the environment, it *may* constitute a source of pollution.

We feel this is a reasonable summary of the thermodynamic-economic position. However, this first definition is incomplete for two reasons. First, it does not encompass the wider social understandings of waste; it does not situate the concept of waste as a wider social phenomenon. Second, it offers no advice on the social mechanisms for coping with waste; indeed, this must, in part, derive from the social understandings of waste.

1.2.4 Waste and Culture

Rather than taking a theoretical-empirical approach to waste, as embodied in thermodynamics and economics, one could instead take a socio-phenomenological position. That is, one could define waste in terms of behaviours, perceptions and the role of such material in the 'lived life'. This is precisely the position of the cultural anthropologist and as Verena Winiwarter notes in Chapter 3, 'waste constitutes a central category of social order'. In particular, waste cannot be dissociated from wider sets of social meanings and social relations. The notion of waste may become linked to notions of dirt/danger/purity, even to 'stickiness'; conversely what one culture may see as 'dirty' waste (e.g. human faeces) another may associate with agricultural and social value.

A consequence of this richer interpretation of waste is that the history of the 'management' of waste begins to require a range of interpretive approaches. If one period of history focuses on waste as dirt, then waste management may become the role of social outcasts (e.g. the 'sweeper' or 'untouchable' castes in earlier periods in India). In Victorian England, the literature of the period (e.g. Charles Dickens' *Our Mutual Friend*) reflects the tension between waste being better 'out of sight', and the entrepreneurial spirit to recycle waste heaps. In the modern world, the range of waste management practices in Western Europe alone demand an analysis embedded in the social meaning of wastes.

In Britain waste seems still to carry traces of earlier times, with most domestic waste collection being in large bins, which do not allow segregation by material type. This material then mainly goes on to landfill or incineration, with rather little material recovery or recycling. Conversely, in Germany waste is diligently sorted by households, and recycling levels are high. It is difficult to believe that two countries with comparable levels of economic 'development' and population density would develop such different waste management strategies on the basis of economic and technical 'rationality'. It seems more likely that the understanding of these differences in practice are better understood through the differing social meanings attaching to waste and waste disposal.

1.2.5 Waste Policy

We began this chapter by suggesting that 'waste is a quintessentially ecological economic issue'. We have tried to support this by noting that understandings of waste derive from thermodynamics, economics and wider cultural analyses. Now we turn to the implications for these understandings of waste for policy.

From thermodynamics, an immediate policy consequence is that waste is something we cannot do without! No waste means no production, which means no consumption and no humans. Put this way, we see that waste is not something we can 'wish away' or ignore.

From economics, we know that waste which constitutes a negative externality cannot be dealt with by the market. If it could, it would not be an externality. Thus policy towards waste requires government intervention; that is, it demands that there *be* a policy.

Finally, from social theory we see that a waste policy cannot be just about 'waste'; it must be about how societies conceptualise and respond to wastes in their multiple social connotations and constructions.

Clearly, waste policy is necessary but not simple. It must be a complex mixture of technologies of waste collection, treatment, reuse and recycling, together with subtle understanding of economic motivations and social and personal tastes and distastes. Given the range of both technical possibilities and social factors, that we observe a wide range of waste management practices around the world should be no surprise.

1.3 THE CONTENTS OF THE BOOK

Having tried to make the case for an ecological economic approach to waste, we now move to a brief description of the contents of this book. As all of the chapters have been referred to above, to a greater or lesser extent, here we offer a brief synopsis of the chapters, and how they attempt to contribute towards a synthesis.

The book is in three parts. Part One tries to set the scene for understanding waste, through considering waste through the thermodynamics of production processes, and through an assessment of the history of waste. Building on this physico-social background, Part Two looks at waste policy, in particular relating to attitudes, economics and the law. Part Three looks at three specific types of waste, municipal, toxic and nuclear.

1.3.1 Chapter 2 – Thermodynamics of Waste Generation

Thermodynamic issues relating to waste have been discussed above, but in summary, this chapter notes that the First and Second Laws of Thermodynamics have strong implications for materials processing, as in production processes. In particular, a necessary result of the production of wanted, low specific entropy goods is the by-production of high specific entropy and probably unwanted wastes. A criticism sometimes made of thermodynamic analysis in ecological economics is that it is often qualitative in nature, but in this chapter Stefan Baumgärtner is able to offer quantitative illustration of his argument, using the increasingly popular concept of exergy.

1.3.2 Chapter 3 – History of Waste

Verena Winiwarter approaches waste from the role of an historical cultural anthropologist, and offers a rich and persuasive discussion of the way the concept of waste has evolved over time and in different cultures. As well as indicating the way the transition from rural to urban societies involved an alteration in the production and perception of wastes, she also seeks to show how waste is intimately connected to the concepts of 'dirt' and 'order'. She then goes on to consider the waste-society relationship at the more micro level, when cultural heterogeneities are recognized. She concludes with an overview of the historical experience of waste generation and treatment.

1.3.3 Chapter 4 – Attitudes to Waste

In the first of the chapters relating to waste policy, Katy Bisson addresses a growing feature in the literature, that of the importance of attitudes to waste. If modern societies are to come to terms with their growing problems of waste generation, new approaches to waste management will be essential. She begins by assessing negative attitudes to waste, with particular focus on the NIMBY (Not In My Back Yard) phenomenon., and contrasts this with the 'deep green' assertion of NIABY (Not In Anyone's Back Yard). She notes that in contrast, rather little is known about the nature, and influences upon, positive attitudes to waste disposal (e.g. recycling). She concludes with a discussion of methods of investigating attitudes to waste, and makes a strong case for the use of the newly emerging Q methodology.

1.3.4 Chapter 5 – Economics of Waste

This chapter by Powell et al., looks at waste from the perspective of economic analysis. However, the authors rather quickly indicate that the 'standard' tools of analysis, such as Pigovian taxes or the assertion of property rights (i.e. Coase's theorem), are of limited utility. Rather, they point out the importance of including institutional and political factors in the analysis. Thus while the economics of waste is often presented as a theoretical issue of simply efficiency, the authors here make a case for a wider understanding of the application of economics, in line with the more pluralistic approach of ecological economics. In particular, they illustrate their analysis by reference to case studies from the UK, relating to both 'waste relations' between companies, and to scenarios for waste management by local authorities.

1.3.5 Chapter 6 – Waste Law

In this chapter David Wilkinson addresses what he sees to be central elements of waste policy: that 'waste' is a useful legal category as currently defined, and that the currently popular notion of the 'waste management hierarchy' is likely to be effective. The discussion begins with a brief historical overview of the development of European waste regulation, and this offers a complementary analysis to that in Chapter 3. He then moves to a discussion of how the term 'waste' has been interpreted in European law, pointing out that the meanings the term has been given are both contradictory, and also not well-founded in economic and production understandings. Similarly, the chapter argues that the waste management hierarchy, while having a certain surface appeal, offers neither a comprehensive nor even fully rational approach to the management of waste streams.

1.3.6 Chapter 7 – Municipal Waste

In the first of the three chapters devoted to specific waste issue, Eduardo Barata gives a comprehensive overview of the issues relating to municipal waste, which is principally the waste households generate and put in their dustbins. He begins with a discussion of the historical development of municipal waste and its treatment, with particular stress on management strategies, and the technical options available (e.g. reduction, recycling, incineration, landfilling, etc.). For each management option, not only are the technical issues detailed, but also the economic and environmental implications are outlined. The chapter concludes by reflecting that, as noted in Chapter 3, municipal waste management is as much a social and political process as a technical and managerial one.

1.3.7 Chapter 8 – Toxic Waste

Toxic waste is the stuff of nightmares, and in this chapter Francis Adeola offers a comprehensive assessment of the nature of toxic waste, the threats it poses to people and the natural environment, and the emerging legal and technical regimes for its management. As these regimes are so geographically diverse, the focus is on US experience and practices, complementing the focus on the European experience in Chapter 6. Following a discussion of the definition of toxic waste, there is an assessment of the hazards it presents and how society interprets and responds to these (including through the already mentioned NIMBY phenomenon). A comprehensive analysis follows, of the classifications of toxic wastes, with a number of case studies, including the infamous Love Canal incident. The chapter concludes with an assessment of the numerous pieces of US legislation addressing the toxic waste problem.

1.3.8 Chapter 9 – Nuclear Waste

In the final chapter, John Proops analyses the issue of nuclear (i.e. radioactive) waste. To situate the discussion, he first outlines the nuclear fuel cycle, and how the 'end' of the cycle is the production of highly radioactive, and therefore extremely dangerous, waste materials. The reason for the production of nuclear waste does not fit simply into the thermodynamic perspective, discussed in Chapter 2, so the physics of nuclear decay is outlined, and there is a portrayal of the extreme complexity of the processes involved, and the great heterogeneity of the nuclear species resulting. The measurement of radioactivity, and how it affects living systems, is outlined, to allow an assessment of the various waste disposal options. In the longer term, the only feasible option seems to be deep burial, though there are great uncertainties associated with disposal problems reaching millennia into the future.

1.4 CONCLUSION

In this chapter we have tried to set the scene for the book as a whole (and we believe that it does, indeed, constitute a reasonably comprehensive and integrated whole).

Of course, attempting to address an issue as broad and multi-faceted as waste in a single volume could lead to a treatment that is too sketchy to be either useful or convincing. We hope that this volume is not guilty of that sin. Its aim is not to be fully comprehensive; rather, as indicated in the opening section of this chapter, the aim is to begin to fill a gap in the ecological economics and technical waste literature. Whether it is successful in its aim will necessarily be judged by whether, as we hope, it serves a stimulus for further research and publication in this area of great theoretical and policy importance.

REFERENCES

Faber, M., J. Proops and S. Baumgärtner (1998), 'All production is joint production – a thermodynamic analysis', in S. Faucheux, J. Gowdy and I. Nicolaï (eds), *Sustainability and Firms. Technological Change and the Changing Regulatory Environment*, Cheltenham: Edward Elgar, pp. 131-58.
Sagoff, M. (1988), *The Economy of the Earth: Philosophy, Law, and the Environment*. Cambridge: Cambridge University Press.

PART ONE

Physical and Historical Perspectives

2. Thermodynamics of Waste Generation

Stefan Baumgärtner[1]

2.1 INTRODUCTION

As waste is undesired and often harmful to the natural environment, why don't we just avoid its occurrence? One possible answer to this question that most economists will give (see Chapter 5) is that the occurrence of waste and its disposal in many instances constitute an external effect, i.e. the consequences of producing and disposing of waste are not internalised in market prices. In this economic view the occurrence of waste is due to a market failure, which could, in principle, be cured by imposing suitable policy measures, such as e.g. Pigouvian taxes or tradable permits on waste.

While the waste problem indeed is to some extent due to a market (and policy) failure, taking a thermodynamic point of view reveals a different relevant aspect of an answer to the question. For, from a thermodynamic point of view the occurrence of waste appears as an *unavoidable necessity* of industrial production. This is the perspective taken in this chapter.

In Section 2.2 the economic process is recast in energetic and material terms. It is described as society's *metabolism*. In Section 2.3 the laws of *thermodynamics* are introduced to provide an analytical framework within which results about society's metabolism may be rigorously deduced in energetic and material terms. In Section 2.4 the laws of thermodynamics are applied to analysing processes of industrial production. It is demonstrated that industrial production is necessarily and unavoidably *joint production*. Therefore, waste outputs are an unavoidable by-product in the industrial production of desired goods. Thus, while waste is shown to be an essential qualitative element of industrial production, the quantitative extent to which waste occurs may vary within certain limits according to the degree of *(in)efficiency* with which these processes are operated. Section 2.5 concludes by linking the thermodynamic considerations on waste to the issue of *sustainability*.

2.2 ECONOMIC METABOLISM AND THERMODYNAMICS

Every process of change far from thermodynamic equilibrium requires low entropy energy. This is the case for natural ecosystems (e.g. a leaf growing on a tree) as well as for the human economy (e.g. the production of metal from metal ore).

2.2.1 Ecosystems: Production, Consumption and Decomposition

In natural ecosystems, the energy to drive processes of change comes almost exclusively from the sun. The transformation of solar radiation into chemical or mechanical energy, in order to sustain a structured non-equilibrium state of plants and animals, requires at least one material cycle. In nature the cycle of synthesis and respiration involves not just one, but usually five different cycles of chemical elements and compounds: water, carbon, nitrogen, phosphorus and sulphur (Ricklefs and Miller, 2000, Chap. 11).

Numerous species of plants, animals and microbes move matter in cycles. According to their role within ecosystems they may be classified as producers, consumers and decomposers (Folke, 1999, pp. 896-98). *Producers* are those organisms which use sunlight as the only source of energy. In the process of photosynthesis they build up complex and energy-rich molecules from simple constituents taken from the soil or the air. Green plants are the most important producers in most terrestrial ecosystems. Animals that feed on green plants or other animals are called *consumers.* They make their living on the chemical energy and nutrients stored in other organisms. The so-called *decomposers*, mainly bacteria and fungi, break up the 'wastes' and the dead material from producers and consumers. They bring the nutrients back into the material cycles. Like consumers, they rely on the chemical energy provided by producers as their source of energy.

As almost all matter involved in processes of transformation in natural ecosystems stays in closed cycles, the dominant form of waste is waste heat. The latter is radiated into space.

2.2.2 Economic Systems: Production, Consumption and Reduction

The human economy, similarly to ecosystems, displays processes of change that require low entropy energy. Important insights into the nature of these processes can be gained by completely abstracting from the one feature that sets economic systems apart from natural ecosystem – human desires, wants and purposes – and focusing instead on the purely material aspect. When referring to this purely material and energetic dimension of the economic process, one may speak of 'industrial metabolism' (Ayres and Simonis, 1994). The term 'metabolism' is borrowed from physiology and denotes, in its original meaning, all of the internal processes of a living organism responsible for its maintenance, reproduction and growth. It comprises the extraction of energy and matter from the organism's environment and the disposal of dissipated energy and degraded matter into that environment. In a metaphorical sense industrial metabolism is then understood as the interconnected system of 'all materials/energy transformations that enable the economic system to function, i.e., to produce and consume' (Ayres and Simonis, 1994, p. xi).

In this view the economic process comprises three different kinds of activities: production, consumption and reduction. These are defined in analogy to the three different kinds of actors in ecosystems (see Section 2.2.1 above). Producers employ low entropy energy to transform raw materials into consumption goods. These are used by consumers to increase their welfare. After use, they constitute waste. While this waste used to be left over, modern industrial economies put more and more effort into reducing the amount of waste, recycling it, or transforming it into forms that are useful as inputs into the production process. All these activities are denoted by 'reduction'.

2.2.3 Economy-Environment Interactions

While there seems to be an analogy between ecosystems and economic systems as far as the role of production, consumption and decomposition/reduction is concerned, there are at least two characteristic differences between natural and industrial metabolism (Ayres, 2001):

- The low entropy energy employed in modern industrial economies is typically not sunlight, as in ecosystems, but energy stored in materials, such as fossil or nuclear fuels.
- Material flows in economies are not in closed cycles, as in ecosystems, but to a large extent they are throughput through the economic system. Materials are taken from some reservoirs outside the economy and in the end are disposed of in different reservoirs outside the economy. As a consequence, economies do not only emit waste heat, as ecosystems do, but they also generate vast quantities of material waste.

For these two reasons, current economies are not at all self-contained but vitally depend on and severely interfere with their natural environment. As this economy-environment interaction is, in the first place, an exchange of energy and matter, the laws of thermodynamics provide a useful analytical framework within which fundamental insights into society's metabolism may be rigorously deduced in energetic and material terms.[2]

2.3 THERMODYNAMICS

Thermodynamics is the branch of physics that deals with transformations of energy and matter (Reif, 1965). Briefly summarised, the fundamental concepts and laws of (phenomenological) thermodynamics can be stated as follows.[3]

2.3.1 Systems and Transformations

With respect to the potential exchange of energy and matter between the inside and the outside of the system under study, one distinguishes between the following types of thermodynamic system:

- *Isolated* systems exchange neither energy nor matter with their surrounding environment.
- *Closed* systems exchange energy, but not matter, with their surrounding environment.
- *Open* systems exchange both energy and matter with their surrounding environment.

A system is said to be in *thermodynamic equilibrium* when there is complete absence of driving forces for change in the system. Technically, the various potentials of the system are at their minimum, such that there are no spatial variations of any of the intensive variables within the system. *Intensive* variables are quantities which do not change when two separate but identical systems are coupled. In contrast, *extensive* variables are quantities whose value for the total system is simply the sum of the values of this quantity in both systems. For example, temperature and pressure are intensive variables while mass and volume are extensive ones. As long as there are spatial variations in, say, temperature within a system, it is not yet in thermodynamic equilibrium, but there exists a potential for change. The equilibrium state is characterised by a uniform temperature throughout the system.

Consider an isolated system which undergoes a transformation over time between some initial equilibrium state and some final equilibrium state, either by interaction with its environment or by interaction between different constituents within the system. If the final state is such that no imposition or relaxation of constraints upon the isolated system can restore the initial state, then this process is called *irreversible*. Otherwise the process is called *re-*

versible. For example, at some initial time a gas is enclosed in the left part of an isolated box; the right part is separated from the left part by a wall and is empty. Now, the separating wall is removed. The molecules of the gas will then evenly distribute themselves over the entire volume of the box. The thermodynamic equilibrium of the final state is characterised by a uniform density of molecules throughout the entire volume. Reintroducing the wall into the isolated system separating the left part from the right half would not restore the initial state of the system. Nor would any other imposition or relaxation of constraints on the isolated system be able to restore the initial state. Therefore, the transformation given by the removal of the wall is an irreversible transformation of the isolated system.[4] Generally, a process of transformation can only be reversible if it does not involve any dissipation of energy, such as through e.g. friction, viscosity, inelasticity, electrical resistance or magnetic hysteresis.

2.3.2 The Fundamental Laws of Thermodynamics

The *First Law of Thermodynamics* states that in an isolated system (which may or may not be in equilibrium) the total internal energy is conserved. This means that energy can be neither created nor destroyed. However, it can appear in different forms, such as heat, chemical energy, electrical energy, potential energy, kinetic energy, work, etc. For example, when burning a piece of wood or coal the chemical energy stored in the fuel is converted into heat. In an isolated system the total internal energy, i.e. the sum of energies in their particular forms, does not change over time. In any process of transformation only the forms in which energy appears change, while its total amount is conserved.

Similarly, in an isolated system the total mass is conserved (*Law of Conservation of Mass*). Obviously, if matter cannot enter or leave an isolated system, the number of atoms of any chemical element within the system must remain constant. In an open system which may exchange matter with its surrounding, a simple *Materials Balance Principle* holds: the mass content of a system at some time is given by its initial mass content plus inflows of mass minus outflows of mass up to that point in time. The law of mass conservation, while often regarded as an independent conservation law besides the law of energy conservation, is actually an implication of the First Law of Thermodynamics. According to Einstein's famous relation $E=mc^2$ mass is a form of energy, but mass can only be transformed into non-material energy, and vice versa, in nuclear reactions. Therefore, neglecting nuclear reactions it follows from the First Law of Thermodynamics that mass and non-material energy are conserved separately.

In any process transforming energy or matter, a certain amount of energy is irrevocably transformed into heat. The variable *entropy* has been defined by Rudolph Clausius (1854; 1865) such as to capture this irrevocable transformation of energy: if a certain amount of heat dQ is reversibly transferred to or from a system at temperature T, then $dS=dQ/T$ defines the entropy S. Clausius showed that S is a state variable of the system, i.e. it remains constant in any reversible cyclic process and increases otherwise. The *Second Law of Thermodynamics*, the so-called Entropy Law, states the unidirectional character of transformations of energy and matter: With any transformation between an initial equilibrium state and a final equilibrium state of an isolated system, the entropy of this system increases over time or remains constant. It strictly increases in irreversible transformations, and it remains constant in reversible transformations, but it cannot decrease.

Entropy, in this view, can be interpreted as an indicator for the system's capacity to perform useful work. The higher the value of entropy, the higher the amount of energy already irreversibly transformed into heat, the lower the amount of free energy of the system and the lower the system's capacity to perform work. Expressed the other way round, the lower the value of entropy, the higher the amount of free energy in the system and the higher the system's capacity to perform work. Hence, the statement of the Second Law of Thermodynamics amounts to saying that, for any process of transformation, the proportion of energy in the form of heat to total energy irreversibly increases or remains constant, but certainly never decreases. In other words, with any transformation of energy or matter, an isolated system loses part of its ability to perform useful mechanical work and some of its available free energy is irreversibly transformed into heat. For that reason, the Second Law is said to express an irreversible degradation of energy in isolated systems over time. At the same time, the economic relevance of the Second Law becomes obvious.

While the notion of entropy introduced to phenomenological thermodynamics by Clausius is based on heat, Ludwig Boltzmann (1877) introduced a formally equivalent notion of entropy that is based on statistical mechanics and likelihood. His notion reveals a different interpretation of entropy and helps to show why it irreversibly increases over time. Statistical mechanics views gases as assemblies of molecules, described by distribution functions depending on position and velocity. This view allows the establishment of connections between the thermodynamic variables, i.e. the macroscopic properties such as temperature or pressure, and the microscopic behaviour of the individual molecules of the system, which is described by statistical means.[5] The crucial step is to distinguish between microstates and macrostates of a system. The *microstate* is an exact specification of the positions and velocities of all individual particles; the *macrostate* is a specification of the thermodynamic variables of the whole system.

Boltzmann assumed that all microstates have equal *a priori* probability, provided that there is no physical condition which would favour one configuration over the other. He posited that every macrostate would always pass to one of higher probability, where the probability of a macrostate is determined by the number of different microstates realising this macrostate. The macroscopic thermal equilibrium state is then the most probable state, in the sense that it is the macrostate which can be realised by the largest number of different microstates. Boltzmann defined the quantity Ω, counting the number of possible microstates realising one macrostate, and related this to the thermodynamic entropy S of that macrostate. He used $S = k \log \Omega$, with k as a factor of proportionality called Boltzmann's constant. Entropy can thus be taken as a measure of likelihood: highly probable macrostates, that is macrostates which can be realised by a large number of microstates, also have high entropy. At the same time, entropy may be interpreted as a measure of how orderly or mixed-up a system is. High entropy, according to the Boltzmann interpretation, characterises a system in which the individual constituents are arranged in a spatially even and homogeneous way ('mixed-up systems'), whereas low entropy characterises a system in which the individual constituents are arranged in an uneven and heterogeneous way ('orderly systems'). The irreversibility stated by the Second Law in its phenomenological formulation (in any isolated system entropy always increases or remains constant) now appears as the statement that any isolated macroscopic system always evolves from a less probable (more orderly) to a more probable (more mixed-up) state, where Ω and S are larger.

Whereas the Second Law in its Clausius or Boltzmann formulation makes a statement about isolated systems in thermodynamic equilibrium only, the study of closed and open systems far from equilibrium has shown (Prigogine, 1962; 1967) that entropy is also a meaningful and useful variable in closed and open systems. Any open system is a subsystem of a larger and isolated system. According to the conventional formulation of the Second Law the entropy of the larger and isolated system has to increase over time, but the entropy of any open subsystem can, of course, decrease. Viewing open systems as subsystems of larger and isolated systems reveals, however, that an entropy decrease in an open subsystem necessarily has to be accompanied by an entropy increase in the system's environment, that is the rest of the larger, isolated system, such that the entropy of the total system increases.

A generalization of the Second Law is possible such that it refers not only to isolated systems. Irrespective of the type of thermodynamic system under study, and irrespective of whether the system is in thermodynamic equilibrium or not, it is true that entropy cannot be annihilated; it can only be created (Falk and Ruppel, 1976, p. 353). This more general, system independent formulation of the Second Law implies the usual formulations for isolated systems. The relevance of the system independent formulation of the Second Law lies in the fact that most real systems of interest are not isolated but closed or open. Hence, the latter formulation is the form in which the Second Law is apparent in everyday life.

2.3.3 Quantification and Application

The entropy concept is essential for understanding how resource and energy scarcity, as well as the irreversibility of transformation processes, constrain economic action (Georgescu-Roegen, 1971; Baumgärtner et al., 1996b). However, it is a very abstract concept and it is notoriously difficult to apply in specific contexts. One of the complications is due to the fact that a system's capacity to perform work depends not only on the state of the system, but also on the state of the system's environment. Therefore, for applications of the fundamental thermodynamic insights in the areas of mechanical and chemical engineering, as well as in economics, it is useful to relate the system's ability to perform work to a certain standardised reference state of its environment. *Exergy* is defined to be the maximum amount of work obtainable from a system as it approaches thermodynamic equilibrium with its environment in a reversible way (Szargut et al., 1988, p. 7). Exergy is also commonly called *available energy* or *available work* and corresponds to the 'useful' part of energy, thus combining the insights from both the First and Second Laws of Thermodynamics. Hence, exergy is what most people mean when they use the term 'energy' carelessly, e.g. when saying that 'energy is used' to carry out a certain process.

The relationship between the concepts of entropy and exergy is simple, as $W_{lost} = T_0 S_{gen}$ (*Law of Gouy and Stodola*), where W_{lost} denotes the potential work or exergy lost by the system in a transformation process, T_0 denotes the temperature of the system's environment, and S_{gen} denotes the entropy generated in the transformation. This means, as the system's entropy increases as a consequence of irreversible transformations according to the Second Law, the system loses exergy or some of its potential to perform work. Exergy, unlike energy, is thus not a conserved quantity. While the entropy concept stresses that with every transformation of the system something useless is created, the exergy concept stresses that something useful is diminished. These developments are two aspects of the same irreversible character of transformations of energy and matter.

As the system might consist simply of a bulk of matter, exergy is also a measure for the potential work embodied in a material, whether it be a fuel, food or other substance (Ayres, 1998; Ayres et al., 1998). The exergy content of different materials can be calculated for standard values specifying the natural environment, by considering how that material eventually reaches thermodynamic equilibrium with its environment with respect to temperature, pressure, chemical potential and all other intensive variables.[6] Taking a particular state of the system's environment as a reference point for the definition and calculation of exergy may be considered as a loss of generality as compared to the entropy concept. However, this referencing seems to be permissible since all processes of transformation – be it in nature or in the economy – are such that:

(i)   all of the materials involved eventually do reach thermodynamic equilibrium with the natural environment, and
(ii) the environment is so large that its equilibrium will not be affected by the particular transformation processes under study.

While both the entropy and the exergy concept yield the same qualitative insights into the fundamentally irreversible character of transformations of energy and matter, the exergy concept is more tangible, as it is directly related to the very compelling idea of 'available work' and it can be more easily quantified than entropy.

2.3.4 The Use of Thermodynamic Concepts in Resource, Environmental and Ecological Economics

In the late 1960s and early 1970s the laws of thermodynamics were found by economists to be concepts with considerable implications for environmental and resource economics (Spash, 1999, p. 418). The Materials Balance Principle was formulated based on the Law of Conservation of Mass as implied by the First Law of Thermodynamics (Boulding, 1966; Ayres and Kneese, 1969; Kneese et al., 1972). In view of the Materials Balance Principle all resource inputs that enter a production process eventually become waste.

At the same time Georgescu-Roegen (1971) developed an elaborate and extensive critique of economics based on the laws of thermodynamics, and in particular the Entropy Law, which he considered to be 'the most economic of all physical laws' (Georgescu-Roegen, 1971, p. 280).[7] His contribution initiated a heated debate on the question whether the Entropy Law is relevant to economics (see e.g. Burness et al., 1980; Daly, 1992; Kåberger and Månsson, 2001; Khalil, 1990; Lozada, 1991; 1995; Norgaard, 1986; Townsend, 1992; Williamson, 1993; Young, 1991; 1994).[8] While Georgescu-Roegen had, among many other points, formulated an essentially correct insight into the irreversible nature of transformations of energy and matter in economies, his analysis is to some extent flawed by wrongly positing what he calls a

'Fourth Law of Thermodynamics' (Ayres, 1999). It may be for this reason that the Second Law and the entropy concept have not yet acquired the same undisputed and foundational status for resource, environmental and ecological economics as have the First Law and the Materials Balance Principle.

But as Georgescu-Roegen's work and the many studies following his lead have shown, the Entropy Law, properly applied, yields insights into the irreversible nature of economy-environment interactions that are not available otherwise (Baumgärtner et al., 1996b). In particular, it becomes obvious that '[g]iven the entropic nature of the economic process, waste is an output just as unavoidable as the input of natural resources' (Georgescu-Roegen 1975, p. 357). Both the First and the Second Laws of Thermodynamics therefore need to be combined in the study of how natural resources are extracted, used in production, and give rise to emissions and waste, thus leading to integrated models of ecological-economic systems (e.g. Faber et al., 1995; Perrings, 1987; Ruth, 1993; 1999). In the following section the basic insights from thermodynamics about waste generation in industrial production processes are recast in a simple framework.

2.4 JOINT PRODUCTION OF DESIRED GOODS AND WASTE

2.4.1 The Thermodynamic View of Production

Production can in the most general way be conceived as the transformation of a number of inputs into a number of outputs. In thermodynamic terms, energy (actually: exergy) and matter are the fundamental factors of production (Faber et al., 1998). From a qualitative thermodynamic viewpoint, each input and each output is characterised by its mass, m, and its entropy, S. In a quantitative thermodynamic analysis it would be more convenient to characterise each input and output by its mass and its exergy (instead of its entropy); this will be done in Section 2.4.3 below. Note that inputs or outputs need not be material ($m>0$) but may be immaterial ($m=0$), e.g. waste heat that occurs as a by-product in producing electricity from fossil fuels. Since both mass and entropy are extensive quantities, it is useful to introduce the ratio of the two, $\sigma = S/m$, for $m>0$ as an intensive quantity. σ is called *specific entropy* and measures the entropy per mass of a bulk of matter irrespective of that bulk's size.[9]

2.4.2 Waste is Unavoidable in Industrial Production

Let us now narrow down the analysis to the particular type of production which is found in most developed countries and which is most relevant as far as economy-environment interactions are concerned. This is what one may call 'industrial' production. For that reason, consider the following toy model of industrial production (Baumgärtner, 2000, Chap. 4).

In typical industrial production processes a raw material is transformed into a final product. The exergy necessary to carry out that transformation is typically provided by a material fuel. As the analysis of the toy model will reveal, it is then unavoidable that a by-product is jointly produced with the desired product. The analysis will also suggest that this by-product may often be considered an unwanted waste. The industrial production process can, thus, be depicted as in Figure 2.1. An example of such an industrial production process is the production of pure iron as a desired product from iron ore as raw material (see e.g. Ruth, 1995). The fuel in that example is coke, and there are slag, carbon dioxide and heat as waste by-products.

Figure 2.1 The thermodynamic structure of industrial production

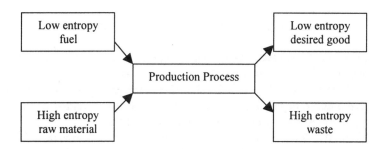

Source: Baumgärtner et al. (2001, p. 366).

The focus on typical industrial production processes justifies building the toy model on the assumption of two kinds of inputs, raw material and fuel, and not more than two kinds of outputs, desired product and by-product.[10] In the notation introduced above, m_j and S_j are the mass and the entropy of the inputs and outputs involved and σ_j is their respective specific entropy (j=raw material, fuel, product, by-product). One may then formally define in thermodynamic terms the notion of industrial production. A process of production is called *industrial production* if and only if it exhibits the following three properties:

(IP1) $m_{\text{raw material}}, m_{\text{product}} > 0,$
(IP2) $\sigma_{\text{raw material}} > \sigma_{\text{product}},$
(IP3) $m_{\text{fuel}} > 0.$

Property IP1 means that the production process essentially consists of a material transformation, i.e. a raw material is transformed into a material desired product. Property IP2 states that the direction of this material transformation is such as to transform a raw material of relatively high specific entropy into a desired product of lower specific entropy. The underlying idea is that most raw materials are still impure and, therefore, can be thought of as mixtures from which the desired product is to be obtained by de-mixing of the different components of the raw material. More generally, desired products are thought of as matter in a more heterogeneous and orderly state than the raw material. From basic thermodynamics we know that such a transformation process requires the use of exergy. Property IP3 states that the exergy input also has mass, i.e. the exergy necessary to carry out the desired transformation is provided by a material fuel, such as e.g. oil, coal or gas.

The constraints imposed on production processes by the two Laws of Thermodynamics can be formalised as follows:

(TD1) $m_{\text{raw material}} + m_{\text{fuel}} \quad = m_{\text{product}} + m_{\text{by-product}},$
(TD2) $S_{\text{raw-material}} + S_{\text{fuel}} + S_{\text{gen}} = S_{\text{product}} + S_{\text{by-product}} \quad \text{with } S_{\text{gen}} \geq 0.$

The First Law (TD1) states that the total ingoing mass has to equal the total outgoing mass since mass (besides energy) is conserved in the production process.[11] The Second Law (TD2) states that in the production process a non-negative amount of entropy is generated, S_{gen}, which is added to the total entropy of all inputs to yield the total entropy of all outputs.

Within the framework of that toy model, one can show that the two thermodynamic constraints TD1 and TD2, together with properties IP1, IP2 and IP3, imply that either the mass $m_{\text{by-product}}$ or the entropy $S_{\text{by-product}}$ (or both) of the second output is strictly positive (Baumgärtner, 2000, p. 77). This means, the occurrence of a by-product is necessary and unavoidable in every process of industrial production. In economic terms, one may speak of *joint production*, as the desired product and the by-product are necessarily produced together (Baumgärtner et al. 2001).

The intuition behind this result is the following. One obvious reason for the existence of joint outputs beside the desired product is simply conservation of mass as demanded by the First Law of Thermodynamics. If, for instance, pure iron is produced from iron ore with a carbon fuel, the desired product, which is pure iron, does not contain any carbon. Yet, the carbon material from the fuel has to go somewhere. Hence, there has to be a joint product containing the carbon. But there is another reason for the existence of joint products besides and beyond conservation of mass, and that is the generation of entropy according to the Second Law of Thermodynamics. Think of a production process where all of the raw material and the material fuel end up as part of the desired product, e.g. the production of cement. In that case the First Law alone would not require any joint product. But since the desired product has lower specific entropy than the raw material, and there is some positive amount of entropy generated by the process, there is a need for a joint output taking up the excess entropy. In that case, as in the example of cement production, the high entropy joint product is simply heat.

In most cases of industrial production both of these reasons – the one based on the First Law and the one based on the Second Law – hold at the same time. Therefore, the joint product is typically a high entropy material. Due to its high entropy it will most often be considered useless and, therefore, an undesired waste. However, one should be careful to note that the classification of an output as 'waste' carries a certain value judgment, which cannot be inferred from thermodynamics alone.[12]

2.4.3 Thermodynamic (In)Efficiency of Production

The thermodynamic analysis in the previous section has demonstrated that the existence of a high entropy joint product is necessary and unavoidable in every process of industrial production. In reality, however, much of the waste currently generated is obviously avoidable. Yet this observation is not in contradiction to the result derived in Section 2.4.2 above. While the toy model was based on the assumption of thermodynamic efficiency, current technology and production practices are to a large extent thermodynamically inefficient. As a consequence, while a certain amount of waste is necessary and unavoidable for thermodynamic reasons, the actual amount of waste produced with current technologies is expression of an inefficiency. Thermodynamic considerations, in particular the exergy concept (see Section 2.3.3 above), which is based on both laws of thermodynamics and refers explicitly to matter as well, can tell us exactly what amount of waste is due to inefficiency and may, in principle, be reduced (e.g. Bejan et al., 1996; Brodyansky et al., 1994; Creyts, 2000; Dewulf et al., 2000).

In this section, industrial production is analysed in exergy terms with regard to thermodynamic (in)efficiency. While the analysis in the previous section was qualitative, the efficiency analysis in this section will be quantitative. For that reason, we turn in detail to one particular step in the industrial production process introduced above. In the production of pure iron from iron ore, the first step is to extract the ore from the deposit. In the next step, the ore is separated by physical means into iron oxide and silicates. The third step, which we shall analyse in detail in this section, then consists of chemi-cally reducing the iron oxide to pure iron.[13] This reduction requires exergy. It is typically provided by burning coke, which, for the purpose of this analysis can be taken to be pure carbon. So, in the terminology of Section 2.4.2 the desired product of this transformation is pure iron (Fe), the raw material is iron oxide (Fe_2O_3) and the fuel is carbon (C). As a waste joint product in this reaction, carbon dioxide (CO_2) is generated. The chemical reaction in this production process may be written down as follows:

(CR1) $2 Fe_2O_3 + 3 C \rightarrow 4 Fe + 3 CO_2$.

The exergy values and molecular weights of the chemicals involved in the reaction are given in Table 2.1.

*Table 2.1 Exergy values and molecular weights of the different chemicals
involved in the reduction of iron ore to pure iron*

Chemical	Molecular Weight	Exergy (kJ/mole)
Fe	56	376
Fe_2O_3	160	16
C	12	410
CO_2	44	20
O_2	32	4

Source: Szargut et al. (1988, Appendix, Table I.).

As one sees, the desired product Fe has a much higher exergy (i.e. lower specific entropy) than the raw material Fe_2O_3. It is the relatively high exergy content (i.e. low specific entropy) of the fuel C that provides the exergy for this transformation to happen. The waste CO_2 is then characterised by low exergy content (i.e. high specific entropy).

2.4.3.1 Mass balance
The chemical reaction equation (CR1) is correct in terms of the mass balance: all atoms of an element that go into the reaction come out of the reaction as well. Conservation of mass is the reason for the existence of the joint product CO_2. Producing four moles[14] of Fe, thus, entails three moles of CO_2 as waste. That makes 0.75 moles of waste CO_2-emissions per mole of Fe produced (corresponding to 0.59 kg CO_2 per kg of Fe) for mass balance reasons alone.

2.4.3.2 Thermodynamic efficiency
Checking the reaction equation (CR1) with the exergy values given in Table

2.1 reveals that while the reaction equation is written down correctly in terms of the mass balance, it is not yet correct in energetic terms. For, in order to produce four moles of Fe with an exergy content of 4x376 = 1504 kJ one needs the input of at least 1504 kJ as well. (Remember that exergy cannot be created, but always diminishes in the course of a transformation due to irreversibilities.) But three moles of C only contain 3x410 = 1230 kJ. Therefore, one actually needs more than three moles of C to deliver enough exergy for four moles of Fe to be produced from Fe_2O_3. We compensate for this shortage of exergy on the input side by introducing one additional unit of the exergy source C. The reaction equation should, thus, be written down as follows to obey both laws of thermodynamics:

(CR2) $2 Fe_2O_3 + 4 C + 1 O_2 \rightarrow 4 Fe + 4 CO_2$.
              (32)   (1640)   (4)   (1504)   (80)

The numbers in brackets below each input and output give the exergy content in kJ of the respective amounts of inputs and outputs. On the input side one mole of oxygen (O_2) has been added to fulfill the mass balance with the additional mole of C involved. This oxygen comes from the air and enters the transformation process when carbon is burned.

From reaction equation (CR2) we see that the exergy supplied to the reaction by its inputs now suffices to yield the exergy of the outputs. As (almost) no exergy is lost in the reaction, i.e. the exergy of the inputs equals (approximately) the exergy of the outputs, this corresponds to a thermodynamically 100 per cent efficient and reversible transformation, in which no entropy is generated at all. In mass terms, reaction equation (CR2) tells us that even in thermodynamically ideal transformations of Fe_2O_3 into Fe, four moles of CO_2 are generated as material waste when producing four moles of Fe. That makes one mole of waste CO_2-emissions per mole of Fe produced (corresponding to 0.79 kg CO_2 per kg of Fe). This amount is the minimum waste generation required by the two laws of thermodynamics, as shown in Section 2.4.2 above to necessarily exist.

2.4.3.3 Thermodynamically inefficient production
In real industrial production processes, the exergy content of carbon of 410 kJ/mole is never put to work with an efficiency of 100 per cent. Detailed data on pig iron production in real blast furnaces in Poland (Szargut et al. 1988, Table 7.3), where coke is burned together with atmospheric oxygen, imply that the efficiency of exergy conversion is only about one third, or some 33 per cent. This means that out of one mole of C one obtains only 137 kJ instead of the ideal value of 410 kJ. As a consequence, in order to deliver the exergy necessary to carry out the chemical reaction one needs to employ at

least twelve moles of C. The reaction equation for a transformation that is only 33 per cent efficient in energy conversion would thus read:

(CR3) $2 Fe_2O_3$ +   12 C   + $9 O_2$ → 4 Fe + 12 CO_2.
        (32)   (4920×0.33=1624)   (36)   (1504)   (240)

We see that due to the inefficiency in energy conversion the amount of material fuel which is necessary to drive the transformation has tripled. In order to produce four moles of Fe with a 33 per cent efficiency, one needs 12 moles of C (CR3) instead of just four moles in the efficient case (CR2). As a consequence, the reaction generates 12 moles of CO_2 (CR3) instead of just four moles in the efficient case (CR2). That makes three moles of waste CO_2-emissions per mole of Fe produced (corresponding to 2.36 kg CO_2 per kg of Fe), with only one mole due to thermodynamic necessity (see the discussion of CR2 above) and two moles due to thermodynamic inefficiency.

From this analysis one might conclude that roughly two thirds of the waste currently generated in iron production is due to thermodynamic inefficiency, while one third is actually necessary for thermodynamic reasons. Therefore, even increasing thermodynamic process efficiency to the ideal value of 100 per cent will not reduce the amount of waste to zero, but only to one third the amount currently generated.

2.4.3.4 Finite-time/finite-size thermodynamics

Pointing to the thermodynamic inefficiency of a real production process, and how it implies the occurrence of large amounts of waste, seems to suggest that the amount of waste can easily be reduced by increasing the thermodynamic efficiency at which the process is carried out. However, there are good reasons why this form of inefficiency may actually be desired.

The analysis so far has been entirely based on concepts and methods from ideal equilibrium thermodynamics, which means that a level of 100 per cent efficiency in this framework is reached by operating processes in a completely reversible way between one equilibrium state and another equilibrium state, resulting in zero entropy generation during the process. But that requires that the process is basically left alone to self-evolve spontaneously. It, therefore, also requires a very long time (in the limit even infinitely long) for the process to be completed.

Recent developments in the applied field of engineering thermodynamics (e.g. Bejan et al., 1996; Bejan, 1997) have addressed the circumstance that chemical and physical processes in industry never happen in a completely reversible way between one equilibrium state and another equilibrium state. Rather, these processes are enforced by the operator of the process and they are constrained in space and time. This has led to two extensions of ideal equilibrium thermodynamics:

(i)   There now exist a number of methods for modelling and optimisation of flow systems, i.e. systems that are in states of internal non-equilibrium. Internal gradients of temperature and pressure drive internal heat and mass currents. Consequently, the development of such systems is necessarily characterised by irreversibility.

(ii) Models now account for global constraints on the system, e.g. finite spatial sizes, finite times of operation or particular properties of the material. These models, thus, give more realistic representations and predictions of actual thermodynamic systems in industry.

Both developments are known under the name of finite-time/finite-size thermodynamics.

From the point of view of finite-time/finite-size thermodynamics it appears that the minimum exergy requirement and minimum waste production in chemical or physical processes is considerably higher than that suggested by the ideal equilibrium thermodynamics analysis carried out so far. The reason for the increased exergy requirement (which entails an increased amount of waste at the end of the process) lies in the fact that chemical and physical transformations are forced to happen over a finite time by the operator of the production plant, which necessarily causes some dissipation of energy. In the language of the toy model of Section 2.4.2 above, this shows in a strictly positive amount S_{gen} of entropy generated in the process. While the finite-time consideration is not very relevant for the example of reducing iron oxide to pure iron in blast furnaces – a process that is typically not intentionally forced to be completed over shorter time-spans than when left alone – it is a very relevant consideration for many other production processes, especially in the chemical industry.

An example which demonstrates how large S_{gen} can actually be, is the enrichment of uranium (Balian, 1991, pp. 347-48, 383-85). In the production of enriched uranium the actual exergy input is larger than the theoretical minimum calculated from ideal equilibrium thermodynamics by a factor of 70 million! This huge factor is entirely due to a huge S_{gen}. At Eurodif factory, the French enriching plant from which the data are taken, the process of enriching by isotope separation is realised by gas diffusion through a semipermeable membrane. An ideal process realisation would require letting the gas diffuse in thermodynamic equilibrium, which would take an infinite timespan. In order to carry out the process in finite time, diffusion is enhanced by building up a pressure difference between the two sides of the membrane. Then, the process of diffusion is no longer an equilibrium process. Instead, it is irreversible and $S_{gen} > 0$. A comparison of the ideal separation process and the real process realisation shows that the huge irreversible loss of energy in the actual separation process is entirely due to the dissipation of energy in the many compressions and decompressions which are necessary to run the separation process under a pressure difference and, thus, in finite time. This dissipated energy leaves the process as waste heat.

2.4.4 The Thermodynamic Properties of Waste

In the previous parts of Section 2.4 we have seen that the occurrence of joint products is necessary and unavoidable in industrial production processes. Yet the quantitative amount in which they occur may vary according to the degree of thermodynamic (in)efficiency with which the process is carried out. The sheer amount of waste by-products (measured in mass terms) may be the most obvious result from a thermodynamic analysis of production. But beyond that, the thermodynamic view also allows statements about the properties of this waste. From the simple toy model of industrial production analysed in Section 2.4.2 above it is obvious that, in some sense, high entropy may be seen as the fundamental characterisation of waste (Faber, 1985). This idea has been operationalised by Kümmel (1989), who defines an aggregated measure for pollution as the rate of increase in entropy per unit volume of the biosphere where this increase occurs.

On the other hand, it is important to distinguish between high entropy waste in the form of heat and in the form of waste materials.[15] The former may be considered a minor problem since it can, in principle, be radiated into space.[16] It is only the latter which accumulates in the biosphere, thus causing major environmental problems. Waste materials, however, might cause environmental problems not because of their high entropy, but – just the opposite – because their entropy is not yet maximal. In other words, it is the exergy still contained in waste materials, i.e. the potential to initiate chemical reactions and perform work, which makes these wastes potentially harmful to the natural environment (Perrings, 1987; Ayres and Martinás, 1995; Ayres et al., 1998).[17]

2.5 CONCLUSION: THERMODYNAMICS AND SUSTAINABLE ECONOMIC METABOLISM

Although the two examples studied in Section 2.4 (reducing iron oxide to iron and the enrichment of uranium) are rather specific, the insights from the analysis of these examples are fairly general and hold for industrial production processes at large. The basic result is that, from the thermodynamic viewpoint, waste is an unavoidable and necessary joint product in the industrial production of desired goods. Thermodynamic analysis also allows one to quantify the amount of waste which – beyond the thermodynamic minimum required – is due to inefficiencies. There are three major reasons for the occurrence of large amounts of excessive material waste from industrial production:

1. The first reason is the *thermodynamically inefficient performance* of current technologies when it comes to the conversion of exergy, which is a necessary factor of production in all production processes. This inefficiency not only considerably increases the need for fuel beyond the minimum exergy requirement as given by the laws of thermodynamics; it also increases the amount of material waste generated far beyond the thermodynamic necessity. This holds, in particular, for carbon dioxide emissions when carbon (e.g. coal or coke) or carbohydrates (e.g. oil or natural gas) are used as a fuel.

2. The second reason is the use of a *material fuel* at all. The fuel – carbon in our example – only serves to provide the exergy for the chemical reaction. The carbon material itself is actually neither wanted nor needed in the reaction. Since mass is conserved, the fuel material has to go somewhere after its exergy content has been stripped off. And that makes the waste.[18]

3. The third reason is the operation of industrial production processes under *non-equilibrium conditions*, in order to have them completed in finite time. The shorter the time-span within which one wants the process to be completed, the more energy will irreversibly be dissipated. First of all, this leads to an increase in the minimum exergy required to operate the process in finite time, which also increases the waste heat released from the process. And as long as the exergy to drive the process is provided by a material fuel, this also increases the amount of material waste produced.

With these insights, what is the role of thermodynamic analysis for conceiving sustainable modes of society's metabolism? The analogy between ecosystems and economies, which has been sketched on thermodynamic grounds in Section 2.2 above, seems to suggest that the answer is as simple as (e.g. de Swaan Arons and van der Kooi 2001, p. G54):

(i)   do not use material fuels as a source of exergy, but only sunlight;
(ii) keep matter in closed cycles, i.e. let heat be the only true waste; and
(iii) carry out all transformations thermodynamically efficiently.

However, one important caveat seems to be in place. Thermodynamics is a purely descriptive science. That means, it only allows one to derive statements of the kind 'If A, then B'. In particular, it is not a normative science. By itself, it neither includes nor allows value statements (Baumgärtner, 2000, pp. 65-66) or statements of the kind 'C is a good, and therefore desirable, state of the world, but D is not'.[19] In contrast, sustainability is essentially a normative issue (Faber et al., 1995; Faber et al., 1996, Chap. 5). Sustainability is about the question 'In what kind of world do we want to live today and in the future?', thus, inherently including a dimension of desirability. A purely descriptive science alone, like thermodynamics, cannot give an answer to that question.

Thermodynamics, however, is necessary to identify clearly the feasible options of development and their various properties, before a choice is then made about which option to choose based on some normative criteria. That choice requires a valuation or, more generally, a normative judgment of the different options at hand. In particular, it involves an assessment of the different joint products generated by society and of the potentially harmful consequences when emitting them into the natural environment. It is therefore necessary not only to know the energetic and material basis of society's metabolism – both current and feasible alternatives – but also to link these thermodynamic aspects to the human perception and valuation of commodity products and waste joint products. This includes, *inter alia*, considering different attitudes towards waste, as expressed earlier in history (see Chapter 3) or prevalent in today's societies (see Chapter 4), as well as the economic valuation of waste (see Chapter 5).

The role of thermodynamics for conceiving sustainable modes of societal metabolism, therefore, is relative but essential. Thermodynamics is necessary to identify which options and scenarios of resource use and waste generation are feasible and which are not. It, thereby, contributes to making informed choices about the future.

REFERENCES

Ayres, R.U. (1998), 'Eco-thermodynamics: economics and the second law', *Ecological Economics*, **26**, 189-209.

Ayres, R.U. (1999), 'The second law, the fourth law, recycling, and limits to growth', *Ecological Economics*, **29**, 473-83.

Ayres, R.U. (2001), 'Industrial ecology: wealth, depreciation and waste', in H. Folmer, H. Landis Gabel, S. Gerking and A. Rose (eds), *Frontiers of Environmental Economics*, Cheltenham: Edward Elgar, pp. 214-49.

Ayres, R.U. and L.W. Ayres (eds) (2002), *A Handbook of Industrial Ecology*, Cheltenham: Edward Elgar.

Ayres, R.U. and A.V. Kneese (1969), 'Production, consumption, and externalities', *American Economic Review*, **59**, 282-97.

Ayres, R.U. and K. Martinás (1995), 'Waste potential entropy: the ultimate ecotoxic?', *Economie Appliquée*, **48**, 95-120.

Ayres, R.U. and U. Simonis (1994), *Industrial Metabolism: Restructuring for Sustainable Development*, Tokyo: United Nations University Press.

Ayres, R.U., L.W. Ayres and K. Martinás (1998), 'Exergy, waste accounting, and life-cycle analysis', *Energy*, **23**, 355-63.

Balian, R. (1991), *From Microphysics to Macrophysics, Vol. I*, Heidelberg: Springer.

Baumgärtner, S. (2000), *Ambivalent Joint Production and the Natural Environment. An Economic and Thermodynamic Analysis*, Heidelberg: Physica.

Baumgärtner, S. (2001), 'Thermodynamic and economic notions of efficiency', Contribution to the Symposium *Sustainable Processes and Products*, 30 May 2001, Delft University of Technology, Department of ChemTech.

Baumgärtner, S., H. Dyckhoff, M. Faber, J. Proops and J. Schiller (2001), 'The concept of joint production and ecological economics', *Ecological Economics*, **36**, 365-72.

Baumgärtner, S., M. Faber and J. Proops (1996a), 'Entropy: A unifying concept for ecological economics', in Faber et al. (1996: Chap. 6).

Baumgärtner, S., M. Faber and J. Proops (1996b), 'The use of the entropy concept in ecological economics', in Faber et al. (1996: Chap. 7).

Beard, T.R. and G.A. Lozada (1999), *Economics, Entropy and the Environment. The Extraordinary Economics of Nicholas Georgescu-Roegen*, Cheltenham: Edward Elgar.

Bejan, A. (1997), *Advanced Engineering Thermodynamics*, 2nd ed., New York: Wiley.

Bejan, A., G. Tsatsaronis and M. Moran (1996), *Thermal Design and Optimization*, New York: Wiley.

Berry, R.S., P. Salamon and G.M. Heal (1978), 'On a relation between economic and thermodynamic optima', *Resources and Energy*, **1**, 125-37.

Boltzmann, L. (1877), 'Über die Beziehung eines allgemeinen mechanischen Satzes zum zweiten Hauptsatz der Wärmetheorie', *Sitzungsberichte der Kaiserlichen Akademie der Wissenschaften in Wien, Abt. 2*, **75**, 67-73.

Boulding, K.E. (1966), 'The economics of the coming spaceship Earth', in H. Jarrett (ed.), *Environmental Quality in a Growing Economy*, Baltimore: Johns Hopkins University Press.

Brodyansky, V.M., M.V. Sorin and P. Le Goff (eds) (1994), *The Efficiency of Industrial Processes: Exergy Analysis and Optimization*, Amsterdam: Elsevier.

Burness, H.S., R.G. Cummings, G. Morris and I. Paik (1980), 'Thermodynamic and economic concepts as related to resource-use policies', *Land Economics*, **56**, 1-9.

Callen, H.B. (1985), *Thermodynamics and an Introduction to Thermostatics*, 2nd ed., New York: Wiley.

Clausius, R. (1854), *Fortschritte der Physik*, **10**.

Clausius, R. (1865), 'Über verschiedene für die Anwendung bequeme Formen der Hauptgleichungen der mechanischen Wärmetheorie', *Annalen der Physik*, **125**, 353-400.

Creyts, J.C. (2000), *Use of Extended Exergy Analysis as a Tool to Optimize the Environmental Performance of Industrial Processes*, Ph.D. Thesis, Berkeley: University of California, Department of Mechanical Engineering.

Daly, H.E. (1992), 'Is the entropy law relevant to the economics of natural resources? Yes, of course it is!', *Journal of Environmental Economics and Management*, **23**, 91-95.

Dasgupta, P.S. and G.M. Heal (1979), *Economic Theory and Exhaustible Resources*, Cambridge: Cambridge University Press.

de Swaan Arons, J. and H.J. van der Kooi (2001), 'Towards a metabolic society: a thermodynamic view', *Green Chemistry*, **3** (4), G53-G55.

Dewulf, J., J.M. Mulder, M.M.D. van den Berg, H. Van Langenhove, H.J. van der Kooi and J. de Swaan Arons (2000), 'Illustrations towards quantifying the sustainability of technology', *Green Chemistry*, **2** (3), 108-14.

Erkman, S. (1997), 'Industrial ecology: an historical view', *Journal of Cleaner Production*, **5** (1-2), 1-10.

Faber, M. (1985), 'A biophysical approach to the economy: entropy, environment and resources', in W. van Gool and J.J.C. Bruggink (eds), *Energy and Time in the Economic and Physical Sciences*, Amsterdam: North Holland.

Faber, M., F. Jöst and R. Manstetten (1995), 'Limits and perspectives on the concept of sustainable development', *Economie Appliquée*, **48**, 233-51.

Faber, M., R. Manstetten and J. Proops (1996), *Ecological Economics: Concepts and Methods*, Cheltenham: Edward Elgar.

Faber, M., H. Niemes and G. Stephan (1995), *Entropy, Environment and Resources: An Essay in Physico-Economics*, 2nd ed., Heidelberg: Springer.

Faber, M., J. Proops and S. Baumgärtner (1998), 'All production is joint production – a thermodynamic analysis', in S. Faucheux, J. Gowdy and I. Nicolaï (eds), *Sustainability and Firms. Technological Change and the Changing Regulatory Environment*, Cheltenham: Edward Elgar, pp. 131-58.

Falk, G. and W. Ruppel (1976), *Energie und Entropie. Eine Einführung in die Thermodynamik*, Heidelberg: Springer.

Folke, C. (1999), 'Ecological principles and environmental economic analysis', in J.C.J.M. van den Bergh (ed.), *Handbook of Environmental and Resource Economics*, Cheltenham: Edward Elgar, pp. 895-911.

Georgescu-Roegen, N. (1971), *The Entropy Law and the Economic Process*, Cambridge/MA: Harvard University Press.

Georgescu-Roegen, N. (1975), 'Energy and economic myths', *Southern Economic Journal*, **41**, 347-81.

Graedel, T. (1995), 'Industrial ecology: some definitions', in R. Socolow, C. Andrews, F. Berkhout and V. Thomas (eds), *Industrial Ecology and Global Change*, Cambridge: Cambridge University Press.

Huang, K. (1987), *Statistical Mechanics*, 2nd ed., New York: Wiley.

Kåberger, T. and B. Månsson (2001), 'Entropy and economic processes – physics perspectives', *Ecological Economics*, **36**, 165-79.

Khalil, E.L. (1990), 'Entropy law and exhaustion of natural resources: Is Nicholas Georgescu-Roegen's paradigm defensible?', *Ecological Economics*, **2**, 163-78.

Kneese, A.V., R.U. Ayres and R.C. d'Arge (1972), *Economics and the Environment: A Materials Balance Approach*, Washington: Resources for the Future.

Kümmel, R. (1989), 'Energy as a factor of production and entropy as a pollutian indicator in macroeconomic modelling', *Ecological Economics*, **1**, 161-80.

Kümmel, R. and U. Schüssler (1991), 'Heat equivalents of noxious substances: a pollution indicator for environmental accounting', *Ecological Economics*, **3**, 139-56.

Landau, L.D. and E.E. Lifshitz (1980), *Statistical Physics*, 3rd ed., Oxford: Pergamon.

Lozada, G.A. (1991), 'A defense of Nicholas Georgescu-Roegens's paradigm', *Ecological Economics*, **3**, 157-60.

Lozada, G.A. (1995), 'Georgescu-Roegens's defence of classical thermodynamics revisited', *Ecological Economics*, **14**, 31-44.

Mayumi, K. (2001), *The Origins of Ecological Economics. The Bioeconomics of Georgescu-Roegen*, London: Routledge.

Mayumi, K. and J.M. Gowdy (eds) (1999), *Bioeconomics and Sustainability. Essays in Honor of Nicholas Georgescu-Roegen*, Cheltenham: Edward Elgar.

Norgaard, R.B. (1986), 'Thermodynamic and economic concepts as related to resource-use policies: synthesis', *Land Economics*, **62**, 325-28.

Perrings, C. (1987), *Economy and Environment: A Theoretical Essay on the Interdependence of Economic and Environmental Systems*, Cambridge: Cambridge University Press.

Prigogine, I. (1962), *Introduction to Non-Equilibrium Thermodynamics*, New York: Wiley.

Prigogine, I. (1967), *Thermodynamics of Irreversible Processes*, New York.

Reif, F. (1965), *Fundamentals of Statistical and Thermal Physics*, New York: McGraw-Hill.

Ricklefs, R.E. and G.L. Miller (2000), *Ecology*, 4th ed., New York: W.H. Freeman.

Ruth, M. (1993), *Integrating Economics, Ecology and Thermodynamics*, Dordrecht: Kluwer.

Ruth, M. (1995), 'Technology change in the US iron and steel production', *Resources Policy*, **21**, 199-214.

Ruth, M. (1999), 'Physical principles in environmental economic analysis', in J.C.J.M. van den Bergh (ed.), *Handbook of Environmental and Resource Economics*, Cheltenham: Edward Elgar, pp. 855-66.

Spash, C. (1999), 'The development of environmental thinking in economics', *Environmental Values*, **8**, 413-35.

Szargut, J., D.R. Morris and F.R. Steward (1988), *Exergy Analysis of Thermal, Chemical, and Metallurgical Processes*, New York: Hemisphere Publishing.

Townsend, K.N. (1992), 'Is the entropy law relevant to the economics of natural resource scarcity?', *Journal of Environmental Economics and Management*, **23**, 96-100.

Williamson, A.G. (1993), 'The second law of thermodynamics and the economic process', *Ecological Economics*, **7**, 69-71.

Young, J.T. (1991), 'Is the entropy law relevant to the economics of natural resource scarcity?', *Journal of Environmental Economics and Management*, **21**, 169-79.

Young, J.T. (1994), 'Entropy and natural resource scarcity: a reply to the critics', *Journal of Environmental Economics and Management*, **26**, 210-13.

Zemansky, M.W. and R.H. Dittman (1997), *Heat and Thermodynamics: An Intermediate Textbook*, 7th ed., New York: McGraw-Hill.

NOTES

1 I am very much indebted to Jakob de Swaan Arons (Delft University of Technology, The Netherlands) for what I learned from him about engineering thermodynamics. Helpful comments by John Coulter, Jakob de Swaan Arons, Malte Faber and John Proops on an earlier draft are gratefully acknowledged.

2 The field of *Industrial Ecology* (Ayres and Ayres, 2002; Erkman, 1997; Graedel, 1995) has recently emerged, with the aim of redesigning the economic system such as to follow the insights from ecosystems about sustainable metabolism. The key idea is to 'close the material cycles' within the economic system, thereby reducing the intake of material natural resources from the environment and the disposal of material waste into the natural environment. See Section 2.5 below for an important caveat concerning that endeavour.

3   For a comprehensive introduction to (phenomenological) thermodynamics see Callen
     (1985), Reif (1965) or Zemansky and Dittman (1997). Baumgärtner et al. (1996a) and
     Baumgärtner (2000, Chap. 3) give an introduction to thermodynamics for economists.
4   Note that this does not mean that the initial state of the system can never be restored.
     However, in order to restore the system's initial state, the initially isolated system has to be
     opened to the influx of energy. For instance, the initial state could be restored by removing
     the system's insulation and performing work on the system from the outside, e.g. by pressing
     all the molecules into the left part with a mobile wall that is initially at the right hand end of
     the system and from there on moves left.
5   Balian (1991), Huang (1987) and Landau and Lifshitz (1980) give an introduction to
     statistical mechanics.
6   Exergy values for many materials are typically calculated for an environmental temperature
     of 298.15 K and pressure of 101.325 kPa and can be found in tables, such as e.g. in Szargut
     et al. (1988; Appendix).
7   The works of Georgescu-Roegen are surveyed in a number of recent volumes (e.g. Beard
     and Lozada, 1999; Mayumi, 2001; Mayumi and Gowdy, 1999) and a special edition of the
     journal *Ecological Economics* (Vol. 22, No. 3, 1997).
8   See Baumgärtner et al. (1996b) for a summary of that discussion.
9   If one doubled a bulk of matter, then the two extensive quantities m and S would double as
     well while the ratio of the two, $\sigma = S/m$, would remain constant.
10   This assumption may be relaxed. It may be assumed that there are a number of additional
     inputs and outputs besides the ones mentioned in the text. The joint production result is not
     altered by the assumption of additional inputs or outputs.
11   One should actually distinguish between different chemical elements, as the mass of each
     element is conserved separately. This can easily be taken into account by introducing an
     additional index for the chemical element (see Baumgärtner, 2000, pp. 72ff.). While this
     inflates the notation, it does not change the fundamental result.
12   For a review of various attempts to construct a so-called 'entropy theory of value', and a
     refutation of these endeavours see Baumgärtner et al. (1996b).
13   I am grateful to Jakob de Swaan Arons for introducing me to the exergy analysis of this
     example.
14   A *mole* is the amount of a chemical which is given by the molecular weight in grammes. For
     example, CO_2 has molecular weight 44, so one mole of CO_2 is the amount of CO_2 that
     weighs 44 grammes.
15   Kümmel and Schüssler (1991) have suggested using heat equivalents for characterising
     different material pollutants. These heat equivalents are defined as the amount of heat that is
     inevitably produced when cleaning the environment from the respective pollutant or avoid-
     ing the occurrence of the pollutant altogether. Waste heat may thus be considered to be the
     ultimate form of waste.
16   Of course, waste heat that is directly released into ecosystems may cause harm to these
     systems, e.g. when heating up surface waters. Also, the ability to radiate heat into space may
     be impaired by the greenhouse effect that is caused by certain greenhouse gases in the
     Earth's atmosphere and further aggravated by anthropogenic emission of these gases.
17   The view that the 'waste exergy' of by-products can be seen as a measure for potential harm
     done to natural ecosystems, to be sure, is limited. It does not take into account the (eco-)
     toxicity of some inert materials, nor does it take into account purely physical effects of inert
     materials, e.g. global warming due to the carbon dioxide emitted into the atmosphere.
18   Note that, since the primary goal of carrying out the transformation studied in Section 2.4.3
     (cf. reaction equations CR1, CR2 and CR3) is to split Fe_2O_3 into Fe and O_2, the minimal
     way of doing that would be: $2\ Fe_2O_3$ + direct exergy $\rightarrow 4\ Fe + 3\ O_2$. The exergy necessary
     to achieve the splitting of Fe_2O_3 into Fe and O_2 could, for instance, be delivered by solar
     energy directly. Without any material fuel the amount of material waste would be consid-
     erably reduced. With four moles of Fe there would be three moles of O_2 jointly produced.
     That makes 0.75 moles of waste O_2 emissions per mole of Fe produced (corresponding to
     0.43 kg O_2 per kg of Fe). However, running the chemical process in this direct way, i.e.

powered by solar energy instead of material fuel input, would require technologies very different from the ones we are currently using.

19 This holds even for the notion of *thermodynamic efficiency*, which is a purely technical notion. It may be questioned that thermodynamic efficiency is a desirable property from the point of view of normative economics, i.e. whether thermodynamic efficiency is a necessary condition for economic efficiency, even when economic efficiency includes concerns for resource scarcity and environmental quality (see e.g. Berry et al., 1978; Dasgupta and Heal, 1979, Chap. 7; Baumgärtner, 2001).

3.   History of Waste

Verena Winiwarter[1]

3.1 INTRODUCTION

Viewed from the vantage point of cultural anthropology, waste constitutes a central category of social order. Historically speaking, what is considered as waste changes with changes in social order. Seen from a material viewpoint, waste is the final output of social metabolism; its composition and amount depend on the quality and quantity of the input. Changes in social metabolism, hence, are reflected in changes in waste, and thus determine how dangerous wastes will be. The way social systems deal with waste depends on the interplay of cultural concepts and material objects. Decisions about disposal, sewage, incineration and recycling of wastes in their respective social context cannot be understood without considering both the material and the cultural contexts of waste.

This environmental historian's view of waste is dominated by an interest in the material flows that lead to waste and the controversies in dealings with waste, seeking possible explanations for the facts of historical developments. The history of waste management technology, or the detailed course of events in adopting and revising such technologies, is important but cannot figure prominently in such a short overview.

The use of theories in history differs from that in economics or biology, in that historians seek to construct plausible narratives out of historical events with the aid of theoretical concepts, but they cannot conduct experiments. Three theoretical approaches, besides the underlying concept of social metabolism, are used in this overview. Human attitudes towards order have to be considered to understand the cultural relevance of waste. Combined with a concept of the dynamics of waste, using such an approach allows one to see a general pattern in the history of waste. Cultural theory offers a framework to analyse conflicts over waste management on a more general level, defining social groups by means of their attitudes towards nature. The three frameworks complement each other and allow for a more general understanding of the waste issue throughout history.

Sustainability in the ecological sense is a balance between the amounts and qualities of the output of social systems and nature's capacities to re-naturalise this output. Waste poses a problem to sustainability by what has consciously been termed the 'overexploitation' of natural sinks. The quality and quantity of wastes we experience today is unparalleled in history; however, the way we deal with waste has historical and cultural origins. To explore them can help us to understand the current situation and its challenges.

3.2 WHAT IS WASTE?

According to the Oxford English Dictionary, the noun 'waste' has three distinct meanings. The OED cites the first documented use, in 1200, had 'waste' (spelled exactly as today) denote uninhabited or sparsely inhabited and uncultivated land. The useless expenditure or consumption of goods, time or money, was considered a waste from the late thirteenth century onwards. The third category of meanings, 'waste matter' or 'refuse', is first documented in 1430. The synonym 'rubbish' is first documented a little earlier, in 1392-93. The oldest references to waste, and therefore also the oldest documented perception of waste as a distinct phenomenon, date back more than half a millennium in the English language. But wastes have existed longer than that. Ever since the Neolithic transformation, sedentary humans have left waste-pits for archaeologists to explore, so waste seems an inevitable by-product of human societies. We now call all matter 'waste' that has been dumped, because there was no use for it and no interest in its storage, instead of naming it more particularly, night-soil, rubble, debris, worn-out shoe or chicken bone.

Waste is what is left over. Waste can be what annoys us, what stinks. Waste is what is rendered worthless, matter in the wrong place, an obstruction and challenge to environmental movements and policy makers. Anyone who changes natural systems inevitably produces wastes (see Chapter 2). Hunter-gatherer societies produce only small amounts of waste, and most of it can easily be recycled, as they are not intervening in nature on a large scale. Archaeologists, experts on human leftovers, find broken or lost stone tools, arrowheads and bones as the waste of such societies. Jewellery and cult objects found in Neolithic graves do not count as waste, as they have been placed there on purpose and not to get rid of them. Human excrement is seldom fossilised, and due to the low population densities of such societies, it does not often figure in archaeological records. Hunter-gatherers had no reason to gather their excrement, as they did not undertake agricultural operations such as manuring. The example of hunter-gatherers shows clearly that the amount and composition of wastes are characteristic of the specific mode of production of a society. The type of input from nature into society determines what is left over at the end, i.e. determines output. In understanding waste, societies need to be described not only in terms of their cultural or political systems, but also as material entities that channel material and energy flows. They can be described as having a metabolism, just like individual organisms. Using the concept of social metabolism, and coupling this idea with the notion of modes of production (or subsistence), gives a useful concept to describe waste systematically and to understand its change over time (Fischer-Kowalski and Haberl, 1993; Weisz et al., 2001).

3.3 HOW HISTORIANS LOOK AT WASTE

Waste has not figured as a central problem in the historical sciences. Economic history and cultural history have touched upon certain facets of the theme, but only with the advent of environmental history did waste gain attention as a research topic in its entirety (e.g. Melosi, 1981; Tarr and Dupuy, 1988).

3.3.1 Waste and Economic History

The economic history of waste closely parallels economic history at large. We encounter waste as an embedded part of the subsistence economies of agricultural societies. Waste materials were and are considered as potentially recyclable, which can be and are to a high degree re-inserted into production processes (Kuchenbuch, 1989).

Agricultural production underwent a process of commodification in more densely populated areas where urban centres developed at an early date. Two perceptions and concepts of waste begin to become distinct in the Mediterranean in classical antiquity; the valuation of waste begins at the same time as its recognition as a sanitary problem. Excrement and other wastes produced by urban dwellers translated into costs for the communities and demanded administrative and technical solutions. For the municipality of Rome, by far the largest city in the Mediterranean during antiquity, waste management figured high on the agenda and was a major cost factor. At the same time, agricultural textbooks showed an awareness of the necessity of manuring and even elaborate on the varying qualities of dung produced by different animals. The two parallel threads, 'urban' and 'rural', co-existed for a long time.

A dung-heap in seventeenth century England could be part of a bequest, its value listed in shillings and pence (King, 1992).

Wastes can be considered a raw material and resource within the framework of (agricultural) primary production. But within the secondary, artisan-dominated urban sector of pre-modern society they are a sanitary problem and a nuisance, often being considered a threat to the aesthetic quality of cities. The economic history of industrialisation includes a history of new qualities of wastes, as well as being characterised by a pronounced increase in the quantity of waste. The economic history of industrial wastes is conceptualised as a history of externalised – and later on partially internalized – costs due to regulatory interventions (Reith, 1998). From the economic historian's perspective, waste neatly fits into the general trend of tertiarisation of the economy. Not the product itself, but the provision of services around it, its orderly disposal, becomes the value-adding factor of a new sector of economy built around wastes in late twentieth-century industrial society. Wastes reflect the general structure of the economy. Looking at them from an economic point of view does not offer fresh insights, but just adds to the general picture.

3.3.2 Waste and Urban History

Urban history is the historical sub-field where references to waste are most abundant. Due to the concentration of manufacturing and consumption in urban areas, the waste problems associated with these activities become apparent earlier than in rural areas. But people in rural settlements also issue regulations out of sanitary and aesthetic concerns. These concerned human excrement, wastes arising from the butchering of animals, dead animals in general, ashes (which were also used in soaps) and items that were considered hazardous waste, such as the straw bedding of a deathbed (Jaritz and Winiwarter 1994; Winiwarter, 2001). In smaller settlements, regulation was easier, dumping space was available and waste needs less regulatory effort. Historians are mainly confined to contested terrain in their sources, as the obvious and easy was usually not written about, at least not as often as the complicated and conflicting. So historians find less material in rural areas. In addition, urban administrations have a tendency to keep written records on more issues, and their archives are better preserved and better known. Therefore, sources on rural waste problems are relatively scarce, but it would be a misconception to think that waste was exclusively an urban problem prior to industrialisation.

The quality and amount of waste depends on the mode of production of a society. Furthermore, the mode of production determines the potential value of wastes. European agricultural economies conceptualised (urban) waste as a problem rather than a resource, because of the relative abundance of animal manure. Agriculture in Europe was dominated by a mixed farming regime, with arable, pasture and grazing animals that served not only as a source of milk, meat and wool, but also as a nutrient pump from grazing ranges to the arable fields. The dung they produced was as valuable a resource as the other products that could be extracted from them. In such circumstances, human excrement from the cities was not considered a prime resource for agriculture. Japanese and Chinese towns, in contrast, relied on the supply of human excrement. Therefore, collection and transportation of nutrients from the cities back to the agricultural areas is economically feasible. Due to the very limited supply of animal manure in their agricultural systems, the rice-growing Asian agriculturalists needed not only to collect human excrement, but also to recycle such materials as oil-cake residues and ashes to fill the nutrient gap. The European solution came at a cost, because the production of manure via animals is an expensive solution in energetic terms. In solar based societies, energy means area, so the area needed to feed one person in Europe was much higher than in Asia, due to the extra area needed to produce animal fodder. Nutrient supply via animals greatly enlarges the social metabolism, as the throughput of cattle and pigs has to be added to that of humans. Enlarging the metabolism on the input side increases output also. More and different materials could be produced, such as parchment from pig skins, woollen undergarments for armour from sheep, etc., but new forms and thus new problems of waste inevitably arose.

Japanese city-dwellers from the sixteenth to the twentieth centuries could sell their excrement with sizeable gains (Hanley, 1987) and they, as well as their Chinese counterparts, did not have to bother about waste disposal (Netting, 1993). Cities in Asia were far more hygienic places than most European ones and water pollution due to faecal matter, one of the recurrent European problems, was almost unknown. Excrement was waste in Europe but recyclable in Asia. Epidemics, life expectancy in cities and demographic patterns, all depended to some degree on how human faeces was conceptualised and dealt with.

European cities became cleaner places with time. Nevertheless, urban wastes are a far more important problem nowadays than ever before, due to the fact that more than half of humankind are city-dwellers these days, and this proportion is still increasing. The major amount of wastes is produced in urban agglomerations nowadays. The urban waste problem becomes even more pressing when the relative scarcity of space for dumps and landfills in densely populated areas is considered.

3.3.3 Waste and Cultural History

The dumping of waste as the accepted solution to the problem should not be considered as a 'natural' way of dealing with wastes. Moving to cultural history we see the changing patterns of human relations to waste interpreted as part of 'The Civilizing Process' (Elias, 1969). The sensory perception of nuisances and its change over time has been researched widely, including recently for Vienna (Payer, 1997). The connection between cleanliness (the absence of dirt and wastes) and social discipline imposed on the lower classes has been a theme of cultural and social history as, e.g. described for Berlin (von Saldern, 1994).

Urban centres (at least in Europe) are cleaner today than they were in the Middle Ages – or dirtier, if one takes a different approach. The problem lies in comparing apples with oranges: The stink of horse-dung in the streets cannot easily be compared with the less perceptible but more toxic motor vehicle exhausts or other industrial air pollutants. What exactly was and is meant by 'clean' changes as well as the material ramifications of waste production, and therefore the perception of a specific treatment as adequate or inadequate also changes.

Cultural anthropology offers insights into different concepts and perceptions of cleanliness, order and dirt, thus enabling one to understand the cultural connotations of waste.

3.4 ORDER, DIRT AND VALUES

On an abstract level, the importance of waste for the analysis of human culture becomes even more apparent. A society's ways of dealing with waste should be considered a central attribute, because the creation of order is a central aim of all cultures and waste is the inevitable by-product of order. Cultural anthropologists have dealt with waste as a cultural category, in particular with the relationship between waste and order.

Mary Douglas, in her 1966 study on 'Purity and Danger', offered two definitions of dirt. The first is a spatial one, defining dirt as 'matter out of place'. This implies that matter does indeed have a 'right' place, it implies some kind of order; dirt is an offence against order. All cultures create order out of the chaos of the primeval world, and cultures can be understood as systems to establish order. Items found in the wrong place, according to the concept of order to which a culture adheres, are considered to be pollutants. To pollute, therefore, can be conceived as a threat to order. Our practices in handling refuse are indebted to this basic idea. Rubbish is a threat to order as long as it has not been dumped into a sanitary landfill. Landfills are considered non-polluted places, as the residue of the social metabolism has found its assigned niche in space there. Why waste sites are considered a 'solution' to the waste problem can be explained with Mary Douglas' idea. Following her, we need to consider landfills as a successful creation of order. This is a cultural achievement, which can explain their acceptance as a solution, despite it being quite clear that to dump material in a designated area is not a 'solution', just a transfer.

Just how threatening an object of 'waste' is, depends on its intrinsic properties. Apart from categories that have come to denote industrial societies' forms of waste, such as radioactive waste, hazardous waste or infectious waste, predominantly one attribute makes wastes a threat; it is their 'stickiness'. Sticky wastes can adhere to objects of value or persons, persistently pollute them and hence threaten the borderlines between the human body and its environment. Threats to the borderline of the human body are the strongest ones in any culture, and crossing them (e.g. with a surgical instrument) is a taboo even in our culture, which still tries to control doctors by having them swear an oath before allowing them to practice. Mary Douglas' suggestion is to take the stickiness into account when studying waste; pieces resulting from tearing a sheet of paper are less nauseating and obscene than wet, sticky or slimy wastes, which pollute the person encountering them. Mary Douglas' two concepts of waste, the spatial and the material-haptic, allow a plausible explanation for the cultural attitudes towards waste that are reflected in waste management policies and technologies (Douglas, 1966).

But Douglas has nothing to offer to help understanding the 'career' of objects, the product cycle of items from 'new' to 'used' to 'waste' and back into the antique shop or newly decorated home. Michael Thompson's 'Rubbish Theory' focuses on this theme (Thompson, 1979). He suggests one differentiate three categories of objects, one of which is hidden. These are the *transient*, the *permanent* and the *hidden*. Most items of everyday use are perishable, transient. Such objects turn into waste when they have reached the threshold of usability. The end of usability can be determined both culturally ('out of fashion') and materially ('broken'). Objects vanish into the rubbish pits and dumps, they are forgotten, and there is no point in discussing them. So waste could be considered the final destination, the output, the culde-sac of matter that has left society. But, Thompson argues, some of the rubbish objects are re-transferred into society by a process of valuation (which runs concurrent with a process of restoration) and are lifted up into the category of the permanent, the enduring. Henceforth they are treated as if their material properties would inherently make them enduring and permanent. But a closer look shows that permanence is mainly a cultural construction. St. Paul's Cathedral is not long-lived because of its construction, but because society is willing to invest a sizeable amount of money in its longevity. Such amounts of money are not invested in other buildings considered to be transient, which renders such buildings dilapidated and moves them into the rubbish category. Some might be elevated from there to reappear again in society as in a painstakingly renovated, fashionable old-building neighbourhood.

Within the hidden category of rubbish each object can undergo two kinds of transitions. It may continue to be rubbish and therefore be destroyed in the end, burnt in an incinerator or be disintegrated by the combined forces of physical and biological agents in a landfill. Alternatively, it can be elevated into permanence and be conserved. Differences between social groups within a society are constituted (partially) by differences in their attitudes towards objects. Some groups tend to interpret the majority of objects as being transient, whereas others rescue objects from rubbish and invest in their permanence. An important part of the dynamic of societies at large can be explained by the transfer of objects between these categories. Studies of culture, according to Thompson, need to focus on rubbish rather than set it aside.

3.5 POSSIBLE WAYS OF DEALING WITH WASTE

This brief history of waste will conclude with a survey of social principles of waste management followed by several paradoxical insights derived from a focus on rubbish. The correct and accepted way of dealing with waste changes with time. It can be considered correct to wait for high water in the adjoining river to empty the privy during the night. It can be considered correct not only to burn rubbish, but to burn it at temperatures that transform the residue into a glassy substance, which is more or less sterile and therefore hygienically acceptable. Who approves of which kind of rubbish management, at what time and place, depends on the concept of nature and of possible dangers subscribed to by those in charge of waste management decisions.

To take a closer look, we need to move from the cursory concept of 'society' that has been used so far, to a more elaborate concept that takes social heterogeneity into account. Groups within a given society differ (also) in the way they deal with waste. We all know those who drink out of an aluminium can in the metro and simply leave the empty can. And we know those who recycle each piece of paper, even if it is the size of a postage stamp, and hold their re-usable linen shopping-bags up as banner of waste minimisation against consumer society. People within every neighbourhood differ greatly in their attitudes to waste, and we can safely assume that societies in the past were not completely uniform either. Dealing with waste is an epitome of our dealing with nature as the 'other' of society in general. Cultural theory, a framework developed by cultural anthropologists, suggests one differentiate (for current societies) between four different concepts and patterns of behaviour: *individualist, egalitarian, hierarchist* and *fatalist*. It should have become clear that one man's waste can be another's treasure. Likewise, the four groups differ in their approaches to waste.

Hierarchists conceive of society as being isomorphic to nature, and as the two are connected like an image and its mirror, pollution is understood as a perturbation of social order mirrored in nature. Polluted natural objects have to be brought back to an orderly condition, and if this is not possible, nature has to be changed to match the new social order. This can be done, as nature is reparable. If acid rain changes lakes into acid, one can add lime to repair the problem. To solve a waste problem, a hierarchist will establish and assign criteria to sort wastes; e.g. write up taxonomic lists of hazardous wastes, detailing the correct handling, legal procedure and licensing of landfills.

Indvidualists subscribe to the original Mary Douglas concept, considering waste as matter in the wrong place. Costs involved in dealing with such misplaced matter will be dealt with by the market, an institution individualists conceive of as the most powerful force for order. Emission certificates and eco-labeling for products that help minimising waste are typical individualist solutions. Eco-labelling, public audits and the like will enable consumers to act as regulators in the market-driven system.

Egalitarians believe that natural laws are rules that apply also to humans. Therefore, society needs to be changed in order to adapt better to nature. Sufficiency, abstinence from consumption, and minimising interventions to nature are the rules that follow from the egalitarian world-view. Waste is a result of the social disorientation of consumer society and waste problems can be solved only by radically changing society.

The three approaches, different as they may be, have something in common, nevertheless. They all suppose that individuals have an ability to learn, and they fundamentally believe in the feasibility of change and order.

Fatalists are convinced that there is nothing to learn, but that there are many things one simply has to cope with, without being able to change them. Fatalists accept risks as inevitable and as they are the ones who do not protest but comply, they are just as relevant for environmental policies as the other groups (Thompson, 1994).

The methods of waste management a society adopts depend on four factors.

- Which of the above groups prevails at a given time.
- Who dominates in power relations.
- How waste management institutions function.

- The prevailing conceptualisation of risk and danger.

Waste management history can be understood by analysing these four factors.

3.6 HIGHLIGHTING DARK SPOTS: A VERY BRIEF HISTORY OF WASTE MANAGEMENT

A comprehensive history of waste, anecdotal rather than analytical, has appeared in German (Hösel, 1987). The new approach taken hereafter is to emphasise the connection between the input and the output of social metabolism in terms of quantity and material qualities. Concepts of danger applied to wastes merit mention also, as they constitute an important ramification for management decisions. The composition and amount of waste depend on the way of life of consumers (Weisz et al., 2001). The same holds true for industry in terms of the methods of manufacture and the perceived state of the art, because wastes are largely dependent on procedures and processes. Communities face an ever-changing mix of materials and substances making up their wastes. Many of the difficulties encountered in waste management are due to the object of regulation being subject to rapid changes, changes that are faster than an administration can handle.

Individuals in European settlements during the Middle Ages washed away a small part of the human excrement they produced in watercourses. Rubbish pits were commonly used for the combined collection of excrement and all other kinds of wastes. Pits used by artisans, such as tanners or butchers, can be identified in the archaeological record due to their different composition, but this is a phenomenon confined to specialised urban quarters (Keene, 1992). The major part of wastes could easily be used as manure, even if this were done only from time to time. Pollution of drinking water due to leaking cesspools was one of the most pertinent problems of waste disposal. Faecal matter was ubiquitous in urban areas, and the stink of the cities would certainly be unbearable to modern noses. Kitchen residues were fed to pigs living in the backyards, and the streets – prior to the fourteenth century mostly unpaved – changed into stinking swamps during rains, with the smell being provided by draught animals' droppings (Dirlmeier, 1986). All of these 'inconveniences' were registered, complained about and even regulated, but not physically dealt with by administrations. Wastes were considered a private affair for a long time.

The miasmatic theory of pollution, originating in antiquity, was revived in the eighteenth century. Its basic idea is that exhalations (called miasmas) are agents and transmitters of diseases. Deodorants were perceived as an adequate solution to hygienic problems in miasmatic theory. In most cases, however, visible, smelly wastes were transferred to designated places, places that quickly became 'banned' and functioned as the perilous living spaces of liminal or outcast individuals or groups (Reid, 1993). The differences between the developments in Germany and the more centralised France have been investigated in detail by Keller (1998).

In the nineteenth century cleanliness, tidiness and order became important objectives of the bourgeoisie. They influenced the waste management practices, which were mainly focused on outward appearance: visible pollutants were battled against, invisible ones were not an issue. A connection was drawn between the purity of water and air and the moral qualities of the inhabitants of quarters; tidiness (under the principle of visibility) was hence considered an important accomplishment in establishing social order.

The history of waste management offers insights into the paradoxical nature of historical developments and changes. Sanitary reform in Southern New England in the nineteenth century offers a case in point. Miasmatic theory led to a public battle against water pollution by industry. For some time, this battle against industrial interests was quite successful, but then miasmatic theory came under considerable scientific pressure by the new bacteriological paradigm. The concept of the inherent danger of wastes changed completely. Stinking pollutants that poisoned fish were no longer considered dangerous; human faecal matter with its content of bacteria became the new culprit. A river totally poisoned by industry and hence completely devoid of fish was considered 'clean' according to the system of order brought about by bacteriological theory. There were no scientific arguments available against chemical pollution; toxicological theories were in their infancy. So, with the aid of the better scientific theory, industrial interests won. For the next decades, communities had to busy themselves with excrement rather than trying to regulate industrial effluents. The scientifically unsound miasmatic theory resulted in a practice much more environmentally sound than the one fostered by bacteriological theory. Only the development of toxicology could in the end change things for the better. One ought to consider the role of scientific knowledge in the conflict between communities and industry in nineteenth century New England as a cautionary tale against wide-eyed belief in the power of natural sciences (Cumbler, 1995; cf. Hamlin, 1990; Hamlin, 1993).

Back to Europe. A history of waste cannot be written without mentioning the year 1842, which saw the publication of Edwin Chadwick's 'Report on The Sanitary Condition of the Labouring Population of Great Britain'. It quickly became the leading authority on sanitary issues for the next decades (ed. Flinn, 1965).

In these decades, more than just the concept of waste changed. Urban domestic waste underwent a profound change with the diffusion of the water closet, as human excrement from now on was washed away into adjacent rivers and streams and no longer constituted part of solid or semi-solid household waste.

Collection and distribution of human excrement on to fields had been less a priority in Europe than in Asia, but the more advanced agricultural operations became, the more pressing became the need for nutrient supply. Agricultural economists received strong support from geostrategic experts, who argued the necessity to feed populations from domestic production, in order not to be vulnerable. Guano, a natural fertiliser from bird droppings mined in Peru and Chile, was imported in increasing quantities to supply European agriculture with nitrogen and phosphorus, while human excrement was lost to the sea. Contemporaries were industrious in devising ways to overcome what was now perceived as a major drawback. To name but one example, a pneumatic system for collection, the Liernur system, was implemented in the Netherlands, but even concentrated urban excrement was too expensive to be a feasible solution (Winiwarter, 2001). The fetid irrigation problem arising from the distribution of sewage sludge on agricultural land would be the next development, proving that urban sewage was a hard-to-handle nutrient carrier (Hamlin, 1994), but around 1900 fertiliser advocates were still quite confident that human excrement could be a valuable resource, if only technical devices could be invented to harvest this nutrient source.

Apart from human excrement, a second major factor determining the composition of waste, is the prevailing kind of domestic heating. Around 1900, residues from room heating, ashes and slag, accounted for 60 per cent of the total weight of domestic waste in Germany. An additional 20 to 25 per cent was organic matter, basically swill and gardening residues, the small remaining amount consisted of paper, cardboard, glass and metals. Most paper and other combustibles were burnt in household stoves. Synthetic organic materials did not yet exist. Therefore domestic waste had a high density (about $0.5 \mathrm{kgL}^{-1}$), and a very low calorific value. In addition, to add to technical problems, domestic waste composition fluctuated seasonally. According to early twentieth century sources, the German town of Aachen produced daily about 0.6 kg per capita. New York inhabitants around the same time produced 1.5 kg per capita daily (Keller, 1998).

The decades around 1900 saw a fierce battle between municipal politicians from urban areas and their immediate hinterland. The choice was between hygienically sound waste treatment by incineration, the urban solution, versus recycling of wastes after sorting, including the use of the organic matter (not human faeces, but compostable organic matter) as manure, the solution advocated by rural community leaders. The battle between the advocates of nutrients versus those of calories and hygiene as the main concern, was still going on while dramatic changes in waste quantity and composition were underway. The new food processing industry developed, delivering preserved foods and the first ready-made foodstuffs to households, to meet the needs of the families of factory workers. Changing eating habits changed waste composition, and glass and metal content increased. Farmers, who had been able to use the greater part of urban wastes as fertiliser on their land until the end of the nineteenth century, saw a deterioration of waste quality. Scraps of metal and splinters of glass constituted a threat to draught animals on the fields. Outbreaks of cholera, a result of drinking water pollution by faecal matter in German towns, changed the perception of waste mainly into a threat to hygiene.

Consequently, incineration euphoria characterises the next period in waste management history. The first incinerators were built in England around 1870, with more than 200 in operation in 1904. Sorting and recycling (which included fertiliser) versus burning seemed to be the two options for German towns. But by the later 1910s the landfill, the cheap alternative to incineration, had silently been adopted in the majority of towns, an option the earlier discussion had never even considered (Lindemann, 1992).

Urbanisation in the United States set in at a later date. Therefore, developments were different from those in Europe, as Martin Melosi has shown in his studies. US communities could build their own waste policies on British experience, and scientific theories on contagious diseases were already more advanced. Some of the cities in the US were therefore able to avoid the pitfalls encountered by European municipal administrations (Melosi, 1981; Melosi, 2000).

The two World Wars led to an economy of scarcity during which the waste issue almost disappeared. Everything that could be recycled was recycled. Incineration was close to impossible, as domestic heating had returned to pre-industrial customs, leaving almost no combustible material in the waste bins.

In Germany, the scarcity of raw materials of all kinds led to a policy of recycling. National Socialist organisations were successful in campaigning against wasteful living. Like many other National Socialist policies, the waste collection was over-administered and, as in other cases, the Nazi government had expelled the Jewish population which had previously been in charge of the recycling sector. Scrap and rummage merchant shops, which had had a wide network of collectors at their command, were shut down and Nazi administrators had to set up new structures to perform their tasks. The greatest problem in collection and sorting was the ever-increasing shortage of labour. Only by drawing on school pupils could the system be maintained during the war years. Schools administered collection programmes, schoolyards functioned as collection centres, and a system of pressures and incentives ensured the efficiency of pupils as collectors (Huchting, 1981).

After World War II, the German Democratic Republic installed a system of recycling that is considered exemplary from today's point of view. Resource scarcity led to an emphasis on collection and recycling. Although detailed studies on this topic are still absent, one can safely assume that the GDR planned its system drawing on National Socialist collection and recycling systems as the model.

'Bulky household waste' as a distinct category is relatively new, found in Germany no earlier than 1970. With the diffusion of a consumer society lifestyle, large items such as old furniture were regularly discarded en masse and, as Michael Thompson pointed out, would be partially re-inserted into the economy as durable, pertinent, valuable goods via the fleamarket, the second-hand store and later the antique shop. Christian Pfister and others have described what they call the 1950s syndrome, the increase in private consumption and the full diffusion of consumer-oriented lifestyle. This increase in goods can be traced not only on the input side, but also by looking at output (Pfister, 1995). Garbage archaeology opens a way to look at our material culture from the bottom up, and results have been impressive (Rathje and Murphy, 1992).

The 1950s syndrome brought about not only increasing amounts of waste, but also a change in kind. A variety of synthetic materials, from shopping bags to tights and flowerpots, became abundant in domestic waste in the next decades. Together with the increasing amount of paper in the waste bin, they made a renaissance of incineration possible, as wastes then contained enough combustible materials.

For the first time in history, chlorinated hydrocarbons, like the commonly known and widely used PVC (polyvinyl chloride), became part of domestic waste, creating a new environmental hazard when burnt, namely Dioxin. The hazardous waste incinerator, the epitome of end-of-the-pipe technology, can also serve as an example to look into the inner logic of the recent history of waste management; it is costly, and only a partial solution. Communities have to face NIMBY (Not In My Back Yard) activists preventing them from building the needed facilities. Siting has become the most difficult part of erecting a facility. The residual clinker is incombustible hazardous waste that needs to be stored safely, and prevented from entering biogeochemical cycles. And the economically feasible solution that has been developed is debatable and disputed as well. Instead of having to pay for the dumping on a suitable sanitary landfill, the residues can be 'recycled', as the advocates of the idea will have it, to be used as filling material in abandoned mines. This procedure is not considered 'dumping', therefore not regulated as heavily and is thus much cheaper. 'Bergversatz', the German term, has not yet found an English translation, but the practice will probably spread.

3.7 CONCLUSION

Waste management is a tedious but important job, and a growing part of the tertiary sector of the economy. Regulations often lag behind waste developments, and in some cases green rhetoric is used to cover up dirty secrets. The solution to the waste problem lies on the input side of society, where its causes lie. This will require a general re-design of social metabolism. Such changes are unlikely, but not impossible; to bring them about, co-operation is inevitably needed. Any feasible solution will need the combined efforts of regulating hierarchists, economising individualists, concerned egalitarians and fatalists willing to live with waste treatment facilities in their backyard.

The development of waste law is dealt with in Chapter 6. As legal regulations are one form of representation of collective perception, they are valuable sources for the cultural connotations of waste, and for most of history the most widely available and abundant sources for a history of waste. The development of ordinances and laws often lags behind social reality, as has been pointed out. But the legal system can serve as an indicator for society at large in terms of conceptualisation of the world, and especially the environment. The German laws regulating wastes are no longer called waste laws, but are part of a larger body called circular flow economy laws; 'Gesetz zur Förderung der Kreislaufwirtschaft und Sicherung der umweltverträglichen Beseitigung von Abfällen', in effect since 1996 (Ormond, 1998). The concept of waste in these texts is that of a 'special case', not the inevitable outcome in an economy that minimises their use of natural sinks. Changes in concept have been important for changes in practice throughout waste history, as has been outlined above. Whether the circular flow concept will be successful in guiding new practices has yet to be determined, but in the distant future the OED might well contain a note in its article 'waste' that the term has gone out of use with a pointer to words like 'recyclable', 'circular flow products' or others beyond the imagination of the wasteful historian of the twentieth century consumer society.

REFERENCES

Cumbler, J.T. (1995), 'Whatever happened to industrial waste? Reform, compromise, and science in nineteenth century southern New England' *Journal of Social History*, **29**, 149-71.

Dirlmeier, U. (1986), 'Zu den Lebensbedingungen in der mittelalterlichen Stadt: Trinkwasserversorgung und Abfallbeseitigung', in B. Herrmann (ed.), *Mensch und Umwelt im Mittelalter*, Stuttgart: dva, pp. 150-59.

Douglas, M. (1966), *Purity and Danger*, London: Routledge.

Elias, N. (1969), *Über den Prozess der Zivilisation. Soziogenetische und psychogenetische Untersuchungen*, Frankfurt: Suhrkamp.

Fischer-Kowalski, M. and H. Haberl (1993), *Metabolism and Colonization. Modes of Production and the Physical Exchange between Societies and Nature*, IFF-Schriftenreihe Soziale Ökologie **32**, Vienna: Department of Social Ecology.

Fischer-Kowalski, M. and H. Weisz (1999), 'Society as hybrid between material and symbolic realms: towards a theoretical framework of society-nature interaction', *Advances in Human Ecology*, **8**, 215-51.

Flinn, M.W. (ed.) and E. Chadwick (1965), *Report on The Sanitary Condition of the Labouring Population of Great Britain (1842)*, Edinburgh: Edinburgh University Press.

Hamlin, C. (1990), *A Science of Impurity. Water Analysis in Nineteenth Century Britain*, Berkeley: University of California Press.

Hamlin, C. (1993), 'Between knowledge and action: themes in the history of environmental chemistry', in S.H. Mauskopf (ed.), *Chemical Sciences in the Modern World*, Philadelphia: University of Pennsylvania Press, pp. 295-321.

Hamlin, C. (1994), 'Environmental sensibility in Edinburgh, 1839-1840: the "Fetid Irrigation" controversy', *Journal of Urban History*, **20** (3), 311-39.

Hanley, S.B. (1987), 'Urban sanitation in preindustrial Japan', *Journal of Interdisciplinary History*, **18** (1), 1-26.

Hösel, G. (1987), *Unser Abfall aller Zeiten. Eine Kulturgeschichte der Städtereinigung*, München: Kommunalschriften-Verlag J.Jehle.

Huchting, F. (1981), 'Abfallwirtschaft im Dritten Reich', *Technikgeschichte*, **48** (3), 252-73.

Jaritz, G. and V. Winiwarter (1994), 'Wasser. Zu den historischen Mustern eines Problembewußtseins. Annäherungen anhand der historischen Umweltdatenbank Österreichs' *Mitteilungen des Niederösterreichischen Landesmuseums*, **8**, 163-74.

Keene, D. (1982), 'Rubbish in medieval towns', in A.R. Hall and H.K. Kenward (eds), *Environmental Archaeology in the Urban Context* (Research Report No. 43), Council for British Archaeology: London, pp. 26-30.

Keller, R. (1998), *Müll - die gesellschaftliche Konstruktion des Wertvollen. Die öffentliche Diskussion über Abfall in Deutschland und Frankreich*, Opladen/Wiesbaden: Westdeutscher Verlag.

King, W. (1992),'How high is too high? Disposing of dung in seventeenth-century Prescot', *Sixteenth Century Journal*, **23** (3), 443-57.

Lindemann, C. (1992), 'Verbrennung oder Verwertung: Müll als Problem um die Wende vom 19. zum 20. Jahrhundert', *Technikgeschichte*, **59** (2), 91-107.

Kuchenbuch, L. (1989), 'Abfall. Eine stichwortgeschichtliche Erkundung' in J. Calließ, J. Rüsen and M. Strignitz (eds.), *Mensch und Umwelt in der Geschichte* (*Geschichtsdidaktik* **5**), Pfaffenweiler: Centaurus, pp. 257-76

Melosi, M.V. (1981), *Garbage in the Cities. Refuse, Reform and the Evironment, 1880-1980*, Chicago: The Dorsey Press.

Melosi, M.V. (1988), 'Technology diffusion and refuse disposal: the case of the British Destructor', in J.A. Tarr and G. Dupuy (eds.), *Technology and the Rise of the Networked City in Europe and America*, Philadelphia: Temple University Press, pp. 207-25.

Melosi, M.V. (2000), *The Sanitary City. Urban Infrastructure in America from Colonial Times to the Present*, Baltimore: Johns Hopkins University Press.

Netting, R.M. (1993), *Smallholders, Householders. Farm Families and the Ecology of Intensive, Sustainable Agriculture*, Stanford: Stanford University Press.

Ormond, Th. (1998), 'Der Kreislauf des Abfallrechts', *Forum historiae iuris*, http://data.rewi.hu-berlin.de/FHI/articles/9810ormond.htm (26-01-02).

Payer, P. (1997), *Der Gestank von Wien. Über Kanalgase, Totendünste und andere üble Geruchskulissen*, Wien: Döcker.

Pfister, Ch. (1995), 'Das 1950er Syndrom - Die umweltgeschichtliche Epochenschwelle zwischen Industriegesellschaft und Konsumgesellschaft', in J. Sieglerschmidt (ed), *Der Aufbruch ins Schlaraffenland. Stellen die Fünfziger Jahre eine Epochenschwelle im Mensch-Umwelt-Verhältnis dar?* (Special Issue 2), Environmental History Newsletter: Mannheim, 28-71.

Rathje, W. and C. Murphy (1992), *Rubbish! The Archaeology of Garbage*, New York: Harper Collins.

Reid, D. (1993), *Paris Sewers and Sewermen. Realities and Representation*, Harvard: Harvard University Press.

Reith, R. (1998), Internalisierung der externen Effekte. Konzepte der Umweltgeschichte und die Wirtschaftsgeschichte, in G. Bayerl and W. Weber (eds), *Sozialgeschichte der Technik. Ulrich Toitzsch zum 60. Geburtstag (Cottbuser Studien zur Geschichte von Technik, Arbeit und Umwelt 7)*, Münster: Waxmann, pp. 15-24.

Von Saldern, A. (1994), 'Wie säubere ich einen Linoleumboden?', in Berliner Geschichtswerkstatt (ed.), *Alltagskultur, Subjektivitaet und Geschichte: zur Theorie und Praxis von Alltagsgeschichte*, Münster: Westfaelisches Dampfboot, pp. 235-53.

Tarr, J.A. and G. Dupuy (1988), *Technology and the Rise of the Networked City in Europe and America*, Philadelphia: Temple University Press.

Tarr, J.A. (1994), 'Searching for a "sink" for an industrial waste: iron making fuels and the environment', *Environmental History Review*, **18** (1), 9-24.

Tarr, J.A. (1996), *The Search for the Ultimate Sink. Urban Pollution in Historical Perspective*, Akron, OH: University of Akron Press.

Thompson, M. (1979), *Rubbish Theory. The Creation and Destruction of Value*, Oxford: Oxford University Press.

Thompson, M. (1994), 'Blood, sweat and tears. Guest editorial', *Waste Management and Research* **12**, 199-205.

Weisz, H., M. Fischer-Kowalski, C. Grünbühel, H. Haberl, F. Krausmann and V. Winiwarter (2001), 'Global environmental change and historical transitions', *Innovation: The European Journal of Social Science Research*, **14** (2), 117-42.

Winiwarter, V. (2001), 'Where did all the waters go? The introduction of sewage systems in urban settlements', in C. Bernhardt (ed.), *Environmental Problems in European Cities in the 19th and 20th Century (Cottbuser Studien zur Geschichte von Technik, Arbeit und Umwelt 14)*, Münster: Waxmann, pp. 105-19.

NOTES

1   The work for this chapter was conducted during a Hertha Firnberg research fellowship of the Austrian Science Foundation, Grant No. T-45-HIS. Suggestions and corrections by Herwig Weigl and John R. McNeill, as well as by the editors, are gratefully acknowledged.

PART TWO

Waste Policy

4.   Attitudes to Waste

Katy Bisson

4.1 INTRODUCTION

It is well documented that more integrated and sustainable waste management systems are needed (DETR, 2001). A number of EU and national level
objectives are in place to divert waste from unsustainable landfill to other
management methods, such as incineration, recycling and waste reduction.
However, there are barriers to the more sustainable practices of recycling and
reduction, including:

- market failure, where the prices of goods do not match their environmental resource value;
- government failure, where the policies in place encourage inefficient and
  unsustainable practices; and
- institutional or societal failure, where a lack of public awareness blocks a
  move towards more pro-environmental behaviour.

This chapter looks at the area where government and institutional failure
overlap. Here, it is necessary to understand the public's attitudes to waste, as
this is critical in raising public awareness. The two arenas of failure need to
be developed hand-in-hand, as raising awareness without providing an
adequate infrastructure will not produce the much-needed increase in recycling rates. What are needed are both a more motivated society and an
infrastructure to facilitate the behaviours they may wish to exhibit.

So far, rather little is known about the factors that influence waste management behaviour. As a consequence, we need to understand the behaviours
that produce waste; the reasoning behind actions such as recycling and waste
reduction; and the reasons for the opposition to certain aspects of waste
management, so as to achieve more acceptable, sustainable waste management policies.

This chapter will discuss both negative and positive attitudes to waste and its management. Section 4.2 will discuss negative attitudes to waste, such as feelings and actions of opposition to waste management facilities and explore the concept of 'NIMBY', questioning whether it alone is sufficient to explain oppositional attitudes and behaviours. Section 4.3 explores positive attitudes to waste, in particular the extrinsic and intrinsic motivations behind such actions as recycling and reduction, and possible facilitators and barriers to such activities. Sections 4.4 and 4.5 discuss the importance of understanding attitudes to waste, the various discourses on waste, and analyse the various qualitative and quantitative methods used to uncover attitudes to waste. Finally, one particular method of examining attitudes is discussed, not only in relation to waste but also to other areas of environmental policy and ecological economics.

4.2 NEGATIVE ATTITUDES TO WASTE

The disposal of waste poses important challenges. As the shift away from landfill continues and we move towards more recycling, reuse and reduction, there arises a need for more facilities, such as recycling plants and 'Energy from Waste' plants. Therefore, the public will become more involved in such matters, as they will have to bear more of the costs of waste management, such as closer involvement in recycling through source separation. Also, there will be more opportunities and incentives to take part in reuse and reduction schemes. There is already a degree of public awareness about waste disposal, recycling programmes and the presence of waste disposal facilities. Disposal awareness has been heightened by an increased awareness of general environmental issues and by popular media accounts of community concerns towards waste facility siting. With the increased need for such facilities, there will need to be not only a raised public awareness of waste management, but also a higher degree of public confidence, especially in safety, justification and fairness.

4.2.1 Opposition to Waste Facilities

Public opposition to waste disposal facilities, especially towards landfill sites, stems from a number of attitudinal variables. The source of this opposition has been often characterised as 'Not In My Back Yard'[1] (NIMBY), which stems from people within the host community perceiving an imbalance between the benefits they will receive as hosts, and the costs they will have to bear. Communities may voice concerns over physical dangers, environmental impacts, aesthetic effects, a drop in property values, and facility control.

Opposition therefore occurs when the community is reluctant to accept the perceived risks and costs, especially if they seem to be unable to influence the decision.

NIMBY concerns are rational and need to be addressed through open, personal dialogue at the early planning stages of a facility's development, so as to avoid a lack of knowledge fuelling the public's perception that the risks are unreasonably (and unrealistically) high. Risk perception and risk communication are fairly new areas of research and in the past, with regard to waste, have dealt with public opposition to hazardous and industrial facilities. Opposition has often been misinterpreted as people fearing what they do not understand, with 'experts' knowing the real risks and the public overestimating them. Therefore, early risk communication focused on convincing the public that the risks were low and could be reduced further by predictable and controllable technology and science (Beder and Shortland, 1992, p. 154). Meanwhile, environmentalists portrayed a view of technology as being unpredictable and uncontrollable and the media, not being able to discern who was correct, dwelt on this polarisation and conflict, and so opposition continued (ESART, 2001). NIMBY, wrongly therefore, has come to symbolise an irrational response of the general public, rather than the multiplicity of reasons why people may not want a facility in their locality.

If it is assumed that not all of the stakeholders can evaluate real risks, then one of two types of risk communication may be employed. One type is based on the rationalist 'information deficit model' (Owens, 2000, p. 1141), where the aim is to convince the public to accept something which they think they do not want. The second form of risk communication gives all of the stakeholders sufficient information so that they may readily understand and take part in decision-making. The first method imparts knowledge and this, while worthwhile for its own sake, does not necessarily lead to an acceptance of the proposed scheme. In fact, this method can lead to a distrust of scientists and experts, as they often appear to be merely engaging in a public relations exercise. In this approach, the public are frequently regarded as a homogeneous group, who simply need to be better informed so that they may change their opinions to more 'objective points of view'. But while the public may not understand all of the scientific complexities, they do understand 'the complexities of commercial imperatives, are sceptical about politics and distrustful of the competence and impartiality of regulatory frameworks' (ESART, 2001, p. 18).

The second method, however, avoids 'expert monopolies of information' and tries to ensure that all affected groups are equally represented, and that no one has dominance, thus facilitating the achievement of a consensus through a fair process with justifiable outcomes. Problems should be framed to encompass human behaviour rather than simply 'science', and to involve experiences or the potential for personal impact (Thompson and Rayner, 1998). Therefore, to impart an understanding of the science alone is not enough to resist opposition. As Beder and Shortland (1992, p. 148) state:

> ... the debate over risks ... has tended to focus on technical factors and neglect social and political factors ... (this) to some extent reflects the desire of governments and experts to limit debate to areas that give mainstream groups the advantage over their opposition in terms of access to information and public credibility.

Unless policies are sensitive to the everyday contexts in which individual attitudes and behaviours are situated, policies are unlikely to produce the desired effects. When changes in behaviour are needed, new knowledge is not enough, as the constraints on the capacity for effective action, for example the cultural norm of consumption, are not amenable to simple fixes (Owens, 2000, p. 1146).

4.2.2 NIMBY or NIABY?

The NIMBY model has been shown only partially to explain public behaviour and attitudes. There have also been examples of exceptions to NIMBY, such as NIABY, 'not-in-*anyone's*-back-yard' (Lober and Green, 1994, p. 34). NIABY suggests that not only do some people not want a facility near to them, but they feel that it should not be constructed anywhere. This suggests that there may be a wider variety of variables influencing attitudes than just self-interest. Empirical studies have investigated the relationship between distance from the facility and opposition (Lindell and Earle, 1983), the perception of need rather than desire for compensation alone, issues of self-interest and individualistic values, and the perception of risk (Slovic, 1987).

When faced with the possibility of a 'locally-undesirable-land-use', or 'LULU', the public, especially the host community, is likely (almost by definition) to be in opposition. The public's perception of risk, however, seems to be far greater than that supported by the evidence supplied by science, risk assessments, policy makers and government. The perception and acceptance of risk depend on many factors, such as:

- social and cultural factors (Slovic, 1987, p. 281);
- whether the risk is old, or new and therefore not well known;
- whether the hosts are uncertain, or feeling threatened due to lack of knowledge; and
- the demographic characteristics of the host community, such as their age, sex, education and employment.

Some hold that community opposition reflects exaggerated fears, such as contamination of ground and surface water, nuisance from litter, traffic and visual intrusion, and the devaluation of property. Fears seem increased by closer proximity to the facility, as citizens see unwanted effects dissipated with distance.

When considering how to effect useful and appropriate policies for siting waste disposal facilities, one can consider incentives. An incentive refers to a 'strategy which involves a compensatory offering (the stimulus) to an individual, group, or region in exchange for consent to site and operate a disposal facility' (Bacot et al., 1994, p. 231). As Inhaber (1992, p. 57) discusses, incentives should not be regarded as bribery, which is usually in pursuit of an illegal act, is always done secretly and is always targeted. In contrast, incentives would lead to socially approved action and would be publicly and widely made. Incentives may be economic, involving money for education or infrastructure or direct tax credits, or they may be operational, allowing citizen participation. People's attitudes may be influenced by self-interest and concerns of equity in their share of costs and benefits, so incentives may succeed. However, as Portney (1985, p. 88) illustrates, if people's assessment of risk is underestimated, then economic incentives will hold little bargaining power. Financial compensation alone may underestimate the magnitude of people's assessed risk, as these might be be so great that virtually no reasonable amount of compensation can have a significant impact.

If citizens have fears over waste facility siting, then attempting to overcome these perceived fears may mitigate the opposition. There needs to be consideration given to the fact that economic incentives alone may not be enough. Attitudes may be altered *ex post*, especially if the actual experience of the facility does not match the expectations (Okeke and Armour, 2000, p. 151). However, while the attitudes to the facility *ex post* are a function of the experience of operation, attitudes *ex ante* are a function of the expected outcomes. Such expected outcomes may be 'context-related', being defined by the background within which the siting of the waste facility is to take place. This may include the environmental and historical context in which policies operate. It can also include familiarity and perceptions of need, which may reflect familiarity with the technology or the facility.

The attitudinal variables may also be 'process-related', where they are associated with the process of the siting and often include trust. This may be trust of institutions, of central or local government, of private companies, and even perceptions of fairness during the process. Trust influences people's perception of fairness and so procedural equity is an important consideration, whether it is in self-interest, that is for more benefits, or whether it is relational, that is, affecting group status (Lober, 1995).

Many NIMBY disputes feature conflict of one sort or another. The conflict may be between different parties over the conceptualisation of the risk, or over conflicting values. It is important to establish exactly what the conflict is about. Conflict may arise from misconceptions, such as 'displaced conflict', where the parties fail to identify the real reasons for their differences. Alternatively, the source of conflict could be 'false conflict', where there is no objective basis for rejection; this may be rectified with information or education (Focht and Lawler, 2000, p. 107).

4.3 POSITIVE ATTITUDES

Little is known about the factors that influence waste management behaviour and how individuals' attitudes affect this behaviour. However, there has been a growing body of research on attitudes to 'environmentally significant behaviour', 'pro-environmental behaviour' and 'environmentally responsible behaviour'. Such research focuses on the factors that may influence attitudes and behaviour, such as the characteristics of the recycler, possible influences on recycling behaviour, such as the costs and benefits, and barriers to recycling.

4.3.1 Environmentally Significant Behaviour

There are various types of 'environmentally significant behaviour'. One may be such that it directly causes an environmental change, for the better or worse, such as toxic waste dumping. Another may 'shape the context in which choices are made that directly cause environmental change' (Stern, 2000, p. 408), such as supporting policies, willingness to pay for environmental protection or committed activism. Both of these types of environmentally significant behaviour are 'impact-orientated' and can make a large difference to the environment. Other types of environmentally significant behaviour are 'intent-orientated' and, as Stern (2000, p. 409) describes, these may include 'private-sphere environmentalism', such as purchasing recycled goods. These behaviours will have a large impact on the environment only in the aggregate.

Interventions to change environmentally significant behaviour must take account of the various types of behaviour and the many possible influencing variables. Many environmentally significant behaviours are matters of habit and routine, or are affected by income. Some people may act in a pro-environmentally manner without the intent, such as being keen to save money rather than resources. On the other hand, some may intend to act pro-environmentally but may not achieve the desired impact, for example recycling without appropriate segregation. Therefore, pro-environmental predisposition not only depends on the pro-environmental attitude, but also on the actor and the context. Pro-environmental attitudinal variables may include beliefs, morals, personal capabilities or outside influences, such as incentives or support. Some of these variables therefore relate to the actor (intrinsic) and others to the context (extrinsic).

4.3.2 Intrinsic and Extrinsic Factors

Recent research has studied the roles of motives in recycling and waste reduction behaviour. Studies on the motives behind waste reduction are relatively few; however, the motivations which have been identified include:

- factors influencing purchase decisions;
- altruistic feelings for society and the environment; and
- 'future orientation', i.e. the extent to which people are concerned for the future and its association with the actions people take in the present (Ebreo and Vining, 2001, p. 427).

It should be noted that there are significant differences between waste reduction and recycling as activities, and also between their antecedents and correlates. Recycling activities are familiar to people while waste reduction is not so familiar, nor is it so frequently practised. Waste reduction is also altruistic behaviour. Therefore, to appeal to people to reduce their waste, in campaigns one needs to focus on promoting and emphasising the environmental justifications and concerns for the future (Ebreo and Vining, 2001).

Many studies have examined the motivations behind reduction and, even more, recycling, both in terms of extrinsic and intrinsic means. Extrinsic means may include behavioural intervention, especially in the initiation of a new behaviour, while intrinsic motivations may involve encouraging people to initiate and maintain environmentally responsible behaviour.

4.3.3 Intrinsic Motivations

It is often considered that people decide to recycle after 'weighing up the pros and cons', comparing the gains of recycling against the efforts required. However, it is more likely that the main attitude is based on morality (Thogersen, 1996) and so one should appeal to people's intrinsic values and beliefs. As the environment is a public good, altruistic motives are needed for individuals to act significantly[2]. Intrinsic factors, that is variables internal to the individual, may then include a sense of morality (Van Liere and Dunlap, 1978; Thogersen, 1996), where an agent holds concern for the welfare of others, or values fairness and justice. Intrinsic factors also include responsibility, (Arbuthnot et al., 1977; Granzin and Olsen, 1991), frugality, 'making a difference' (De Young, 1986), and personal satisfaction in avoiding waste. Such behaviour may arise from a need to conform to social expectations or traditional behaviour.

Environmental attitudes, values, perceptions and knowledge are also considered intrinsic motivations, whether they concern the general environment or are specific to the waste problem. Environmental attitudes may be related to the environment in general or to the waste problem specifically, although it is often the case that attitudes are specific, and so should be targeted as such. Personal value is also an important intrinsic motivator, whether it is valuing frugality, prosperity or simply collective action (De Young, 1986). Perception can also influence behaviour, sometimes in a negative way; for example, the perception of the difficulties involved in recycling, such as cost and effort. Finally, knowledge is also an important intrinsic motivator; that is, knowledge via awareness or from the receipt of information.

4.3.4 Extrinsic Motivations

Extrinsic factors associated with recycling that have been (weakly) identified include socio-demographic variables (income, age, gender, education, home-ownership) (Vining and Ebreo, 1990; Oskamp et al., 1991; Margai, 1997). Margai (1997, p. 772) proposes that well-educated families from suburban homes are more likely to recycle, while Oskamp et al. (1991, p. 515) discuss the importance of owning one's own home, and living in a single family house, on the relative ease of recycling. Chung and Poon (1996, pp. 215-24), found that while most people support the idea of waste recycling, the participation rate is lower. However, this rate is higher among certain groups, for example housewives, who are more aware of the possible recyclable proportion of household waste, and are more likely to be the person to perform the task.

Situational variables also influence behaviour; antecedents may be prompts and incentives, while consequences may be rewards and punishments (Schultz et al., 1995). Incentives and prompts have been seen to influence recycling behaviour (Hopper and Nielsen, 1991) although they do not create long-lasting behavioural changes (De Young, 1986). Although intrinsic motivations (such as altruism or environmental concern) may be significant reasons for recycling, especially if basic economic and survival needs have been met, non-recyclers would find convenience and monetary rewards to be important influences on their behaviour, especially as a stimulus to beginning recycling (De Young, 1990, p. 72). Studies have shown, however, that changes in behaviour do not last when an economic incentive is withdrawn (De Young, 1986). So for long-term changes in behaviour, incentives need to be ongoing. It should not be assumed that general environmental concern will lead to recycling, and so campaigns should be focused directly on recycling, rather than on environmental consciousness. Margai (1997, p. 773) suggests that participation in source reduction and other activities 'exists in almost every demographic group if the resource needs, capabilities and concerns are understood'.

The correlation between intention and actual behaviour is often low; perhaps suggesting that while people *mean to be* environmentally responsible, there is a discrepancy between this and the recycling they actually perform. A major source of pressure on individuals' recycling behaviour may include social pressures, either by encouraging dialogue or changing attitudes (Tucker, 1999, p. 63). Recycling by friends and neighbours influences recycling, especially in stimulating participation in kerbside recycling programmes (Oskamp et al., 1991, p. 517). Hopper and Nielsen (1991) discuss how positive social pressures can enhance community recycling, and how negative influences could prevent recycling behaviour, even if the attitudes are favourable. People will recycle more when they are exposed to behavioural modification techniques, but this stimulus is often insufficient to sustain behaviour.

4.3.5 Internal and External Facilitators and Barriers

Facilitators enable one to recycle. Internal facilitators include the awareness of the importance of recycling, and so related barriers may, for example, involve consumer ignorance and the perception of recycling as inconvenient. External facilitators and barriers may include the time, money and effort needed to store and transport material for recycling. If the common facilitators and barriers are recognised, then suitable strategies may be adopted, tackling internal barriers through education and improving the social image of recycling. Barriers to recycling need to be minimised, even if there are sufficient incentives in place, to avoid sporadic recycling or deflection from recycling.

Thogersen (1996, pp. 558-59) suggests that recycling may depend on social norms (external) in the introductory phase and on personal norms (internal) after recycling has been in effect for a longer period. He further suggests that if an economic incentive is offered to compensate for the costs associated with recycling behaviour, the 'framing of the behaviour in the mind of the actor may change in a way that weakens or destroys the moral obligation'. One must identify the root of people's incentives and barriers to recycling to avoid assuming the nature of their environmental behaviour.

4.4 ATTITUDES AND ENVIRONMENTAL POLICY

Many factors have been identified that influence individuals' attitudes and behaviour. Internal motivations depend on altruism and, as such, are long-lived, being sustained by the self, whereas utilitarian incentives are more short-lived. Guagnano et al. (1995, p. 699) suggest that instead of trying to view individuals as either internally or externally motivated agents, the influencing variables should be integrated. By emphasising either internal interventions, such as education, or external interventions, such as regula-tions or taxes, policies may inevitably 'fall short because they neglect the critical insights provided by the other perspective'.

Some research suggests that trying to change environmental attitudes is futile, for several reasons. Firstly, attitudes are deep-rooted traits, and the link between attitudes and behaviour is quite weak, as shown by the difference between attitudes to recycling and the actual participation rates. More im-portantly, however, the change needs to be made at a 'higher' level; that is, at the institutional or governmental level, rather than a personal or individual level. As Stern (2000, pp. 407-24) suggests, it is important to tackle both the social infrastructure and individual attitudes, by providing methods of facili-tating people's desires to act in pro-environmental ways.

Effective behavioural change may occur if there is a combination of the following intervention types:

- moral appeals to values, to change beliefs;
- education and information, to change attitudes; and
- changes in incentives, to affect expectations and behaviour.

At the local level, policies need to appreciate the public's attitudes towards recycling and promote strategies that will allow participation to 'make a difference'. Such strategies should involve the presence of an initial motiva-tion, a method to enhance already-existing participation, the provision of information to change misconceptions, and the presentation of reasons for commitment.

4.5 INVESTIGATING ATTITUDES TO WASTE

Waste has historically been considered with a negative connotation, as something that needs to be disposed of. More recently, there has been a contextual shift in how we view waste, from a disregard of waste to the recognition of its health implications, to the acceptance of the need to collect and process waste. As Redclift (1996, pp. 146-47) discusses, the language we use to describe waste and its management provides an indication of the value we place on waste. The processes that cause the production of wastes, and the capacity of the environment to act as a 'sink' for such wastes, are embodied in our language, our ways of thinking and our actions. We may deny the connection between our actions and the consequences, because we do not wish to see them. We try to avoid changes in the social behaviour that drives the production of waste. The waste disposal options in place often do not require substantial change in consumer behaviour, nor do they require reorganisation of the infrastructure at the household, commercial, industrial or waste management level (Redclift, 1996, p. 154). Reactive solutions, such as Energy from Waste, have certain advantages compared to landfilling, such as gains in space, but they do not solve the inherent problems of the production of waste.

The waste crisis is perhaps due to the part played by human behaviour often being ignored, and waste being seen as something that is spontaneously generated, not as something that we generate as part of our lifestyle. Waste cannot be successfully understood, managed or legislated, if it is separated from the behaviours that produce it. We need not only accurate, objective data on waste production, and scientific data on waste management, but also information on behaviour and attitudes, because waste is the product of human behaviour.

4.5.1 Discourses on Waste

A discourse is a way of seeing and talking about something (Dryzek, 1990). For example, waste may be regarded by some as an environmental problem which may be easily 'solved' by small personal actions. Others may see waste as something beyond their control. While others may regard waste as unimportant when compared to other environmental issues, such as global warming. Therefore, a discourse is a set of attitudes on a particular topic. It is individual and subjective, and may change over time, yet a discourse may also be shared between individuals.

4.5.2 The Methods Employed to Understand Waste Discourses

Attitudes are often explored through qualitative research methods, such as interviews, or quantitative research methods, such as surveys and questionnaires; however, there may be problems with both methods. Attitudes may be difficult to communicate, and even if qualitative interviews generate useful information from discussions, this is not always amenable to rigorous statistical methods. Conversely, quantitative questionnaires and survey analysis are statistically rigorous but they do not really *explore attitudes*; rather they explore how people respond to certain questions. Here, researchers may (inadvertently) impose their own attitudes, by guiding respondents with loaded questions. An alternative to these approaches is *Q Methodology*, which involves a combination of both qualitative and quantitative research analysis. It openly examins individuals' subjectivity, while maintaining a quantitative aspect with statistical procedures to examine the discourses revealed.

4.5.3 Q Methodology

Q methodology[3] seeks to identify attitudes, by providing a way to study the subjectivity of individuals (i.e. their points of view), with a combination of both qualitative and quantitative research analysis. It involves both the examination of subjectivity and the use of rigorous statistical procedures, in this case correlation and factor analysis.

There are many differences between Q Methodology and more usual questionnaire or survey analysis, the fundamental difference being that Q has a distinct approach to measurement. More specifically, it does not use measures pre-specified by the researcher, nor does it require large numbers of participants to achieve valid results. The range of attitudinal topics that can be studied using Q methodology is almost unlimited, but typical examples include representations of social objects (selves, others); understandings (social issues, cultural artefacts); and policies and strategies (e.g. towards social issues).

> What these all have in common is that they are socially contested, argued about, and debated; in other words, matters of taste, values and beliefs about which a limited variety of alternative stands are taken (Stainton Rogers, 1995, p. 180).

4.5.4 The Application of Q Methodology to Environmental Policy and Ecological Economics

Current methods employed in environmental policy involve little research on what makes policies socially acceptable. Q methodology may aid environment policy by exploring how people conceptualise environmental problems. Most environmental attitude research is grounded in social psychology or a search for the demographic correlates of environmental concern (Kalof, 1997, p. 101). However, environmental attitudes may not apply to the entire population, and so methods must be employed to detect differences in attitude structures, rather than assuming homogeneity. As Q methodology is one of these methods, its applications to environmental issues have grown in recent years. (For a discussion of Q and its application to a range of environmental issues, see Addams and Proops, 2000).

Q methodology is particularly well suited to the examination of attitudes on any complex and socially contestable issue, such as how individuals think about waste. Until we know what discourses exist on waste, i.e. the way people think and talk about waste, it will be impossible to plan socially acceptable waste policies. Q methodology is a tool for policy analysis, as it provides an insight into how people think about waste, and how it positions itself in their other concerns, whether they be other environmental issues or even their day-to-day lives. Q also has the possibility of providing policy makers with a framework for analysing the polarisation and/or overlap of attitudes of stakeholders in advance of commencing policy dialogue (Focht and Lawler, 2000, p. 115). Q is a unique method of identifying similarities among individual attitudes. It does not use pre-specified methods, but allows the 'constructions' rather than the 'constructors', or participants, to be the focus of study (Stainton Rogers, 1995, p. 180). It allows for not only the identification of collective understanding, but for discoveries that are possibly unanticipated.

4.6 CONCLUSION

To be able to move towards a more sustainable waste strategy, we need to introduce more socially acceptable waste policies. To achieve this we must not only raise public awareness of the importance of waste policy, but also improve our own understanding of the discourses which exist on waste.

Generalisations have, wrongly, come to exist on what the public think and feel about waste, whether in regard to their 'irrationality' over facility proposals, their reluctance to participate in recycling schemes, or their preference for virgin products over recycled goods. There are a multiplicity of reasons why people feel the way they do over waste and its management. The public should not be regarded as an homogeneous group; instead of trying to view individuals as either internally or externally motivated agents, the possible influences on behaviour should be integrated.

It should also be recognised that increasing awareness alone is not enough. There are huge constraints on the capacity for effective action, the cultural norm of consumption being the most obvious obstacle. There needs to be change made at a higher level, such as in institutions or government. We need to tackle both individual attitudes and the (social and physical) infrastructure, by providing methods of facilitating people's desires to recycle and reduce their waste.

Effective changes in recycling may occur if there is a combination of moral appeals to values, education and information to change attitudes, and changes in incentives to affect expectations and behaviour. By understanding more fully the attitudes that exist towards waste, policies may be designed to involve an initial motivation, enhance already-existing participation, and retain commitment. Current methods employed in environmental policy involve little research on what makes policies socially acceptable. Q methodology is a tool which can provide the framework that is lacking in current environmental policy, to provide insights into how the public conceptualise waste and to allow a fuller understanding of each others' needs for both policy makers and stakeholders.

REFERENCES

Addams, H. and J. Proops (2000), *Social Discourse and Environmental Policy: An Application of Q Methodology*, Cheltenham: Edward Elgar.

Arbuthnot, J., R. Tedeschi, M. Waymer, J. Turner, S. Kressel and R. Rush (1977), 'The induction of sustained behaviour: through the foot in the door technique', *Journal of Environmental Systems*, 6, 354-67.

Bacot, H., T. Bowen and M.R. Fitzgerald (1994), 'Managing the solid waste crisis: exploring the link between citizen attitudes, policy incentives and siting landfills', *Policy Studies Journal*, **22** (2), 229-44.

Beder, S. and M. Shortland (1992), 'Siting a hazardous waste facility: the tangled web of risk communication', *Public Understanding of Science*, **1** (2), 139-60.

Brown, S.R. (1980), *Political Subjectivity: Applications of Q Methodology in Political Science*, New Haven: Yale University Press.

Brown, S.R. (1993), 'A primer on Q Methodology', *Operant Subjectivity*, **16**, 91-138.

Brown, S.R. (1996), 'Q Methodology as the foundation for a science of subjectivity'. Q archive list, http://facstaff.uww.edu/cottlec/Qarchive/.

Chung, S.S. and C.S. Poon (1996), 'The attitudinal differences in source separation and waste reduction between the general public and the housewives in Hong Kong', *Journal of Environmental Management*, **48**, 215-27.

Department of Environment, trade and the Regions (DETR) (2001), *Waste Strategy 2000 for England and Wales*, London: HMSO.

De Young, R. (1986), 'Some psychological aspects of recycling: the structure of conservation satisfactions', *Environment and Behaviour*, **18**, 435-49.

De Young, R. (1990), 'Recycling as appropriate behaviour: a review of survey data from selected recycling education programs in Michigan', *Resources, Conservation and Recycling*, **3**, 253-66.

Dryzek, J. (1990), *Discursive Democracy*, Cambridge: Cambridge University Press.

Environmental Services Association Research Trust (2001), *Public Confidence in Waste Management-The ESART Project*, ESART Research Report E/008, www.esart.org.

Focht, W. and J.J. Lawler (2000), 'Using Q Methodology to facilitate policy dialogue', in H. Addams and J. Proops (eds), *Social Discourse and Environmental Policy: An Application of Q Methodology*, Cheltenham: Edward Elgar.

Granzin, K.L. and J.E. Olsen (1991), 'Characterising participants in activities protecting the environment: a focus on donating, recycling and conservation behaviours', *Journal of Public Policy and Marketing*, **10**, 1-27.

Guagnano, G.A., P.C. Stern and T. Dietz (1995), 'Influencing attitude-behaviour relationships: a natural experiment with curbside recycling', *Environment and Behavior*, **27**, 699-718.

Hopper, J.R. and J.M. Nielsen (1991), 'Recycling as altruistic behaviour: normative and behavioural strategies to expand participation in a community recycling program', *Environment and Behaviour*, **23** (2), 195-220.

Inhaber, H. (1992), 'Of LULUs, NIMBYs and NIMTOOs', *The Public Interest*, **107**, 52-64.

Kalof, L. (1997), 'Understanding the social construction of environmental concern', *Human Ecology Review*, **4** (2), 101-6.

Lindell, M. and T.C. Earle (1983), 'How close is close enough: public perceptions of the risks of industrial facilities', *Risk Analysis*, **3** (4), 245-53.

Lober, D. and D. Green (1994), 'NIMBY or NIABY: a logit model of opposition to waste facility siting', *Journal of Environmental Management*, **40**, 33-50

Lober, D. (1995), 'Why not here? The importance of context, process, and outcome on public attitudes toward siting of waste facilities', *Society and Natural Resources*, **9**, 375-94.

Margai, F.L. (1997), 'Analysing changes in waste reduction behaviour in a low-income urban community following a public outreach program', *Environment and Behavior*, **29** (6), 769-92.

McKeown, B. and D. Thomas (1988), *Q Methodology*, New York: Sage Publications.

O'Hare, M. (1977), 'Not on my block you don't: facility siting and the importance of compensation', *Public Policy*, **25**, 407-58.

Okeke, C.U. and A. Armour (2000), 'Post landfill siting perceptions of nearby residents: a case study of Halton landfill', *Applied Geography*, **20**, 137-54.

Oskamp, S., M.J. Harrington, T.C. Edwards, D.L. Sherwood, S.M. Okuda and D.C. Swanson (1991), 'Factors influencing household recycling behaviour', *Environment and Behavior*, **23** (4) 494-519.

Owens, S. (2000), 'Engaging the public: information and deliberation in environmental policy', *Environment and Planning*, **32**, 1141-48.

Portney, K.E. (1985), 'The potential of the theory of compensation for mitigating public opposition to hazardous waste treatment facility siting: some evidence from five Massachusetts communities', *Policy Studies Journal*, **14** (1), 81-89.

Redclift, M. (1996), *Wasted: Counting the Costs of Global Consumption*. London: Earthscan.

Schultz, P.W., S. Oskamp and T. Mainieri (1995), 'Who recycles and when? A review of personal and situational factors', *Journal of Environmental Psychology*, **15** (2), 105-21.

Schwartz, S.H. (1973), 'Normative explanations of helping behavior: a critique, proposal, and empirical test', *Journal of Experimental Social Psychology*, **9**, 349-64.

Schwartz, S.H. (1977), 'Normative influences on altruism', in L. Berkowitz (ed.), *Advances in Experimental Social Psychology*, New York: New York Academic Press.

Slovic, P. (1987), 'Perception of risk', *Science* **236**, 280-85.

Stainton Rogers, R. (1995), 'Q Methodology', in J. Smith, R. Harre and L. Van Langenhove (eds), *Rethinking Methods in Psychology*, New York: Sage.

Stephenson, W. (1953), *The Study of Behaviour: Q-technique and its Methodology*, Chicago: University of Chicago Press.

Stephenson, W. (1977), 'Factors as operant subjectivity', *Operant Subjectivity*, **1**, 3-16.

Stern, P.C. (2000), 'Toward a coherent theory of environmentally significant behavior', *Journal of Social Issues*, **56** (3), 407-24.

Thogersen, J. (1996), 'Recycling and morality', *Environment and Behavior*, **28** (4), 536-59.

Thompson, M. and S. Rayner (1998), 'Cultural discourses', in S. Rayner and E. Malone (eds), *Human Choice and Climate Change, The Societal Framework, Vol. 1*, Columbus, OH: Battelle Press.

Tucker, P. (1999), 'Normative influences in household waste recycling', *Journal of Environmental Planning and Management*, **42** (1), 63-82.

Van Liere, K.D. and R.E Dunlap (1978), 'Moral norms and environmental behaviour: an application of Schwartz's norm-activation model to yard-burning', *Journal of Applied Social Psychology*, **8**, 174-88.

Vining, J. and A. Ebreo (1990), 'What makes a recycler? A comparison of recyclers and nonrecyclers', *Environment and Behavior*, **22** (1), 55-73.

Vining, J. and A. Ebreo (2001), 'How similar are recycling and waste reduction? Future orientation and reasons for reducing waste as predictors of self-reported behavior', *Environment and Behavior*, **33** (3), 424-48.

NOTES

1   'Not-in-my-back-yard' evolved from the term 'not-on-my-block-you-don't' (O'Hare, 1977).

2   For more details see Schwartz's (1973; 1977) 'moral norm-activation theory of altruism'.

3   For an introduction to Q Methodology (invented by Stephenson (1953; 1977)) readers may find useful Brown (1980; 1993; 1999), McKeown and Thomas (1988) and Stainton Rogers (1995).

5. Economics of Waste

Jane Powell, Kerry Turner, Michael Peters and Barbara Strobl

5.1 INTRODUCTION

All human activity results in the generation of waste that can harm the environment (see Chapter 2). However careful management of waste can limit the damage done to the environment and conserve scarce resources. The sustainable management of waste involves having regard for the future environmental and economic consequences of today's waste management decisions. It includes taking into account in an integrated way the full environmental cost of products and policies, in addition to the economic cost.

If the cost of waste management options reflected their true social cost, then market forces could achieve the optimal mix of waste management options in efficiency terms. However, due to market and information failure this is usually not the case. The overall result is that levels of waste minimisation and recycling are too low and the levels of waste generation and disposal are too high. This situation is compounded by the lack of a co-ordinated waste management policy that is as efficient, effective and fair as is practicable.

In their quest for a sustainable waste management system, many countries have a 'waste hierarchy' (as discussed in Chapter 6) to indicate their preferred waste management options. The hierarchies invariably place waste minimisation first, followed by re-use and recovery of materials, and then energy generation. However, there have been a number of challenges to the assumed ranking of management options within the waste hierarchy. In particular, the substantial environmental benefits that arise from recovering energy from waste could result in incineration being preferred to recycling. However, uncertainties and psychological factors complicate the picture. The environmental and health costs of the associated toxic gaseous emissions are difficult to quantify precisely and there is considerable public opposition to incineration, signifying issues of the lack of trust and accountability felt by the public. Conversely, although recycling has significant public support the environmental benefits of recovering some materials may not always exceed the environmental costs involved in the separate collection, reprocessing and transportation of secondary materials.

The financial cost of recycling post-consumer (household) waste can be considerable, however this cost does not reflect the environmental and social costs and benefits. The benefits of recycling are well known; conservation of resources; savings in landfill space and emissions associated with landfill and incineration; energy savings in manufacturing and in the transport of waste. Nevertheless, post-consumer recycling also has social costs. Materials for recycling need to be collected, sorted and transported to often distant processors. Transport can involve health and safety aspects and environmental pollution. In addition, there are social costs and attitudinal problems associated with source-separating recyclables and storing them at home, plus the noise and litter that may accompany neighbourhood recycling centres. Social benefits include the 'feel-good' factor arising from participation in recycling activities, and the educational value of 'saving' resources. In order to assess these costs and benefits, a methodology is required to quantify and compare the environmental consequences of different environmental options.

5.2 WASTE MANAGEMENT EVALUATION

Lifecycle assessment (LCA) is an environmental management tool that was originally developed to measure the environmental impacts of products or materials but it can be equally applied to services such as waste management (Powell et al., 1997). It is used to quantify the environmental inputs and outputs of a product or process throughout its lifetime, from the mining of raw materials, through production, distribution, use and re-use or recycling, to final disposal. The two main stages of an LCA are the inventory analysis and the impact assessment. The inventory analysis involves the quantification of environmental inputs and outputs at each stage of the lifecycle, in terms of energy and materials inputs, and emissions to air, water and solid waste. In order to include an allowance for recycling in an LCA, the system is credited with the emissions that are displaced by using secondary instead of primary materials. In a similar manner, when energy is recovered from an energy-from-waste facility an allowance is also made for the emissions attributed to the displaced energy.

The purpose of the impact assessment is to aggregate and evaluate the potential environmental impacts identified in the inventory. Initially, the impacts are attributed to impact categories and are then aggregated on the basis of equivalency factors. Unless the outcome is obvious, values or weights are then attributed to the impacts according to their relative importance. The weighting factors can relate to legislative standards, policy aims, or can be estimated with the guidance of either a panel of experts or a cross section of interested parties (Powell et al., 1997). Various 'valuation' methodologies can be used, including expert judgement based approaches or more inclusionary procedures. A set of widely accepted valuation coefficients have not yet been established, as there is considerable controversy over the different valuation methodologies.

One method, the economic damage approach, allows the comparison of impacts on a common monetary scale. Economic valuation methodologies are concerned with estimating the monetary value that individuals place on goods and services. A 'value' can be revealed by a consumer's behaviour, or preferences derived through surveys in terms of their 'willingness to pay' or 'accept' compensation; or by the use of dose-response relationships and replacement costs (Turner et al., 1993). Economic damage values are available for a number of environmental and social impacts, including gaseous emissions, road congestion, and casualties from road traffic accidents. They can then be incorporated into a decision-aiding procedure such as cost-benefit analysis (CBA).

CBA involves the identification and quantification in monetary terms of the costs and benefits relating to a particular plan, programme, project or decision in order to determine if it will produce a net gain or loss in economic welfare for society as a whole. Traditionally, environmental impacts were described in qualitative terms alongside or within the CBA. Environmental economics has attempted to extend CBA into social cost-benefit analysis by estimating monetary values for the unpriced effects of projects upon society and the environment. In this way environmental information has been incorporated directly in the CBA decision-making framework on a common basis with other costs. There will always, however, be environmental gains and losses in CBA that cannot reliably be valued in this way (Bateman et al., 1993; Turner, 2000a).

An alternative approach, multicriteria evaluation (MCE) (Powell, 1996), has also been used to appraise alternative waste management options. MCE potentially allows a more comprehensive comparison of the different impacts using their original data, measured in cardinal numbers, qualitative terms or binary terms. It also facilitates the comparison of monetised and non-monetised environmental and social costs and benefits. Ranking methods are used to give qualitative impacts a numeric value. To overcome the problem of aggregating different units, a relative scale is applied where the most preferred option for each criterion scores 100 and the least preferred 1. The relative importance of each criterion is signalled via weights. A scoring approach using experts, stakeholders or the general public, can be used to obtain weightings. Sensitivity analysis can then be used to determine the effect of varying the weights on the outcome of the analysis. All decision-making aids should nevertheless be treated with caution. They should be as transparent as possible and are no substitute for the democratic process. But given constrained budgets and the need for strategic resource allocations, some technical analysis is vital.

5.3 THE INSTITUTIONAL CONTEXT AND POLITICAL ECONOMY

Given thermodynamic realities, any industrial activity (raw materials processing, production and distribution) will, depending on scale, location and prevailing technologies, generate a waste stream requiring disposal to the ambient environment. The waste disposal process has the potential to impact detrimentally on a range of receptors. An externality exists when an activity by one individual or group affects the utility level (either positively or negatively) of others, without this being the clear intention of the initiating agent. Policy makers, economists and practitioners continually strive to establish effective ways to mitigate the detrimental effects of these externalities, by assisting industry in the improvement of its waste management and overall environmental performance.

The institutional setting in which economic transactions take place conditions the form and the magnitude of the costs involved in such arrangements. Thus environmental externalities and their costs are related to the internal structure of the actual transaction arrangement in operation – markets or other arrangements (Pearce, 1998). The clear distinction in environmental economic theory between polluter and sufferer, and the assumption of value neutral policy appraisal, are both in practice highly questionable (Vatn and Bromley, 1997).

Contemporary externality theory's two main doctrines – the Pigovian school and the Coasean school – are both open to criticism on these grounds. The Pigovian approach makes the polluter liable and imposes an emissions/discharge tax on the polluter, to internalise the externality and establish an efficient level of pollution. The Coasean approach focuses on the possibility of bargaining solutions between economic agents. It is assumed that externalities are reciprocal and, in a world of zero transaction costs, the efficient 'bargaining' solution is determined on the basis of which agent can change behaviour most cheaply. In both approaches the rights and duties involved in a given pollution problem are assumed to be given *a priori* (Pearce and Turner, 1990).

In the real world, externalities appear outside the sphere of defined property rights and are often not recognised until long after the initial emission/discharge of the pollutants (Vatn and Bromley, 1997). Rights and duties concerning victims of pollution and compensation must therefore be established *ex post* by government. The greater the separation in time and space between pollution emission/discharge and a recognised impact on a receptor, the lower the coincidence between the cause of the pollutant release and the cause of the realised damage impact. The 'rights' and 'wrongs' of the situation are then laid down by societal norms and enacted through established institutions (determining what is internal and what is external).

Vatn and Bromley (1997) have concluded that the very rules of market allocation, requiring atomistic individual economic agents (protected by tailored private property rights), only serve to ensure that the potential for externality generation is always present. The market's operation increases the number of borders of interaction among economic agents, pushing up transaction costs and the risk of externality effects. It is also the case that not all externalities are necessarily either purely unintended by-products of economic activity, or intentional cost shifting tactics by producers. But the latter motivation may become even more apparent in the future, as new cost-shifting possibilities appear with the intensification of global industrial and financial competition (Turner, 2000a).

Traditionally, externalities have been tackled by legislation and taxation. But more recently voluntary initiatives have emerged as a supplementary policy instrument in this regard, attracting considerable interest including in schemes involving waste minimisation (Russell and Powell, 1999). Of particular interest in this context is the extent to which recovered materials from the waste stream might be utilised in the production process, thus reducing net environmental impacts and dependency on primary material inputs.

5.3.1 Industry and Environmental Regulation

The relationship between corporate activities and the environment are neither simple nor unidirectional. As environmental pressure in many industrialised countries increases, corporations are striving towards the 'compliance plus' approach to environmental management, where anticipation of new regulations and up-take of innovative strategies will place them ahead of evolving requirements. Porter (1990) has further advanced this theme by putting forward the concept of 'first mover' advantage from which firms anticipating changes in environmental regulations may benefit, gaining internal cost reductions, new markets and enhanced public image (Arora and Cason, 1996; Cavaliere, 2000).

5.3.1.1 In-plant and inter-plant recycling flows

It is possible to distinguish between 'primary' and 'secondary' industries on the grounds of raw material input. The first category utilises primary natural resources and the latter utilises recycled material inputs (secondary materials). In practice, plants in many industries make use of a mixture of primary and secondary material inputs. For example, the chemical and allied industries evolved as an inter-related set of activities designed to take advantage of the by-product streams generated at various points in the chemical transformation process. This has enabled a high level continuity of in-plant recycling (Turner, 2000b).

Private reclamation industries that concentrate their efforts on the recycling of only certain types of waste flows, also play a key role in secondary industrial activity. For example, in the chemicals sector certain used chemicals are collected from their generation points by the reclamation industry, reprocessed and then sent back to the original waste-generating plant, or sold to other plants capable of utilising the recovered and often degraded chemical. Clearly, the physical characteristics of these types of waste stream (preferably high mass, relatively low contamination, good homogeneity and concentrated location) combine to offer financially profitable opportunities for the would-be reclaimer and/or in-plant recovery unit. These characteristics also underpin an international trade in secondary materials (Grace et al., 1978; van Buekering, 2001). In fact, the reclamation business is dominated by the 'grade structure-end use' relationship. The lower the grade of the potentially recyclable material (i.e. because of unfavourable physical characteristics such as high levels of contamination or small mass), the more expensive is the collection and processing system and the more limited are the end uses available. Financial costs are therefore more likely to outweigh financial revenues in such lower-grade recycling activities. The recycling of municipal solid waste (MSW) is a good example of this problem (as discussed in Chapter 7).

Industrial waste generators, whether they dispose of their own waste or pay for waste contract services, typically pay less than the full social cost of waste disposal. In the absence of government intervention in the form of an environmental quality protection/management policy, materials or energy recovery will take place, theoretically, up to the level where the marginal cost of an additional unit of recycled material or energy just equals its market value in a reclaimed condition (Turner, 2000b). Both the recovery costs (collection plus processing costs) and the value of the recovered item will be subject to change over time.

For this reason, lower-grade recyclable materials arising in small amounts in scattered locations, and with only limited end uses, are problematic from both a financial profitability and economic efficiency perspective. Due to the low market prices paid for inferior grade materials and the high collection system costs, such recycling activities will often involve a financial loss. This loss may not be offset by the environmental gains that are enabled by recycling, including reduced overall resource extraction, processing and energy savings and reduced overall waste and disposal costs.

5.3.1.2 Recycled versus primary material inputs

The extent to which materials and energy recycling is practised (in-plant and/or via external recovery firms) will be a function of the cost of recovered residuals as a raw material input into production, relative to primary raw material inputs. But these relative costs will be determined by a complexity of factors including:

- secondary and primary material market conditions and structure;
- technological innovation in primary and secondary process industries;
- technical advances in primary material extraction;
- end product output specifications;
- government policy on environmental quality protection and, in particular, on final disposal of wastes.

5.3.1.3 Process modifications and product redesign

As environmental quality and waste disposal standards become increasingly stringent during the waste reduction process, firms may be faced with a basic trade-off between process and/or product redesign in order to reduce waste generation, and investments in materials energy recovery systems. Industrial waste generators have been encouraged to reorient their residuals management policy away from end-of-pipe control towards the elimination or reduction of waste at source. One of the principal tenets of this 'cleaner technology' movement has been that environmental protection and profitability goals can be jointly pursued. While there are many opportunities for firms to meet such twin objectives, fundamental waste reduction measures will often prove to be financially unprofitable. It may, however, be the case that promoting a more 'environmentally friendly' image may still bring long-term increases in market share and profits for firms adopting 'cleaner technology'. Certain source reduction measures will prove more and more economically viable as waste disposal costs rise in the long run, and others may even become financially profitable.

Properly designed environmental regulations can trigger innovation that may partially or more than fully offset the costs of complying with them. Relatively lax environmental regulations have stimulated 'end-of-pipe', or secondary waste treatment investment responses. Tougher regulations could force firms to take a new look at their processes and products, with the result that overall resource productivity (eco-efficiency) may improve dramatically (Porter and van der Linde, 1995; Von Weizsacker et al., 1997). Supporters of the Porter hypothesis have deployed two further arguments in support of their case. They argue that tougher environmental regulation is likely to promote an expansion of the pollution control technology industry (external to, but seeking to service the needs of polluting firms). The export potential of this industry is also highlighted, given 'early mover' advantages in international markets, i.e. countries that adopt stricter environmental standards, it is argued, will stimulate firms to provide the necessary technology to reduce pollution; when other countries catch up and want to improve their environmental standards they provide an export market for firms from the country that first improved its ambient environment.

Secondly, in the real world, firms are not always able or willing to function as the textbooks assume and as a result unexploited opportunities for cost savings and improvements in product quality are often present (known as the existence of 'slack' or 'x-inefficiency' in the economy; Leibenstein, 1966). If 'slack' is present and properly designed environmental regulations are introduced, then the firms' capacity for innovation and improvement in productivity terms can be harnessed. Many innovations can partially or more than fully offset the costs incurred. According to Porter and van der Linde (1995), such 'innovation offsets' will be common because reducing pollution is often coincident with improving the productivity with which resources are used.

Large firms can also play a positive role in the promotion of sustainable development, as they speed up the process of diffusing best environmental management practices (environmental audits, policy developments, life cycle analysis, etc.) to firms in their own supply chain and beyond. The scope and magnitude of this ecoefficiency revolution has been the subject of intense debate in the literature (Oates et al., 1994; Schmalensee, 1993; Jaffe et al., 1995).

5.3.2 Dealing with the Externality Problem

Until recently, environmental policy in most countries was dominated almost entirely by direct regulatory measures (OECD, 1997). These are the legal instruments by which governing institutions (at all levels of government) impose obligations or constraints on the actions and behaviour of private firms and consumers in order to protect the environment. Over the last fifteen years or so, these direct 'command and control' (CandC) measures (see Chapter 6) have been slowly supplemented by market-based economic incentive instruments, such as eco-taxes (e.g. the introduction in 1996 of a tax on landfilled waste disposal in the UK). The main types of environmental regulation can be grouped into three categories: command and control in-struments, economic incentive instruments (EIs - also referred to as market-based instruments, or MBIs) and other instruments. The categories and sub-categories of environmental regulatory instruments in OECD countries are presented and discussed below (OECD, 1997; Russell and Powell, 1999).

5.3.2.1 Command and Control (CandC) instruments
These directly regulate behaviour affecting the environment, typically through permit and authorisation procedures relating to the following:

a. the products produced and distributed;
b. the materials used in production;
c. the technologies by which goods and materials are produced;
d. the residuals which are released into the environment;
e. the locations at which production and other economic activities take place.

CandC policies have many properties that have contributed to their popular-ity with governments and regulators. They are simple and direct enabling the setting of clearly defined targets and they also capture society's ethical sensitivity to pollution 'bads' (Field, 1994).

5.3.2.2 Economic instruments
Economic instruments encompass a range of policy instruments that modify behaviour, using financial incentives and disincentives, to improve environ-mental performance. A more widespread and consistent use of EIs has been inhibited by concerns over competitiveness effects, equity effects and oppo-sition from vested interests. The main 'types' of EI are:

a. charges and taxes on emission/discharges, or charges on raw material inputs or products (e.g. packaging), to waste collection and disposal charges;
b. grants and subsidies;
c. fines, etc. for non-compliance;
d. market creation mechanisms, such as recycling credits and tradable permits, desposit-refund systems.

5.3.2.3 Other instruments
A further set or measures aim to improve environmental performance by:

i) improving the supply of information relating to environmental problems and the ways of reducing them, and

ii) raising the level of voluntary commitment, both at an individual organisation and collective level, to modify practices to reduce these problems.

Elements of this approach are to be found in the following examples:

a. environmental planning, environmental impact assessment, lifecycle
   assessment and related extended producer responsibility procedures;
b. voluntary individual and association agreements to promote environmental policy objectives through industry covenants, negotiated
   agreements, self-regulation, codes of conduct and eco-audits;
c. information disclosure schemes (voluntary or compulsory);
d. environmental management systems and environmental audit procedures
   to improve cost-effective compliance with agreed environmental quality
   targets.

Modern day voluntary approaches to environmental management take many
forms, but all build upon the Coase Theorem, maintaining that desirable
outcomes may be achieved efficiently without the need for penalty threats
and economic disincentives (Glasbergen, 1999). The key characteristic of
voluntary initiatives (VIs) is co-operation – the bargainers work together to
reduce degradation and reap the subsequent benefits.

Figure 5.1 Environmental Policy Framework

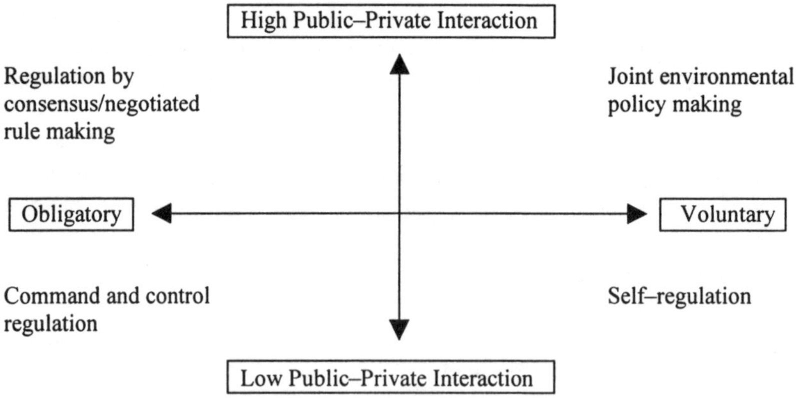

Source: Ingram (1999).

The position of voluntary policy approaches in the overall context of decision
making is worth considering, since process is as important as policy content.
Figure 5.1 is an environmental policy framework, presented by Ingram

(1999), showing different policy instruments and the degree to which they are inherently voluntary/participatory.

In the next section we use a case study approach to highlight some of the important issues facing waste management agencies and the public now and in the future.

5.4. CASE STUDIES

5.4.1 SMEs and Industrial Waste Minimisation

Waste minimisation represents the pinnacle of the UK Government's waste management objectives. In their consultation paper *Less Waste More Value,* it is made very clear that this is the target towards which all efforts concerning the management of wastes should be geared: 'the best way to reduce the impact of waste on the environment can simply be to avoid producing it.' (DETR, 1998: 15). Essentially, the key message is this:

Reduced waste = reduced cost = improved efficiency and a cleaner more sustainable environment.

The reduction of waste generation has been an important and integral component of many large companies' environmental policies for a number of years now – both within the UK and abroad (Coggins, 1996; DTI, 2001). There are numerous well documented case-studies showing the economic and environmental benefits of such initiatives, and encouraging the broader business community to follow suit in the best practice vein (e.g. CEST, 1995; Phillips, 1999). However, the body of evidence from which to draw conclusive arguments on the successful application of waste minimisation techniques for small and medium sized enterprises (SMEs – referring, in the UK, to firms with fewer than 250 employees) is still in its infancy. Drawing on recent research carried out in East Anglia (Peters, 2001), we present here the results of a waste minimisation initiative for SMEs established on an industrial estate in Norfolk to contribute to this body of knowledge.

5.4.1.2 Establishing the waste minimisation initiative for SMEs in Norfolk

The core objective of the research was to determine whether a local-scale waste minimisation voluntary initiative (VI) would be able to break through the common barriers of SME environmental resistance and enable small businesses to address and improve their waste management and environmental performance. It was decided to focus attention on an industrial estate, in the expectation that such a research strategy might well yield the most useful results within a limited time frame. It was also anticipated that the potential for such a business/environment project to produce meaningful outcomes would be improved because of the geographical and local-scale benefits enjoyed by a small number of close-proximity SMEs.

A project proposal was drawn up, the essence of which was to secure a sum of money (£5,000) via the Landfill Tax Credit Scheme, to enable an approved environmental consultant to run a short series of waste minimisation workshops with willing businesses from the industrial estate. The training would be offered free of charge. Recent research has highlighted the potential cost savings, efficiency gains and image benefits that can accrue to both large and small businesses by putting in place strategies for waste minimisation (e.g. DTI, 2001; Phillips et al, 2000). The aim was to deliver these real and lasting benefits to participants, thus contributing to local sustainability and developing a group of environmentally responsible businesses.

This concept was not entirely new or revolutionary. For example, the Groundwork Trust has established certain 'green business parks' in the UK and similar research has been carried out on two industrial estates in Surrey, with some success (Edley and Swan, 1999). It was felt that the research findings would contribute significantly to the steadily growing pool of knowledge on industrial estate approaches to SMEs environmental engagement. The overall approach adopted for the initiative is shown in Figure 5.2.

Figure 5.2 Schematic representation of project strategy

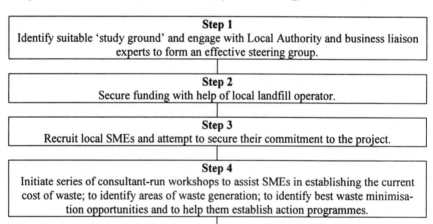

| **Step 1** |
| Identify suitable 'study ground' and engage with Local Authority and business liaison experts to form an effective steering group. |

| **Step 2** |
| Secure funding with help of local landfill operator. |

| **Step 3** |
| Recruit local SMEs and attempt to secure their commitment to the project. |

| **Step 4** |
| Initiate series of consultant-run workshops to assist SMEs in establishing the current cost of waste; to identify areas of waste generation; to identify best waste minimisation opportunities and to help them establish action programmes. |

| **Step 5** |
| Implementation of action programmes and review of project progress. Participants to continue the process of opportunity identification beyond the formal workshop phase. |

5.4.1.3 Agreeing the idea and securing the funding

Co-ordination of certain key players who would enable appropriate contacts to be made, and would be able to attract the necessary funding required, was the single, most important element of the approach. The way in which this co-ordination took place was as follows: first, securing local authority support; second, identifying with their help a suitable industrial estate; and third, contacting a local landfill operator to provide funding via the Landfill Tax Credit Scheme.

The North Walsham Industrial Estate in North Norfolk was chosen, with the advice of the local authorities, as a suitable study area. Recruitment of businesses on the industrial estate was done via letters and follow-up telephone calls, with an initial site visit to carry out the environmental attitudes survey forming the first point of contact. The project had a stated duration of six months, but with the genuine intention of beginning a new culture within the group of businesses, that might be carried on and expanded beyond the official project duration. An approved environmental consultant was contracted to run a series of three interactive waste minimisation workshops with willing businesses on the industrial estate. The main aim was for him to give the businesses the necessary skills to carry out their own simple environmental/waste audit and to guide them through the process of identifying opportunities for improvement. Another central aim was to utilise the collective, innovative capacity of several SMEs to reach imaginative solutions and strategies for individual and collective waste reduction and environmental performance improvement.

Although twelve SMEs expressed an interest and agreed to an initial site visit, it transpired that only three of these actually attended the training workshops. They were:

Company 1: Producers of high quality engraved and decorated glassware for business gift, tourist trade and contract markets.

Company 2: Machine manufacturers. One particular product is designed to fill plastic sheeting with air, sealing the air into small pockets thus creating an effective packaging material.

Company 3: Manufacturers of precision machines and scientific instruments.

Although in some respects this level of attendance was disappointing, the enthusiasm and commitment to the success of the project that these three businesses made, far outweighed the scaled-down nature of the meetings. It is important to point out that all twelve businesses received the information that was covered in the workshops, in addition to receiving invitations to each event. A follow-up visit made by the project facilitator to non-attendees after the first workshop, brought to light time and manpower constraints – rather than a loss of interest – being the primary reason for failure to turn up. As will be discussed further on, the considerable achievements made by the three participants is proof that by working together to reduce waste, small businesses really can make substantial progress.

5.4.1.4 Project achievements

This section describes some examples of key achievements that arose from the voluntary participation of businesses in the workshop sessions and the subsequent take-up of advice and ideas arising from follow-up site visits and corporate action.

- **Process design change to save specialised paper waste at Company 1 (Engraved Glass Manufacturer)**

This involved the purchasing of smaller sheets of paper and reducing margins in the engraving design, resulting in a cost saving and reduced contribution to limited landfill space.

- **Waste exchange initiative between Company 2 and Company 1**

The waste packaging generated by Company 2 used to result in disposal charges and a hiring charge for a compressor and baler to make the waste ready for collection. Company 1 identified this waste as potentially useful packaging material to substitute the polystyrene chips that they had always purchased and used before. This waste exchange scheme therefore enabled considerable cost savings to both companies, reduced contribution to landfill and a reduction of traffic and transport to Company 1's site by the deliverers of polystyrene chips (in addition to a lower demand for this material, which requires a great deal of energy for its production). There was also the beneficial result of reduced noise within Company 2's workshop, as the process of bursting the air pockets with the compressor created a high volume of sound.

- **Legislative compliance and cardboard recycling**

Company 3 has received free professional advice on legislative compliance with regard to appropriate disposal of oil-water mix and acid liquid wastes. They also received a visit from a local recycling expert, who helped them to assess the potential for using the cardboard tubes that were being disposed to landfill.

The common problem of waste cardboard was an area that the District Council wanted to address in the light of the research carried out with the industrial estate. The implementation of a collective recycling scheme to enable shared-cost savings was put forward as a potentially workable strategy.

The businesses involved in this project collectively achieved success in winning an Environment 2000 'Green Oscar' Award from North Norfolk District Council for their participation in this project in July 2000. This Environment Awards Scheme was launched in 1994 to 'encourage groups or individuals undertaking projects that benefit the environment' (NNDC, 2000). It is a good example of the way in which the aims of the local authority can be tied in closely with sensible business progress on environmental performance issues by means of a voluntary policy approach.

The project also received favourable coverage in the local paper (Eastern Daily Press's *The Business*) which is distributed throughout Norfolk and Waveney. This editorial article was an important part of disseminating the achievements of the project to the wider business community in Norfolk.

5.4.1.5 Conclusions
The local-scale industrial estate waste minimisation VI reported here demonstrates the beneficial outcomes that can be realised by all participating businesses. It serves to highlight the type of potential waste and cost reduction opportunities that can be identified when the collective innovation of a group of SMEs is encouraged and guided within the scope of a voluntary project. Savings of this kind – which may well have remained dormant were it not for the initiation and nature of the voluntary initiative – confirm that x-inefficiencies do exist (Porter and van der Linde, 1995). External impetus and guidance seems to be required to start and sustain the process of identifying areas for improvement. This might best be offered by local authorities and associated agencies (e.g. Business Link and Chambers of Commerce) in conjunction with approved consultants at the initial stages. To begin with, funding for such waste minimisation projects is potentially available from the Landfill Tax Credit Scheme, as this research has shown.

It is suggested that an industrial estates approach to reaching and influencing SMEs might constitute an effective and workable strategy for large areas of the UK. The growth in the number of industrial estates across the UK in recent years has provided a large number of potential 'seed beds'. There appears to be no reason why the model tested for this case study could not be replicated elsewhere with possible improvements and modifications.

5.4.2 Lifecycle Assessment at the Regional Scale; Waste Management in Norfolk

In the UK the collection and disposal of household waste is the responsibility of the local authorities. Local waste management is facing the difficult task of complying with several national regulations and targets, implementing them according to set principles, and delivering the most economic as well as the most environmental strategy. The following case study shows that national requirements are not necessarily compatible with the best practical environmental option at the local (regional) level.

Norfolk produces approximately 420,000 tonnes of household waste and over 900,000 tonnes of commercial waste. At present, 86 per cent of household waste is landfilled with the remaining 14 per cent being recycled. Half of the recycled waste is recovered through Household Waste Recycling Centres, with the remainder through a mixture of kerbside collection schemes and bring sites. Norfolk has very few reprocessing facilities and no waste treatment or energy-from-waste plants.

County Councils, regulators and the public all appear to pursue different targets and preferences. Each of these groups has an underlying reason for their preference and would make decisions based on those preferences. Yet, it is still not clear what option ought to be preferred to achieve the 'best' in environmental, economic and social terms. In order to determine the Best Practical Environmental Option for Norfolk, a lifecycle assessment has been undertaken.

5.4.2.1 Lifecycle assessment case study

The lifecycle assessments were conducted using the 1998/99 data as a baseline (Scenario 1), against which four different scenarios were compared:

Scenario 1   14 % Recycling (incl. 5 % Composting), 86 % Landfill
Scenario 2   50 % Recycling (incl. 21 % Composting), 50 % Landfill
Scenario 3   25 % Recycling, 50 % Landfill, 25 % Biogasification
Scenario 4   25 % Recycling (incl. 8 % Composting), 75 % Incineration
Scenario 5   25 % Recycling (incl. 8 % Composting), 75 % refuse derived
                  fuel (RDF)

Scenario 1 reflects the current situation. Three of the remaining four scenarios include approximately 25 per cent recycling (the national target) through increased kerbside collection. The remainder of the waste is disposed of in four different ways, one of which includes further amounts of recycling and composting. Any significant changes, relative to Scenario 1 (the baseline data), are thus easily traced to a certain disposal option.

The software model used in this study is the second edition of 'Integrated Solid Waste Management: A Life Cycle Inventory', developed by McDougall et al. (2001). The model takes into account the replacement of primary resources through the use of recycled material, and the displacement of energy generated by coal-fuelled power station by the energy from energy from waste facilities.

Table 5.1 Results of lifecycle assessment inventory analysis for Norfolk County, UK

		Scenario 1 9% Recycling 5% Composting 86% Landfill	Scenario 2 29% Recycling 21% Composting 50% Landfill	Scenario 3 25% Recycling 25% Biogasification 50% Landfill	Scenario 4 13% Recycling 8% Composting 75% Incineration	Scenario 5 13% Recycling 8% Composting 75% RDF
Materials Recovery Level [%]		6	21	19	13	15
Net Energy Use [GJ]		-129,626	-5,667,875	-5,748,264	-5,001,034	-7,768,952
Emissions to Air [kg]	CO	35,701	-446,932	-455,814	-301,584	-470,716
	CO_2 (non-biogenic)	15,246,358	-69,731,152	-67,043,446	-54,689,449	-257,906,571
	CO_2 (biogenic)	46,447,251	27,999,637	14,314,944	224,662,437	235,101,370
	CH_4	20,112,498	11,326,432	12,223,233	286,852	6,929,366
	NO_x	107,384	-77,723	-117,904	-396,641	-277,954
	N_2O	257	-1,200	195	-398	-507
	SO_x	-9,395	-555,123	-577,911	-951,204	-1,147,29338
	HCl	5,047	-4,569	-8,280	-50,262	-28,718
	HF	1,017	155	-199	2	91
	H_2S	10,237	5,899	6,347	184	3,582
	Dioxins	0.0000001	-0.0000002	0.000001	0.0000192	0.0039
	Particulates	14,973	-158,600	-189,676	-361,131	-521,568
Emissions to Water [kg]	BOD	101,058	79,651	76,804	13,328	14,900
	COD	-464,447	-1,566,102	-1,055,980	-832,743	-831,429
	Suspended Solids	-14,056	-49,554	-94,227	-53,265	-67,971
	TOC	36,888	97,405	67,620	50,815	49,261
	AOX	-5,602	-16,525	-11,362	-8,532	-8,531
	Chlorinated HC	56	38	38	3	4

BOD = Biological Oxygen Demand; COD = Chemical Oxygen Demand; TOC = Total Organic Carbon;
AOX = Adsorbable Organic Halides

Table 5.2 Economic valuation of Norfolk lifecycle assessment

Economic Values EURO/t of waste	Scenario 1 9% Recycling 5% Composting 86% Landfill		Scenario 2 29% Recycling 21% Composting 50% Landfill		Scenario 3 25% Recycling 25% Biogasification 50% Landfill		Scenario 4 13% Recycling 8% Composting 75% Incineration		Scenario 5 13% Recycling 8% Composting 75% RDF	
	low	high	low	high	low	high	low	high	low	high
CO_2 (per kg of C)	0.173	1.039	-0.789	-4.753	-0.759	-4.570	-0.619	-3.728	-2.223	-13.393
CH_4	14.065	25.134	7.921	14.154	8.548	15.275	0.201	0.358	4.846	8.659
N_2O	0.004	0.005	-0.018	-0.023	0.003	0.004	-0.006	-0.007	-0.008	-0.010
PM10	0.373	1.307	-3.964	-13.874	-4.741	-16.592	-9.026	-31.590	-13.036	-45.625
SO_2	0.164	-0.305	-9.712	-18.037	-10.111	-18.777	-16.641	-30.906	-20.072	-37.277
NO_x	0.805	5.368	-0.583	-3.885	-0.884	-5.894	-2.974	-19.827	-2.084	-13.894
As	0.186	-1.241	-0.409	-2.723	-0.455	-3.029	-0.299	-1.990	-0.140	-0.931
Cd	0.000	0.000	0.000	0.000	0.000	-0.001	0.000	0.000	0.004	0.016
Cr VI	0.000	0.000	0.000	0.001	0.000	0.001	0.001	0.004	0.329	2.190
Ni	0.000	0.000	0.000	-0.003	-0.001	-0.004	-0.001	-0.005	0.002	0.010
Dioxins (TEQ)	0.000	0.000	0.000	0.000	0.000	0.000	0.000	0.001	0.019	0.159
Fatalities	0.057	0.057	0.063	0.063	0.062	0.062	0.061	0.061	0.062	0.062
Serious Injury	0.024	0.024	0.027	0.027	0.026	0.026	0.026	0.026	0.026	0.026
Congestion	0.011	0.011	0.012	0.012	0.012	0.012	0.012	0.012	0.012	0.012
TOTAL	15.162	31.398	-7.453	-29.041	-8.298	-33.486	-29.265	-87.591	-32.264	-99.994

The lifecycle inventory results (Table 5.1) consist of a list of emissions to air and water and net energy consumption. Negative energy values indicate a net increase in energy, while negative emission values indicate a net reduction in emissions rather than an increase.

The highlighted value indicates the 'best' option for each individual criterion. In terms of net energy use, the highest gain is made from burning RDF. Scenarios with high levels of recycling (2) and biogasification (3) also recovery high levels of energy. Apart from the baseline case (Scenario 1) the non-biogenic carbon dioxide emissions are negative indicating that more carbon dioxide is displaced, through recycling and incineration, than is generated by the waste management options. The option with the most carbon displacement is scenario 5, with 25 per cent recycling and an RDF plant. The RDF scenario also has the lowest emissions of SO_x and HCl while the high recycling Scenario (2) has low NO_x, N_2O and dioxin emissions.

As can be seen in Table 5.1, there is no clear 'winner' amongst the scenarios. The 'best' option varies according to the different criteria and no one option has a clear lead in achieving the least emissions. Therefore, economic valuation has been used to weigh the various impacts and thus facilitate decision-making.

5.4.2.2 Economic valuation
The results of the economic valuation (Table 5.2) indicate that all scenarios lead to an economic saving apart from Scenario 1 (business as usual). These are summarised in Figure 5.3.

Figure 5.3 Summary of economic valuation of waste management scenarios for Norfolk, UK.

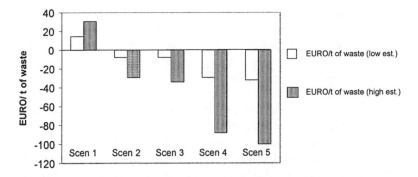

Mass incineration with energy recovery (Scenario 4) yields the greatest benefit, while the production and incineration of RDF (Scenario 5) is the second best option with only slightly less benefits. The current approach,

Scenario 1, is associated with the most costs. The combination recycling/composting scenario reveals a low cost, if the lower economic values are applied, but a slight economic benefit if the higher values are used. This is mainly due to the large differences in high and low economic values for CO_2, PM_{10} and NOx emissions. Generally, the economic valuation for SO_2 and NO_X produces savings due to the displaced energy emissions in incineration processes in Scenarios 4 and 5.

The economic valuation of the lifecycle assessment clearly favours the waste scenarios that recover large quantities of energy. Scenarios that include high levels of disposal to landfill incur high economic costs associated with CH_4 emissions. Recycling also recovers energy through the replacement of primary with secondary materials, however currently not as much material can be recycled as incinerated. A scenario that recycled large quantities of materials and incinerated the remainder would probably have a greater environmental benefit than the scenarios that were used. However, high levels of recycling in Norfolk would probably result in insufficient waste to justify the construction of a large incineration plant.

5.4.2.3 Discussion

The result of the LCA and its subsequent analysis shows the discrepancy between UK regulations and the Best Practical Environmental Option. Instead of high recycling rates, the incineration of RDF and mass incineration turns out to be the most preferred methods of waste management in Norfolk. However, a lifecycle assessment cannot reveal all of the advantages and disadvantages of the different scenarios. Certain aspects are impossible to quantify, but critical in an overall evaluation of the system. The following areas of assessment also need to be taken into consideration:

The results of the economic valuation need to be treated with care, as monetary values do not exist for all of the impacts and some of those that are available vary considerably according to the studies they are based on. Therefore, although the results are a good guide to the environmental impacts of the different waste management options, the assessment is limited by the number of impacts that can be included.

The implementation of each scenario happens in different time frames. The construction of new facilities is preceded by a lengthy planning and consultation process, accompanied by local environmental and economic impacts of its own. The process of planning and building such a facility could turn out to be too lengthy and costly, especially if national and EU targets are to be met. The increase of collection and recycling rates also depends on the extent of public participation.

A further problem with incineration is its inflexibility. There can be up to 10 years lead-time in building a large incinerator, and they can then be in operation for at least 20 years. Waste quantities have to be projected for that time and any fluctuations can reduce the efficiency of the plant. The waste quantity needs to remain relatively fixed and discourages waste minimisation and recycling efforts.

Although energy from waste may be environmentally beneficial, it is very unpopular with the general public in the UK. The concerns over toxic emissions are not entirely scientifically proven and therefore are not reflected in the economic values. However, this does not invalidate the concerns of individuals, particularly those living in close proximity to an existing or proposed waste incineration plant.

Increases in the public participation in recycling schemes depends on an extensive education program (see Chapter 4). In addition the inconvenience and time taken by the participating public in different scenarios needs to be taken into consideration as the public are expected to sort, collect and sometimes transport recyclable materials. There are also implications linked to the need for adequate storage facilities.

The LCA assumes that all of the recovered materials can be reprocessed and sold. However, this may not always be the case. The market for secondary materials is extremely volatile making long term planning difficult. This uncertainty over prices deters many investors, resulting in slow developments in this area.

5.5 WASTE MANAGEMENT FUTURES

In the UK the predominant historic method for the disposal of solid waste has been landfilling. The extractive industries have continually created large numbers of potential sites, which appear to offer an effective, and inexpensive, solution to the disposal of waste. This is in marked contrast to the approach adopted in other western countries, which have either involved the development of their waste incineration capacity, feeding the generated heat and power into their district heating systems and national grids, or their respective recycling industries. However, both these options have only enjoyed limited take-up in the UK.

The 1990 Environmental Protection Act (HM Government, 1990) included a requirement to minimise waste disposal, through the promotion of recycling, and introduced higher standards for the disposal of waste. A target was set, specifying the recycling of 25 per cent of household waste by the year 2000. Waste management was also seen as an area of environmental protection that appeared suitable for the introduction of radical new measures and, as such, was deemed a suitable test bed for an economic instrument.

The proposal to introduce a new tax on waste disposed to landfill was announced in the Budget of November 1994. In March 1995 a consultation paper was released and comments sought from interested parties. The main objectives of the UK Landfill Tax are to ensure that landfill waste disposal is properly priced, which will promote greater efficiency in the waste management market and to apply the 'polluter pays' principle and promote a more sustainable approach to waste management (HM Customs and Excise, 1995).

The tax was introduced on 1 October 1996. Inert waste, such as construction waste, which does not release greenhouse gases, was taxed at £2 per tonne of waste, while active waste that includes all other types of solid waste was taxed at £7 per tonne. This reflected the higher potential environmental impacts in the form of greenhouse gas releases and the potential for leaching into watercourses. The 1999 Budget increased the rate for active waste to £10 per tonne and introduced a tax escalator to increase the tax on active waste by £1 every year until 2004/2005, when it will be subject to further review. The landfill tax raised £361m in 1997-98, and the increase from £7 to £10 per tonne of active waste was expected to raise another £100m per year. The accelerator is expected to add a further £45 million per year for each future £1 increase (HM Customs and Excise, 1999). This suggests that by 2005, the tax will have raised approximately £4.3 billion.

The introduction of the landfill tax was sweetened by a digression from the orthodox UK Treasury principle of no hypothecation of tax revenues. This involved the establishment of the Landfill Tax Credit Scheme, which has private sector status. Under this scheme any landfill operator can choose to pay up to 20 per cent of their landfill tax dues, as voluntary contributions to an approved Environmental Body of their choice. The landfill operator will receive a 90 per cent tax credit on the contribution. The aims of the scheme are to help reduce reliance on landfill and to compensate those living in the vicinity of landfill sites by 'environmental improvements'.

5.5.1 Assessment of the Landfill Tax

It has been suggested that the landfill tax has failed to meet its two objectives (Brisson and Powell, 2000). The first criticism that landfill waste disposal is not properly priced, is the most easily dismissed. When the landfill tax was first introduced, its level was based on estimates of those externalities that could be valued in a reliable manner, which were associated with landfilling (CSERGE et al., 1993). While the estimates are, of course, open to criticism, no-one has seriously asserted that the landfill tax fails to make a useful attempt to internalise the externalities associated with the landfilling of waste

From a welfare economics perspective, the landfill tax may not represent the 'first best' tax, which produces the optimal level of waste arisings from the point of view of society. But the structure and philosophy of the tax is theoretically sound. The issue can be expressed as one of adjustment, rather than radical reconstruction. So, while the initial level of the landfill tax was based on the best available estimates of the externalities associated with landfill, it will undoubtedly be possible to refine the chosen tax rate in future. Improvements in the reliability of valuation techniques, and in the knowledge of the physical impacts of landfilling of waste, will strengthen the estimates of those external effects currently included, and enhance the opportunity of including external effects omitted from the earlier studies (Brisson and Powell, 2000).

The second criticism appears to be the more substantive, and centres primarily on the failure of the tax to achieve desired reductions in the amount of waste going to landfill, and corresponding increases in the amounts being recovered or recycled. This raises three main issues: first, are the targets appropriate? Second, has the landfill tax had the 'optimal conditions' to achieve its objectives? And finally, is it the most appropriate instrument to attain the objectives?

The question of the appropriateness of the targets reflects the concern that the targets themselves, the desired reductions, are flawed objectives. This is due to the fact that they are not based on any assessment of the actual environmental externalities associated with the landfilling of waste, but appear to have been set as a result of political discussion. The recent EU Landfill Directive maps out the required reduction in the amount of organic waste that can be landfilled in future years, but the path appears to have been based entirely on the perceived political undesirability of landfilling. This is a judgement that reflects the dogma inherent in the waste hierarchy, rather than any rigorous assessment of the costs and benefits of the landfilling of waste.

The second issue, that the landfill tax has not been given optimal conditions under which to work, essentially revolves around the issue of household charges for waste. The introduction of a charging system by local authorities, to provide an incentive to households to reduce waste, is currently prohibited in the United Kingdom. The Select Committee (SCETRA, 1999) advised against introducing unit pricing for household waste services, arguing that the charge would be too insignificant to have any effect, and somewhat contradicting this claim, that an unwanted side effect would be that people would dump waste in neighbours' dustbins. Recently, however, government advisors have recommended that variable charging trials for waste collection should be permitted. A number of schemes that charge households for the waste that they generate have been successfully introduced around the world (Brisson and Powell, 2000).

The final issue is a reflection of the argument that it is not the landfill tax that has failed, but the policymakers in their failure to adopt an instrument appropriate for the objective. Clearly, if the political system sets quantitative targets for the amount of waste that can be landfilled, a tax is not the best way of achieving such targets. Instead, an instrument should be chosen which controls quantity rather than price. If there is a desire to achieve the quantitative target at least cost, instruments such as tradable permits should be considered. And, indeed, this is one of the options the DETR is seeking views on in its consultation document relating to the new Landfill Directive (DETR, 1999).

The landfill tax is a radical and progressive step forward in pursuit of the objective of sustainable waste management. It is based on an assessment of the externalities associated with landfilling, and thus represents an initial step to try to ensure that the price of waste services reflect their social cost. It is undoubtedly capable of further refinement, and it could be accompanied by other complementary measures of the type discussed above, to assist in the attainment of policy objectives.

However, much of the discussion surrounding the efficacy of the tax is not a reflection of the tax itself, but the target of the tax. The increasing focus on diverting large quantities of waste from landfill, particularly after the adoption of the new EC Landfill Directive, only serves to highlight the mismatch between the target and the instrument. However, to the extent that the other stated aim of the landfill tax remains valid, namely to make the polluter pay by internalising the external effects of landfilling waste, the efficacy of the tax is constrained by antiquated dogma. Until the principle of not charging households in direct proportion to the amount of waste they produce, is challenged and overcome, no amount of refinement will allow the attainment of the 'first-best' option in welfare-economic, or social, terms.

5.5.2 Towards an Integrated Waste Management Strategy

Along with a comprehensive and reliable time series data set, the main requirement for a future waste management strategy is a more integrated and strategic decision support process. The framework for one such approach is presented in Figure 5.3. The use of scenarios is central to the overall process. These scenarios need to be formulated on the basis of relevant socio-economic and environmental drivers, which in turn inform both policy makers and other stakeholders. It is important that this information exchange is a two-way process, with the decision support mechanisms being sensitive to inputs from stakeholders and the general public.

Scenarios should be used to place upper and lower bounds on future uncertainty. They have their methodological weaknesses and they should not be interpreted as a way of 'picking winners'. The exercise is more useful as a means of exploring alternative mitigation/adaptation options (see the Norfolk case study). One major advantage of the strategy outlined in Figure 5.4 is that it provides for a more forward looking and flexible approach, given future uncertainties. Thus a strategy over-reliant on incineration carries with it, among other negatives, public opposition problems and the risk that a 'technological lock-in' effect will be stimulated (over 15 to 20 years perhaps).

Figure 5.4   Strategic decision support process: an integrated assessment approach

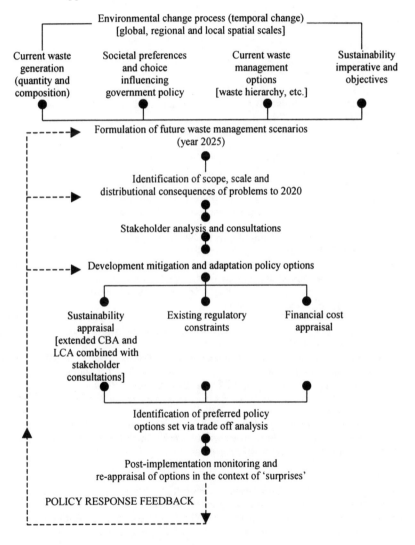

If this were to be the case, a number of newer and more efficient and environmentally effective waste treatment/disposal options may be 'crowded out' and not invested in as soon as they might otherwise be. The strategy in Figure 5.4 provides the opportunity to at least think about 'jumping a technology' and if properly deployed is more inclusionary, with the added benefit of helping to evolve more environmentally aware citizens willing to take some personal responsibility for their waste for the collective good.

REFERENCES

Arora, S. and T.N. Cason (1996), 'Why do firms volunteer to exceed environmental regulations? Understanding Participation in EPA's 33/50 Program', *Land Economics*, **72** (4), 413-32.

Bateman, I.J., R.K. Turner, and S.D. Bateman (1993), 'Extending cost benefit analysis of UK highway proposals: environmental evaluation and equity', *Project Appraisal*, **8** (4), 213-24.

Baumol, W.J. and W.E. Oates (1971), 'The use of standards and prices for protection of the environment', *Swedish Journal of Economics*, **73**, 42-54.

Brisson, I. and J.C. Powell (2000), 'The UK Landfill Tax', in D. Helm (ed.), *Environmental Policy: Objectives, Instruments and Implementation*, Oxford: Oxford University Press.

Cavaliere, A. (2000), 'Overcompliance and voluntary agreements: a note about environmental reputation', *Environmental and Resource Economics*, **17**, 195-202.

CEST (1995), *Waste Minimisation: A Route to Profit and Cleaner Production*, Final report on the Aire and Calder Project, London: Centre for the Exploitation of Science and Technology.

Coggins, P.C. (1996), *Waste Minimisation: Definitions, Measurement and Policy Options*, Northampton: Institute of Wastes Management.

CSERGE, Warren Spring Laboratory and EFTEC (1993), *Externalities from Landfill and Incineration*, London: HMSO.

Department of the Environment, Transport and the Regions (DETR) (1998), *Less Waste More Value*, Consultation paper on the waste strategy for England and Wales, London: HMSO.

Department of the Environment, Transport and the Regions (DETR) (1999), *A Way with Waste: A Draft Waste Strategy for England and Wales*, London: HMSO.

Department of Trade and Industry (DTI) (2001), *Attitudes 2000: A Survey to Assess Attitudes and Barriers Towards Improved Environmental Performance*, Oxford: DTI Envirowise Programme.

Edley, M. and O. Swan (1999), 'Initiating environmental management in small businesses: two different approaches in Surrey', The 1999 Business Strategy and the Environment Conference Proceedings.

Field, B. (1994), *Environmental Economics: An Introduction*, New York: McGraw-Hill.

Glasbergen, P. (1999), 'Tailor-made environmental governance: on the relevance of the covenanting process', *European Environment*, March-April, 49-59.

Grace, R., R.K. Turner and I. Walter (1978), 'Secondary materials and international trade', *Journal of Environment Economics and Management*, **5**, 157-83.

HM Customs and Excise (1999), 'Government support for sustainable waste management', *Press Release CandE*, **5**, 9 March.

HM Government (1990), *This Common Inheritance Britain's Environmental Strategy*, Cmnd 1200, London: HMSO.

Ingram, V. (1999), 'From sparring partners to bedfellows: joint approaches to environmental policy-making', *European Environment*, March-April, 41-49.

Jaffe, A.B., S.R. Peterson, P.R. Portney and R.N. Stavins (1995), 'Environmental regulation and the competitiveness of U.S manufacturing: what does the evidence tell us?', *Journal of Economic Literature*, **33**, 132-63.

Leibenstein, H. (1966), 'Allocative efficiency vs. x-efficiency', *American Economic Review*, **56**, 392-415.

McDougall, F., P. White, M. Franke and P. Hindle (2001), *Integrated Waste Management*, Oxford: Blackwell.

NNDC (2000), *Environment Awards 2000 Information Sheet*, Cromer, Norfolk: North Norfolk District Council.

Oates, W.E., K. Palmer and P.R. Portney (1994), *Environmental Regulation and International Competitiveness: Thinking about the Porter Hypothesis*, Working Paper 94-02, Washington DC: Resources for the Future.

OECD (1997), *Reforming Environmental Regulation in OECD Countries*, Paris: OECD.

Pearce. D.W. (1998), *Economics and Environment*, Cheltenham: Edward Elgar.

Pearce, D.W. and R.K. Turner (1990), *Economics of Natural Resources and the Environment*, New York: Harvester Wheatsheaf.

Peters, M.D. (2001), *Improving the Environmental Performance of Small and Medium Sized Enterprises: An Assessment of Attitudes and Voluntary Action*, PhD Thesis. University of East Anglia, Norwich.

Phillips, P.S., A.D. Read, A.E. Green and M.P. Bates (1999), 'UK waste minimisation clubs: a contribution to sustainable waste management', *Resources, Conservation and Recycling*, **27**, 217-47.

Porter, M.E. (1990), *The Competitive Advantage of Nations*, London: Macmillan.

Porter, M.E. and C. van der Linde (1995), 'Toward a new conception of the environment-competitiveness relationship', *Journal of Economic Perspectives*, **9** (4), 97-118.

Powell, J.C. (1996), 'The evaluation of waste management options', *Waste Management and Research*, **14**, 515-26.

Powell, J.C., D.W. Pearce and A.L. Craighill (1997), 'Approaches to valuation in LCA Impact Assessment', *International Journal of Life Cycle Assessment*, **2** (1), 11-15.

Russell, C.S. and P.T. Powell (1999), 'Practical considerations and comparison of instruments of environmental policy', in J.C.J.M. van den Bergh (ed.), *Handbook of Environmental and Resource Economics*, Cheltenham: Edward Elgar, pp. 307-28.

Schmalensee, R. (1993), *The Costs of Environmental Regulation*, Center for Energy and Environmental Policy Research Working Paper 93-015, Cambridge, MA: Massachusetts Institute of Technology.

Select Committee on the Environment, Transport and Regional Affairs (SCETRA) (1999), *The Operation of the Landfill Tax*, Thirteenth Report, London: HMSO.

Turner, R.K., D.W. Pearce and I.J. Bateman (1993), *Environmental Economics. An Elementary Introduction*, Hemel Hempstead: Harvester Wheatsheaf.

Turner, R.K. (2000a), 'Markets and environmental quality', in G.L. Clark, M.P. Feldman and M.S. Gertles (eds), *The Oxford Handbook of Economic Geography*,

Oxford: Oxford University Press, pp. 585-606.

Turner, R.K. (2000b), 'Waste management', in H. Folmer and H. Landis Gabel (eds), *Principles of Environmental and Resource Economics*, Cheltenham: Edward Elgar, pp. 700-44.

Vatn, A. and D. Bromley (1997), 'Externalities: a market model failure', *Environmental and Resource Economics*, **9**, 135-51.

Van Buekering, P. (2001), *International Trade, Recycling and the Environment: An Empirical Analysis*, PhD Thesis, Institute for Environmental Studies, Vrije Universiteit, Amsterdam.

Von Weizsacker, A., A.B. Lovins and L.H. Lovins (1997), *Factor Four: Doubling Wealth, Halving Resource Use*, London: Earthscan.

6.   Waste Law

David Wilkinson

6.1 INTRODUCTION

In this chapter I wish to look at two of the central tenets of modern environmental policy: first, that waste is a clear and useful concept around which to focus regulatory controls; second, that adherence to the so-called 'Waste Management Hierarchy' is the best way effectively to manage waste problems. The chapter focuses on the European experience and the way European law has developed in addressing the issue of waste.

The remainder of the chapter has the following structure. In the rest of this section I examine the earliest origins of the legal notion of waste. This is followed by a section in which sets out the evolution of the concept of waste in European law, its crystallisation and subsequent loss of clarity. Having shown the legal concept of waste to be currently ambiguous and over-inclusive, I set out, in a further section, an alternative based around 'value'. Finally, the waste management hierarchy, its evolution and shift towards a more sophisticated Best Practicable Environmental Option (BPEO) is explored.

6.1.1 Historical Development of Waste Law from Medieval Controls

The legal concept of 'waste' began with the medieval 'doctrine of waste' (Burn, 1994). The doctrine of waste provides one of the earliest legal embodiments of the twin notions of sustainable development and inter-generational equity. Under the doctrine, a tenant-for-life was prevented from destroying the land, and certain attached items, to the detriment of later owners. The obligation not to commit waste was a tort (civil wrong), independent of any contract or implied covenant that may exist between tenant and landlord. The essential idea behind the doctrine was to share resources equitably between generations and to maintain a minimal stock of certain essential resources for the benefit of future generations. Acts of waste were said to be either 'voluntary' (i.e. positive acts) or 'permissive' (omissions to act). Voluntary waste included pulling down or altering houses, digging pits or mines, detrimental changes in agricultural practice, and cutting timber (i.e. mature trees of a certain girth). Of course, on most readings, sustainable development does not imply absolute resource preservation. Likewise, under the doctrine of waste, a tenant for years was permitted to take wood as well as timber (estovers) for certain essential and immediate purposes. Permissible estovers included wood for fuel or building purposes (house-bote); for making/repairing agricultural implements (plough-bote) and for repairing hedges (hay-bote).

6.1.2 Crystallisation of the Legal Concept of Waste?

In time, the idea of waste as damage gave way to the idea of waste as something of little or no value to be disposed of by a person. European Community laws embodying this new conception of waste arose in the 1970s.

It is interesting to note that the first European Community waste legislation – Council Directive 75/439/EEC on the Disposal of Waste Oils – was not 'environmental' legislation at all, but in fact a resource protection measure in response to the 1973 OPEC oil embargo. The advent of national waste legislation, ostensibly causing non-harmonised economic conditions, prompted a Community response in the form of Directive 75/442/EEC on Waste. The legislative debates during the passage of Directive 75/442/EEC reveal a heated uncertainty and disagreement over the meaning of 'waste' that has dogged this area of environmental law ever since.

The concept of waste used by the Commission in their original proposal for a directive was:

> ... any residue from a production or utilization process and more generally any moveable property which the owner wishes or is obliged to dispose of or which has been abandoned.

> 'Disposal' shall be taken to mean the collection, transport and treatment of waste as well as storage and dumping on or in the soil.

This definition, which the Commission hoped would allow the waste Directive to have the widest possible field of application, was not accepted. Much internal wrangling then took place in the Committee of Permanent Representatives (COREPER) with the following definitions receiving consideration:

- Deletion of the subjective element ('wishes to dispose of') (a Dutch proposal)

- Deletion of 'has been abandoned' (French)
- Deletion of 'is obliged to [dispose of]' (Dutch and French)
- Replacement by: 'any substance or article the methodical disposal of which becomes necessary in the general interest owing to deterioration, wear, contamination or any other material change' (Commission)
- Replacement by: 'any substance or article which requires disposal in the interest of public health or protection of the environment' (Irish)
- Replacement by: 'any moveable property of which the owner disposes (intends to dispose or of which he is obliged to dispose in the general interest' (Germany)
- Replacement by: 'any substance or article which the holder gets rid of; "waste disposal" means collection, transport, treatment of waste; its storage and dumping on or in the soil and also, insofar as possible, its recovery, re-utilization and recycling' (COREPER Chairman)

The range of formulations given above indicates that the notion of waste is hotly contested. There was, in particular, considerable disagreement in COREPER concerning whether items consigned to recycling or re-use should be regarded as waste: a problem which, as we shall see, has continued to bedevil the issue. The Italian delegation, thought that such items should be included and, accordingly, requested deletion of words suggesting that only items subject to processes preliminary to recycling/re-use would be regarded as waste. The German, Danish and UK delegations thought otherwise and eventually it was agreed that the concept of 'recovery' would be incorporated into the definition of 'disposal' itself.

Finally, agreement was reached. The concept of waste, as adopted in the English language text of Directive 75/442/EEC was:

1 (a) 'Waste' means
    any substance or object which the holder disposes or is required to dispose of pursuant to the provisions of national law in force' (Art. 1(a)).

(b) Disposal means
    - the collection, sorting, transport and treatment of waste as well as its storage and tipping above or under ground,
    - the transformation operations necessary for its re-use, recovery or recycling.

This concept of waste ran into some difficulties. There were variations in the interpretation of the term 'dispose' across the EC member states. Also, the definition was not quite congruent with the definitions adopted, at international level, by the Organisation for Economic Cooperation and Development (OECD Council Decision C(88) 90 Final of May 1988) and the Basel Convention on the disposal of hazardous waste. Consequently, in due course, the opportunity was taken to redefine it.

Directive 91/156/EEC, adopted on 18 March 1991, modified Directive 75/442/EEC such that:

1   (a)   'waste' shall mean any substance or object in the categories set out in Annex I which the holder discards or intends or is required to discard.
        The Commission, acting in accordance with the procedure laid down in Article 18, will draw up, not later than 1 April 1993, a list of wastes belonging to the categories listed in Annex I. This list will be periodically reviewed and, if necessary, revised by the same procedure.
    (b)   'producer' shall mean anyone whose activities produce waste ("original producer") and/or anyone who carries out pre-processing, mixing or other operations resulting in a change in the nature or composition of this waste;
    (c)   'holder' shall mean the producer of the waste or the natural or legal person who is in possession of it;
    (d)   'management' shall mean the collection, transport, recovery and disposal of waste, including the supervision of such operations and after-care of disposal sites;
    (e)   'disposal' shall mean any of the operations provided for in Annex II, A;
    (f)   'recovery shall mean any of the operations provided for in Annex II, B;
    (g)   'collection' shall mean the gathering, sorting and/or mixing of waste for the purpose of transport.

Annexes I, IIA and IIB were virtually identical to those previously published by the OECD in its decision of 1988.

At first sight, it appeared that the vexed question of what constitutes waste had been answered, once and for all, by the twin means of the listing of substances and objects in Annex I to the Directive, along with the list of wastes that the Commission was to draw up under Article 1. If only life were so simple!

Surprisingly, and contrary to the wording of Article I, Annex I turned out to have no definitional role. This is because it took the form of a list of categories of substances and objects, the last category of which was 'Any materials, substances or products which are not contained in the above categories'. Such a category clearly includes the whole physical world.

Similarly, the list of wastes (belatedly) produced by the Commission, under its Article 1 mandate, now known as the 'European Waste Catalogue' (EWC), also lacked definitional qualities. This was because, rightly or wrongly, the Commission prefaced the EWC with the following statement:

The inclusion of a material in the EWC does not mean that the material is a waste in all circumstances. The entry is only relevant when the definition of waste is satisfied.

The elimination of Annex I and the EWC leaves only the central term 'discard' (note the subtle change from the previous term 'dispose') and Annexes IIA and IIB. It is, therefore, from these three ingredients that the European legal conception of waste must to be created.

Annex IIA lists a series of disposal operations that, in practice, cover most types of waste disposal operation. Annex IIB lists a similar range of recovery (i.e. reuse, recycling and energy recovery) operations. Neither list, however, purports to be comprehensive.

The first serious attempt to explain the meaning of 'discard', and the relationship between that term and Annexes IIA and IIB, arose in the European Court of Justice (ECJ) case of *Tombesi* (Case C-304/94, together with joined cases C-330/94, C-342/94 and C-224/95, ECJ, 25 June 1997, [1997] CMLR 673). In *Tombesi* the defendants, who had been charged with various waste handling offences, argued that the substances that they had handled were reusable residues and that, therefore, they were not waste.

The Italian court asked the European Court of Justice (ECJ) for its opinion; i.e. whether materials, 'in so far as they are residual, derived from production or consumption cycles in a manufacturing or combustion process' would always be waste and whether certain processes fell outside of Annex II. ECJ judgments are preceded by a detailed 'Opinion' given by an ECJ judge (Advocate General).

In his Opinion for the *Tombesi* decision, Advocate General Jacobs stated that the meaning of 'waste' turned on the meaning of 'discard':

> ... the term 'discard' employed in the definition of waste in Article 1(a) has a special meaning encompassing both the disposal of waste and its consignment to a recovery operation. The scope of the term 'waste' therefore depends on what is meant by 'disposal operation' and 'recovery operation'.

This statement was potentially of the utmost importance since, if correct, the term 'waste' would have become merely short-hand for any object consigned to a disposal or recovery operation. In other words, so long as there had been a disposal or recovery operation there would be no need to find, independently, any act of 'discarding'. We can refer to this as the 'non-substantive' concept of waste. It does seem a little strange, to say the least, however, that the question of what waste is should be determined not by looking at the nature of the material in question, but rather simply by examining the processes to which it has been subject.

The 'non-substantive' concept of waste was given support by a ruling of a UK court in the case of *Mayer Parry Recycling Limited* v. *Environment Agency* ([1999] Env LR 489). Mayer Parry, one of the UK's largest scrap metal reprocessing firms, sought a legal ruling to clarifying the correct approach to be taken by the Environment Agency (EA) in interpreting the concept of 'waste'. The important issue between the parties was whether scrap metals that were subject to various processing operations were 'waste'. Judge Carnworth impliedly backed Advocate General Jacobs' non-substantive approach, by ruling that the case turned on the scope of the term 'recovery' in Annex IIB. Specifically, he ruled, where the metals were subject to pre-processing operations listed in the Annex, they would be waste. On the other hand, where scrap metal was directly re-used without any intervening transformation processes, this did not constitute the use of waste, since direct reuse is not listed in either Annexes IIA or IIB.

Not everyone liked the idea of waste being defined in this 'reverse reasoning' manner. As early as 1994 Waite (1994), anticipating this problem, took the position that the Directive treats 'discarding' as a separate and prior to 'disposal' or 'recovery' and that, therefore, waste cannot be defined simply by the simplistic application of these criteria. Waite also reasoned that the existence of Articles 4 and 8 of the Directive, both of which refer to disposal and recovery of waste, implies prior and separate identification of material as waste; furthermore he observed that the disposal and recovery operations listed in Annex IIA and IIB can be conducted with material other than waste.

In *Arco* (Case C-418/97) the Dutch Supreme Court (the Nederlandse Raad van State) asked the ECJ to determine whether so-called 'LUWA-bottoms' (by-products of a chemical manufacturing process), which are used as fuel in the cement manufacturing process, should be regarded as waste. The ECJ's reply was that the question whether a substance is waste:

> ... must be determined in the light of all the circumstances, regard being had to the aim of the Directive and the need to ensure that its effectiveness is not undermined.

The court added that it is not conclusive in either direction that a substance has been subject to processes listed in Annexes IIA or B. It is also not definitive that the substance in question may be recovered in an environmentally responsible manner for use as fuel without substantial treatment. Nevertheless, such factors are *relevant evidence* to be taken into consideration when such a determination was being made. Specifically, the court added, the fact that the use of a substance as fuel is a common method of recovering waste and the fact that such a substance is commonly regarded as waste can be taken as evidence that the holder has discarded that substance or intends or is required to discard it within the meaning of Article 1(a) of Directive 75/442.

So where does that leave us? Briefly, still in the dark. Whether something is waste depends upon whether it has been discarded (which we already knew) but the ECJ's guidance concerning what is meant by 'discard' is vague to say the least; in *Arco* it said that one should look at all sorts of factors including whether something is 'commonly regarded' as waste and that the question needs to be determined on a 'case by case' basis. Regarded by whom? Are the courts and those involved in the waste industry supposed to employ public opinion research agencies? As for the 'case by case basis', this is normally legal short-hand for 'we haven't got a clue'. It is, therefore, likely that we shall see courts in one EU state ruling that a substance is waste, while those in another state take the contrary view. There is likely to be uncertainty for businesses and environmental regulators alike. Generally, there will be an increase in uncertainty in what is and what is not waste.

6.1.3 Moving to a Value Concept of Waste

The one thing that is clear from the above account is that the concept of waste is much contested, especially when it sought to apply that concept to reusable or recyclable materials. The reason is this: industries feel aggrieved and unnecessarily burdened when they are subject to the plethora of waste laws that exist in relation to objects or materials that are, in essence, just another form of raw material for their processes. They would argue – and it is an argument with which I have much sympathy – that these objects and materials are no more likely to create environmental harm than any other raw material. Indeed, by reutilising what are essentially cast-offs or redundant things, they are solving an environmental problem and ought, on that basis, not to be subject to a waste regulation regime. The heart of the problem lies in the idea that anything that has been discarded should be, by dint of that action, be treated as a potential environmental hazard. This is not true. In fact objects or substances are only likely to treated without care if they are not *valued*. This is why, elsewhere (Wilkinson, 1999) I have argued that if we are to have a concept of waste then it should be one based on the positive notion of value, not on the negative one of discard.

A legal case which illustrates the futility of not using a value approach to waste, is the prosecution in the English case of *Kent County Council* v. *Queenborough Rolling Mill Co. Ltd.* ([1990] Crim LR 813). A third party, who had been contracted to clear broken pottery from a site, offered and supplied that material to the mill company who, in turn, arranged for the broken pottery to be set down on their site to stabilise that land which, being near a river, was liable to subsidence. The mill company was subsequently charged with unlawfully depositing waste without a licence under the Control of Pollution Act 1974. The magistrates concluded that the usefulness of the material on the site precluded its classification as 'waste', and dismissed the charges accordingly. Good sense indeed. However, the Queen's Bench Division (a higher court) overturned that ruling and held that the material in question had been 'waste' for the purposes of the 1974 Act when it was removed from the original site, and that its character was not subsequently changed by its usefulness to the respondents for infill purposes. This decision conflicts with common sense since, regardless of the original owner's intention, the material at the time of its subsequent use, was of obvious value to the rolling mill. Furthermore, being an inert substance, it created no greater environmental hazard than a virgin material that could have been used to stabilise the land instead. Once a substance is in the hands of a holder who values it, there is no longer any good reason to treat it as waste. The fact that the original holder of such a substance has discarded it is, from an environmental perspective, irrelevant. The psychological state of the last holder of a substance is no indicator of the future potential environmental impact of that substance.

In summary, the concept of waste is not only unclear, resting on a case-by-case determination with reference to limitless and unpredictable factors, but it is also inherently flawed, insofar as it seeks to regulate things which are not only not no more hazardous than non-waste, but which are, indeed, part of the solution to the waste problem.

6.2 THE WASTE MANAGEMENT HIERARCHY (WMH)

6.2.1 Why Prioritise?

Since the realisation that the problem of waste exists there have been calls for waste to be dealt with in a strictly prioritised manner. By this I mean the view that in dealing with waste, certain strategies should be applied before others.

6.2.2 Evolution of the WMH

One of the earliest rankings for dealing with the problem of waste is found in the European Commission's 1989 document, 'A Community Strategy for Waste Management' (CEC, 1989). This sets out the following ranking:

1. Prevention
2. Recycling and re-use
3. Optimisation and final disposal
4. Regulation of Transport
5. Remedial Action

For many years this ordering was repeated in a fairly parrot-like manner regardless of the actual desirability of such an approach. In 1994 the UK House of Commons' Environment Committee stated (HCEC, 1994, xxi):

There is broad agreement that methods of waste management can be stated in order of priority in a 'waste management Hierarchy' – with reduction at source as the most favoured option then, in order of desirability, re-use, recovery and disposal ... We are convinced of the fundamental preferability of waste reduction at source. Re-use and recovery (of both energy and materials) are the next best options. The relative merits of energy and materials recovery, however, are finely balanced and will depend very much on the circumstances. Disposal may sometimes be necessary but should be an option of last resort.

Fortunately, recently a welcome degree of sophistication has arisen that that overcomes problems of a such a simplistic approach. The UK government's policy on waste, 'Waste Strategy 2000 (Department of Environment Food and Rural Affairs, 2000) envisages the waste management hierarchy as merely part of an attempt to determine the Best Practicable Environmental Option (BPEO) for any substance or object. BPEO was defined by the Royal Commission on Environmental Pollution in its 12th report (1988, p. 23) as

the outcome of a systematic and consultative decision-making procedure which emphasises the protection and conservation of the environment across land, air and water. The BPEO procedure establishes, for a given set of objectives, the option that provides the most benefits or the least damage to the environment as a whole, at acceptable cost, in the long term as well as in the short term.

This implies that there can be no waste hierarchy that is fixed in stone. Rather, as Waste Strategy 2000 confirms (emphasis added),

The waste hierarchy is a *conceptual framework*, which acts as a guide to the framework that should be considered when assessing BPEO. It can also be a useful presentational tool for delivering a complex message in a comparatively simple and accessible way:

- the most effective environmental solution is often to reduce the generation of waste reduction

- products and materials can sometimes be used again, for the same or a different purpose

- re-use value can often be recovered from waste, through recycling, composting or energy recovered

only if none of the above offer an appropriate solution should waste be disposed of.

The Strategy adds that when considering the BPEO, decision-makers must have regard to international obligations (e.g. the biodegradable municipal waste diversion targets in the Landfill Directive), the national policy framework (including the WMH), and policy guidance at regional and local level.

This entails that (para 3.6):

> ... [t]he concept of BPEO means that local environmental, social and economic preferences will be important in any decision. These may well result in different BPEOs for the same waste in different areas, or even different BPEOs for the same type of waste in the same area but at different times (for example, when the economy is growing or in recession).

All of this implies a degree of insight and flexibility lacking in earlier policy statements. The 'icing on the cake' is the endorsement of multiple criteria analysis (MCA), of which life cycle analysis (LCA) should form a part. All of this is a long way from the WMH's early inflexible origins. Nevertheless, there is still a presumption that generally it is better to produce less waste. To quote again from the Strategy (para 3.7):

> ... the [WMH] ... offers an order which can be used when considering various waste management options, starting with a review of how less waste might be produced. Once this has been carried out, all options in the hierarchy should be considered for each component material within the waste stream, and for waste which cannot be reasonably separated out. For different materials, different options are likely to prove more environmentally effective and economically affordable. Thus the BPEO for a waste stream is likely to be a mix of different waste management methods.

6.2.3 Critique of the Waste Management Hierarchy

The more recent shift, away from a rigid ordering to a looser and more intelligent approach, indicates that the very notion of WMH is flawed. The recent policy statements referred to above reveal that the very notion of a waste management hierarchy is simply an heuristic device to assist in ascertaining the BPEO. It would be far better, in that case, to jettison the unnecessary baggage of WMH and to stick solely with BPEO. The danger of mixing the two concepts is that recipients of WMH waste may still take the view that there is merit *per se* in adhering to a policy of reduction first, recycling next, disposal last, except where BPEO indicates the contrary. There should not be such a presumption. The sole criteria of waste policy should be whether, all things considered, a certain course of action in relation to a particular waste is the best choice for the environment.

Take the case of waste paper for example. The public have long been exhorted to save and recycle this form of mashed compressed wood (e.g. OECD: 1980; Council of the European Communities, 1981). Yet studies show that, due to the problems of pollution from the reconstitution process, along with energy use in the collection and treatment of the material, the benefits of paper recycling are by no means clear-cut (Virtanen, 1993).

6.2.4 Law and the WHM

An examination of law, at International, European and National levels, reveals that, in practice, arrangements for waste management are quite the opposite of the received WMH. When we look at the structure of waste laws, we find that most laws are designed to allow the safe transportation or disposal or wastes; that there are fewer laws that facilitate recycling, and that almost no laws exist that mandate waste minimisation. This is, at first sight, all very strange.

Very few laws oblige the minimisation of waste, which is interesting given that the OECD's (1996) Policy document in this area suggested that wide ranging action should be taken, including:

1. Setting legally-binding waste reduction targets and general measures;
2. Prohibition of certain waste-prone products or waste-prone materials associated with certain products – including controls over use of packaging;
3. Requiring re-use of products and/or requiring products to be manufactured so as to be re-usable;
4. Designing products to have extended life or to result in minimum waste arising at end of product life;
5. Stipulating/facilitating less wasteful manufacturing techniques, through changes in management or processes (including eco-audit and compliance with international standards);
6. Prohibiting toxic substances in manufacturing processes, thereby reducing hazardous waste arising at product grave;
7. Public education and information; and
8. The use of economic instruments

In practice, however, apart from a small number of measures, these calls have remained entirely unheeded. Industries and states remain quite free to decide upon waste minimisation strategies as and when they choose. In fact, attempts by any single state to require products to be lest wasteful would be likely to run foul of free trade rules, such as those that exist under Article 30 of the EC Treaty and the corresponding articles of the NAFTA and GATT Treaties.

Recycling and recovery, on the other hand, has been the subject of a reasonably large number of laws. Most developed states require some, if not all, enterprises to engage in the recycling or recovery of some form of materials. In the EU, for example, Member States are required to achieve quantified recovery targets for packaging under the provisions of the Packaging Waste Directive and for vehicle components under the End of Vehicle Life Directive.

Finally, and in contrast to the two preceding categories, laws governing the disposal of waste are ubiquitous. The EU and the UK have produced several key regulations, including the Waste Framework Directive, the Landfill Directive, the Groundwater Directive and the provisions of part II of the Environment Act 1990.

This picture is interesting: both early and late versions of the WMH point to efforts being focused on essentially preventative measures, while 'law in action' appears to have dealt primarily with the control of waste once it has been produced. The explanation of this discrepancy, I suggest, is that politicians and legislatures instinctively understand the need for adoption of BPEO rather than slavish adherence to any WMH. It is understood – if not expressed – that, in many cases, attempts to reduce, minimise and recycle waste are likely to be expensive without any real environmental benefits over careful control and disposal of waste post-production.

6.3 CONCLUSION

When we combine the discussion of the concept of waste with the waste management hierarchy, we arrive at the following position. First, there is still considerable confusion about what actually constitutes waste. In contrast, there has been a long-felt certainty that the best thing to do with waste can be determined by the application of a fairly simple ranked list of options. It is difficult to agree with either of these outcomes. Waste should be clearly represented as objects or substances that have no value to their current holder. As such it should either be reused as a secondary raw material or, where this is not possible, be treated or subject to processes that will lead to the least environmental harm i.e. the best practicable environmental option.

REFERENCES

Burn, E.H. (1994), *Cheshire and Burn's Modern Law of Real Property*, London: Butterworths.
Commission of the European Communities (1989), 'A Community strategy for waste management', Communication from the Commission to the Council and the Parliament', ref SEC (89) 934 Final.
Council of the European Communities (1981), 'Council recommendation 81/972/EEC of 3 December 1981 concerning the re-use of waste paper and the use of recycled paper', http://europa.eu.int/eur-lex/en/lif/dat/1981/en_381X0972.html.

Department of Environment Food and Rural Affairs (2000) *Waste Strategy 2000 for England and Wales*, http://www.defra.gov.uk/environment/waste/strategy/cm4693/index.htm

HCEC (House of Commons Environment Committee) (1994) *Second Report, Reccling, Volume I*, London: Her Majesty's Stationery Office.

OECD (1980), *Waste Paper Recovery 30 January 1980* http://sedac.ciesin.org/pidb/texts/oecd/OECD-4.07.html

OECD (1996), *Comprehensive Waste Management Policy and the EU Commission's Waste Policy*, com doc (COM(96)399).

Royal Commission on Environmental Pollution (1988) *Twelfth Report: Best Practicable Environmental Option*, London, Her Majesty's Stationery Office

Virtanen, Y. (1993), *Environmental Impacts of Waste Paper Recycling*, London: Earthscan.

Waite, A. (1994), 'Crucial need to understand the meaning of waste', in *Institute of Wastes Management/UKELA Law and the Waste Industry*, IWM/UKELA.

Wilkinson, D. (1999), 'Time to discard the concept of Waste?', *Environmental Law Review*, **1** (3), 172-95.

PART THREE

Specific Waste Issues

7.   Municipal Waste

Eduardo Barata

7.1 INTRODUCTION

Waste management has become a major concern of our times. Worldwide, enormous amounts of residues are being produced, which need to be managed in an economical way, while not compromising the environment and public health. Intensive work is being done in searching for means to reduce the growing amount of waste generated and technologies to discard and dispose of it safely and economically.

This chapter examines some of the issues concerning municipal solid waste generation and management problems, and reviews the most important responses to them.

Section 7.2 sets the limits and the goals of the present study, introducing several general basic issues, such as the concept of municipal solid waste and its empirical importance. The analysis follows with an historical approach to the economic, social and environmental significance of municipal waste management issues. Possible inconsistencies between the strategies presumed by the waste management hierarchy and the integrated approach are highlighted. Despite these potential divergences concerning the municipal waste management systems philosophy, the section closes by stressing that the technologies to handle municipal solid waste economically and safely do exist and are available today.

To offer some guidance on environmentally sound and economically feasible solutions, Section 7.3 examines the most important and widely accepted waste management options (i.e. source reduction, recycling and composting, incineration and other thermal processes, and landfilling). It is stressed that the management of municipal solid waste is not merely an engineering problem, but involves a multiplicity of factors, including environmental, economic and political ones, which quintessentially stress municipal waste management as an issue for ecological economics. Section 7.4 offers some conclusions

7.2 THE NATURE OF MUNICIPAL WASTE

On a regular basis, municipal waste is collected in every municipality in the developed world, and transported to waste processing facilities. The responsibility of carrying out these activities is usually that of the local community authorities.

7.2.1 The Concept of Municipal Waste

Municipal solid waste includes household waste (i.e. waste originating from domestic households) and any other similar substances collected by or on behalf of a 'waste collection authority' (usually the municipality). A distinctive characteristic of this waste stream is that these wastes are produced as part of the daily routine of households and business activity. This definition is relatively complex, being based on at least three separate concepts: waste collection (the municipal collection scheme), waste source (domestic activity of households) and waste type.

The difficulties in dealing with this complexity have resulted in inconsistent applications of the term, making it very difficult to establish direct comparisons between municipal waste management strategies and waste arisings in different countries (EEA, 2000, p. 10). Therefore, in the following, the terms 'daily household and commercial waste', household waste, and municipal waste will be used interchangeably.

7.2.2 The Relative Importance of Municipal Waste

According to the European Environmental Agency (EEA) countries data, municipal waste arisings corresponds to only approximately 10 per cent (150 million tons) of the total amount of the overall waste in these 17 countries (excluding agricultural waste) (EEA, 2000). However, municipal solid waste is highly visible, through daily contact in our residences, commercial establishments and public institutions, and none of us can ignore its presence or our responsibility for its generation. Additionally, household waste has proved to be one of the hardest sources of waste to manage effectively, due to its complex composition and varied sources of generation.

Recently, municipal solid waste management issues appear to have become an important policy problem at a global scale, particularly in the industrialized countries. This is because waste is growing exponentially in quantity, has the potential for polluting land, water and air, and is expensive to deal with properly (Clarke et al., 1999, p. 126). Additionally, the nature of waste itself is also changing, because of development-related changes in consumption patterns.

For decades, the solution of the majority of public authorities worldwide has been simply to burn or bury this waste. It was not until the last 25 years that governments started to give serious thought to the regulation of waste disposal and treatment (Clarke et al., 1999, p. 127), as it became no longer acceptable to discard waste materials without concern for environmental and natural resources issues.

7.2.3 Historical Background

Municipal solid waste management has evolved from primitive origins, through the development of open dumps in ancient Middle Eastern urban developments, as far back as 6000 years ago, to the sophisticated collection and disposal systems that are in use today. However, this evolution has been at different rates in different regions of the globe, and in the developing countries there still exist practices not very different from the Roman open dumps (see also Chapter 3).

A technological approach to solid waste management began to develop in the latter part of the nineteenth century. Water-resistant garbage cans were first introduced in the United States, and sturdier vehicles were used to collect and transport waste. A significant development in solid waste treatment and disposal practices was marked by the construction of the first refuse incinerator in England in 1878 (Gandy, 1994, p. 8). At the beginning of the twentieth century, however, most of the largest cities were still using primitive disposal methods, such as open dumping on land or in water.

Technological advances continued during the first half of the twentieth century, including the development of garbage grinders and compaction trucks. By mid-century, however, it had become evident that open dumping and improper incineration of solid waste was causing problems of pollution and public health. Additionally, particularly during the period since World War II, the production of waste has dramatically increased, reflecting unprecedented global levels of economic activity and increasing affluence. In one estimate for the United States, municipal waste production per capita increased five times over the fifty years period from 1920 to 1970 (Gandy, 1994, p. 1). As a result, improved methods of controlled waste disposal on land were developed, to replace the practice of open dumping and to reduce the reliance on waste incineration. Also, new and more environment-friendly refuse incinerators were designed. These recovered heat energy from the waste and used extensive air pollution control devices to satisfy stringent standards of air quality.

A review of the existing literature (see van Beukering et al., 1999) reveals that a great number of studies on municipal solid waste management have been undertaken. In earlier studies the prime consideration was the quick removal of waste and its destruction, but during the 1970s the debate shifted to issues of waste utilisation. Studies during this time focused on the technical and economic issues surrounding the allocation and utilisation of available resources, and examined existing state-of-the-art resource recovery for managing urban waste.

In the 1980s, environmental concerns began to drive local solid waste planning and management. Additionally, this era brought recognition of the latent landfill capacity crisis (Goddard, 1995, p. 188). Public concern about landfills 'in their back yard' makes solid waste management a major issue for communities, and constitutes a major difficulty in siting new landfill facilities. At the same time, existing landfill capacities appear to be shrinking dramatically (Goddard, 1995, p. 184).

Progressively, municipal solid waste management issues have moved up the public agenda, and during the 1990s the levels of concern and activity by citizens, researchers and governments worldwide reached unprecedented levels (Read et al., 1997, p. 183).

As a result, in the last decade research projects have been promoting an integrated approach to municipal waste management, putting together managerial, environmental, economic and social concerns. This paradigm shift in municipal solid waste management has been stimulated by several major factors, namely:

- Increased rates of municipal solid waste generation associated with increasing costs for disposing of wastes in an environmentally safe manner;
- Growing recognition that conventional approaches (such as 'end-of-pipe' disposal) have become unsustainable in many cities as dumping spaces are becoming hard to acquire and too far away) (Clarke et al., 1999, p. 128);
- The public is more aware of the risks associated with poor waste management practices and increasingly resistant to the locating of new waste management facilities in their vicinities (the NIMBY [Not In My Back Yard] attitude);
- Waste reduction and recycling are now internationally accepted as the basic principles in all waste management systems.

The desire for improved municipal waste management is part of the greater emphasis placed upon environmental issues articulated at the 1992 Earth Summit. In the United Nations 'Agenda 21' document, a number of objectives were set for increasing the sustainability of waste management, including minimisation of waste, stabilisation of waste production, maximisation of environmentally sound waste re-use and recycling, and promotion of environmentally sound waste disposal practices (Read et al., 1997, p. 186). To sum up, in a relatively short time, municipal solid waste management has changed greatly, from a 'dig a hole and bury it' mindset, to the complex notion of 'integrated solid waste management'.

7.2.4. The 'Integrated Approach' versus the 'Waste Management Hierarchy'

According to the 'integrated approach' to municipal solid waste management, decisions on waste handling should take into account economic, environmental, social and institutional dimensions. The economic aspect will always be crucial in any waste management framework. Economic aspects may include the costs and benefits of implementation, and the available municipal budgets for waste management. The environmental dimension may consist of the assessment of local problems (i.e. increased risk of epidemics and groundwater pollution), regional problems (i.e. resource depletion and acid rain), and global problems (i.e. global warming and ozone depletion). Social aspects include employment effects, impacts on human health and ethical issues such as the consent of local people. Finally, concerning the institutional dimension, a special emphasis should be placed on an effective involvement of the main stakeholders, including waste generators, waste processors and government institutions, such as waste managers and urban planners (van Beukering et al., 1999, p. 3).

Therefore, no single and universal solution can be identified that completely answers the question of what to do with our waste. Every community or region has its own unique profile regarding solid waste and should develop its own 'integrated waste management system', taking into account its own local requirements and matching its unique position with the mix of activities that will best serve it now and far into the future.

Nevertheless, the philosophy that has been adopted by most of the world's countries, particularly the industrialised nations, for developing strategies for managing municipal solid waste is based on the 'waste management hierarchy'. This lays primary emphasis on waste prevention, followed in a strictly descending order by the promotion of material recovery (including reprocessing and organic recycling), energy recovery, and then, as the least favoured option, methods of safe final disposal (see Chapter 6).

Briefly, this hierarchy is based on environmental principles which have as the main objective the avoidance of waste generation and its related toxicity. This implies changing production and consumption patterns to reduce the use of disposable, non-reusable materials and packaging. This goal follows a very sensible principle: the easiest (and the cheapest) way to handle waste is not to create it. Besides reducing the total quantity, waste prevention also includes the reduction of environmentally harmful materials in the waste stream.

Where further reduction is not practicable, the opportunity of re-using products and materials should be explored. This involves putting objects and substances back into use, so they do not enter the waste stream, and can be used either for their original or different purposes. The next best alternative is recovering all of the potential residual value from waste, through recycling (material recovery), composting and energy recovery (usually recycling and composting should be considered before recovery of energy from waste). Finally, and only if none of the above offers an appropriate solution, the remaining 'stabilised waste' should be disposed of in an environmentally sound landfill.

Reality does not adhere easily to this environmentally based sequence. In spite of it being generally known that the 'waste management hierarchy' should be understood as a general guideline to achieve the best environmental solution in the long term, it has been subject to strong criticism for various reasons. The main criticism is that its extensive reliance on source reduction and recycling is misguided and expensive. Indeed, although the ranking may indeed be correct in terms of environmental pressure for certain materials, this would not be the case in all circumstances. For instance, it may be better to recycle an old refrigerator rather than reuse it, because its inefficient energy consumption may create more environmental damage than the recycling related burdens (van Beukering et al., 1999, p. 6).

Therefore, many believe that the options should not be ranked in a particular order or hierarchy, but should be considered as a 'menu' of alternatives. Each option can be equally appropriate under the right set of conditions, addressing the right set of waste stream components, according to the framework of an 'integrated waste management approach'.

7.3 MUNICIPAL WASTE MANAGEMENT OPTIONS

7.3.1 Source Reduction

Policy analysts are increasingly recognising the great potential of source reduction in helping to solve the municipal solid waste problem (Lober, 1996, p. 125). Source reduction offers promising economic and environmental opportunities (Fishbein et al., 1994, Section 8.2), as reducing waste before it is generated is an obvious way to avoid financial costs of waste management, to conserve natural resources, and to cut pollution emissions.

Source reduction, or waste prevention, is a proactive approach corresponding to any change in the design, manufacturing, sale, purchase, or consumption of materials, products and packaging, to reduce their amount or toxicity before they become municipal solid waste (USEPA, 1995, Section 5.5). The reduction of the material used in a product, the increase in the lifetime of a product, the substitution of re-usable products instead of single use ones, or the reduction in the overall consumption of goods, are examples of source reduction activities (Lober, 1996, p. 127).

However, source reduction remains a frequently elusive concept. Source reduction, waste prevention, waste reduction, waste minimisation and pollution prevention, are all terms that are regularly used interchangeably. Despite a lack of standard definitions, waste policy analysts consider them to be distinct (Fishbein et al., 1994, Section 8.3). Source reduction and waste prevention are commonly distinguished from waste reduction and waste minimisation. Only initiatives that reduce the amount of waste actually generated are source reduction; anything that happens to waste after it is put out for collection is not source reduction, because the waste must be managed. The difficulties in clearly conceptualising source reduction have led to implementation problems (Lober, 1996, p. 128). Municipal solid waste source reduction plans need to include an explicitly stated source reduction policy, clearly defined goals, and meaningful measurement strategies. The first step should be a comprehensible definition of terms that clarifies what is source reduction, so that it can be differentiated from other waste management options (Fishbein et al., 1994, Section 8.5) (see also Chapter 5).

7.3.1.1 The economics of source reduction programmes

Because source reduction is much broader in scope than recycling or disposal[1], implementing source reduction programmes involves vastly different staff skills and concerns. So, in spite of source reduction not requiring the costly collection and processing operations involved in waste management options, it is not free and it cannot be accomplished without an adequate budget. The costs of source reduction are in the form of up-front investment in data collection, waste audits, legislative development, education, technical assistance, equipment and planning (Fishbein et al., 1994, Section 8.6). The payoff for investment in source reduction is not immediate and is difficult to measure, but it can be very large. It is difficult to measure what has not been produced, and to discern which reductions are due to prevention and which are due to other factors, such as the business cycle or seasonal changes (USEPA, 1995, pp. 5-7). Presently, there is no information on what it would cost to achieve higher levels of source reduction at the household level (Goddard, 1995, p. 186).

Source reduction has come to be recognised as an approach with significant potential to achieve substantial and measurable cost savings. These include avoided collection, transportation and disposal costs, and direct savings in material and supply costs (USEPA, 1993, p. 3). In addition, source reduction is cost efficient in decreasing pollution control and regulatory compliance costs. At the macro-economic level, there is some concern that source reduction might reduce economic growth by decreasing consumption. However, source reduction also offers opportunities for economic gain. Many businesses can enhance their corporate image and become more competitive through source reduction practices and others are finding that products designed for source reduction achieve significant sales (USEPA, 1995, pp. 5-7).

7.3.1.2 Environmental impacts of source reduction

The most valuable benefits from source reduction are for the environment. Source reduction can conserve natural resources and slow the depletion of valuable landfill space. It can also reduce the pollution associated with the manufacture of products. In addition reducing the hazardous constituents in goods can reduce potential management problems with waste, when the products are finally discharged (USEPA, 1993).

To illustrate the environmental impacts of source reduction, it is possible to look at the example of 'climate change', one of the most serious threats facing the world's environment. Source reduction can significantly reduce harmful environmental effects of the release of greenhouse gases into the atmosphere by:

(i)   reducing emissions from energy consumption (e.g. re-using products leads to less energy requirements to retrieve, process and transport raw materials and to manufacture products);
(ii) reducing emissions from waste combustors;
(iii) reducing methane emissions from landfills; and
(iv) increasing storage of carbon in trees (e.g. reduction in the consumption of paper products preserves forests that remove large amounts of carbon dioxide from the atmosphere).

7.3.1.3 Examples of source reduction operations

Source reduction includes a wide variety of activities. Large consumers (governments and organisations) and individuals can promote and practise source reduction for a variety of materials in different settings. For example, 'large consumers' with procurement policies that make source reduction a priority, can achieve a significant impact on the municipal waste stream. Additionally, by implementing source reduction practices, large consumers set an example for the public, and encourage manufacturers to develop less wasteful products and packages which would be available to all purchasers. Other source reduction initiatives include education programmes, legislation and regulatory measures, and economic incentives and disincentives.

Education, technical assistance and promotions are decisive in encouraging source reduction, especially for the residential sector. The consumers' role in source reduction efforts should be emphasised, which might include basing decisions about purchases not only on product attributes and costs, but also on their waste implications (see Chapter 3).

Legislation and regulations governing source reduction are increasing. They have been assuming a variety of forms, such as requirements that businesses conduct waste audits and develop source reduction plans; labelling schemes that give consumers information to encourage less wasteful purchasing decisions; bans on the sale or disposal of specific materials or products; and legislation requiring manufacturers to reduce packaging (Fishbein et al., 1994, p. 8.16).

Economic incentives include, for example, subsidies for repair businesses or reuse organisations, or financial bonuses to communities that reduce the amount of waste sent to disposal (Fishbein et al., 1994, Section 8.17). Examples of economic disincentives to reduce, reuse and refill include the implementation of volume-based rates for waste collection systems, taxes that reflect the disposal costs of packaging material, or taxes on use of virgin materials. Taxes can also be placed on single-use products, to encourage consumers to purchase products that generate less waste.

7.3.2 Recycling

Although it may appear to be a new phenomenon, recycling in one form or another has been practiced for centuries. Horrigan and Motavali (1997, p. 28) illustrate the roots of recycling, noting that metal implements were melted down and recast in prehistoric times. However, the ancient origins of these efforts only illustrate that recycling, as a concept, is being itself recycled to accommodate the exigencies of different times. The fact is that recycling remains an elusive concept about which everyone thinks they have a clear understanding until they began to practise it. There is no common agreement, either in industry or in government, on a consistent and meaningful recycling terminology, which represents a major obstacle to efficiently planning, implementing and assessing the different recycling programmes.

Nevertheless, a widely accepted view is that recycling constitutes 'the beneficial reuse' of products, materials and substances which are at the end of their useful lives and that would otherwise be disposed of. However, it is important to stress that recycling differs from reuse because it includes a processing step (Daskalapoulos et al., 1997, p. 241). Additionally, a proper characterisation of the recycling concept should distinguish between primary and secondary recycling (Daskalapoulos et al., 1997, p. 241). In primary recycling, the products are put back into the same or similar products (e.g. making old glass containers into new glass containers or using old newsprint to create new newsprint). In secondary recycling, discarded materials are reprocessed into other materials or products, in general with less stringent specifications than the original ones (e.g. the use of glass as a road aggregate).

7.3.2.1 Organic waste recycling

For the purposes of recycling, the municipal solid waste stream can be divided into two categories: dry recyclables (comprising e.g. paper, plastics, metals glass and textiles) and organics (consisting mainly of kitchen and garden waste).

Both categories can enter into a process of material recycling, but the methods of treatment of organic materials are likely to be quite specific. Following collection, biological treatments are the clearest alternative for the organic materials fraction. Broadly, organic wastes can be treated in one of two ways (Waite, 1995, p. 35): composting and anaerobic digestion.

Composting is the process by which the material undergoes a controlled biological decomposition in the presence of oxygen, to produce a dry, odourless and stable organic material, which is suitable for a variety of soil conditioning uses[2]. Composting typically takes 50-60 days and reduces the bulk of the original materials by approximately 40-50 per cent. Residential compost programmes are well established in Europe.

Anaerobic digestion is the technique by which the material again undergoes a natural process of decomposition, but in this case in the absence of oxygen[3]. The process generates an energy product (biogas), an organic solid fertiliser and a dilute liquid organic fertiliser. The cost of using anaerobic digestion is generally higher than the alternative of simple composting. However, there are many circumstances where anaerobic digestion can be attractive. Anaerobic digestion uses less land area and has more controllable local environmental impacts than composting, such as odour, flies and vermin, and thus where land is expensive or housing close, anaerobic digestion is an attractive option. In addition, anaerobic digestion generates energy.

7.3.2.2 The mechanics of recycling

Independently of the above considerations, the design of any recycling scheme (the process during which recyclable materials are converted into recycled materials) will evolve according to three consecutive stages: the collection of recyclable materials; the processing of collected materials; and the reprocessing of individual materials. While these activities are usually considered individually, they are mutually dependent. Clearly, the way in which some material is collected will directly affect the ability to sort such material (Waite, 1995, p. 42).

It is possible to distinguish two generic collection approaches:

- bring (or drop-off) systems, which involve householders delivering selected waste materials to designated collection points, where there is a combination of recycling facilities including, for example, glass, can, textile and/or paper banks; and
- kerbside systems, which comprise a range of recyclable materials separated by the householder, placed in a special container or bag and collected at prearranged times from the kerbside[4] (Powell et al., 1996, p. 98).

Each collection method has its own particular characteristics that make it more suitable in some applications and less suitable in others. The choice of the method or methods of collection for recycling is complex, requiring the consideration of diverse factors, such as the types of housing to be serviced, the likely level of public acceptance, and the range of materials to be collected (Waite, 1995, p. 60). To this list must be added the evaluation of the costs of collection.

As bring systems rely on individual householders making the effort to take recyclable materials to a collection point, recovery rates are generally lower than for kerbside collection schemes[5]. In spite of this, they are more common, primarily because they can be introduced on a small scale, they require minimal capital and operation investments and because they can often be self-funding[6]. Kerbside systems tend to be more expensive, mainly because they have to collect the recyclable materials from every household rather than from centralised collection points.

Following collection, the mixture of recyclable materials needs to be separated. This activity is termed processing and can be carried out in a central facility, whose most common designation is the American term of Materials Recovery Facility (MRF).

Manual separation is the simplest approach to material separation and has the advantages of being able to achieve a high degree (and quality) of separation, with a relatively low capital investment. However, it presents the disadvantages of any labour intensive process, i.e. high labour costs and potential performance variation due to tiredness. In addition, there are growing concerns regarding health and safety aspects of manual sorting (Waite, 1995, p. 66). In general, the operating performance of sorting activities can be significantly improved by the appropriate addition of specific automated MRF technologies (e.g. magnetic extraction of ferrous metals).

Beyond the collection and processing of recyclable materials, the process of recycling is not complete until the post-consumer materials are reprocessed, i.e. become new commodities which will return to the market or, eventually, are manufactured into new products.

The lack of stable markets, paying an appropriate price for recyclable materials, is the explanation most often quoted to justify the current low levels of waste recycling (Waite, 1995, p. 162). According to Gandy (1994, p. 30), the contemporary difficulties in maintaining markets for secondary materials are usually attributed to a mismatch between the supply of recycled materials and the demand for recycled products; the competition with virgin materials; and the difficulties of ensuring a consistent supply of sufficiently uncontaminated material in economically-handleable quantities. However, Waite (1995, p. 103) argues that this alleged lack of markets should not be maintained as the key reason why recycling levels are currently so low. The main difficulty in increasing today's level of recycling results from the widespread availability of cheap landfill and while this situation prevails, recycling will not reach its full potential.

7.3.2.3 The economics of recycling

Frequently, the potential of recycling schemes to generate a profit from the sales of processed materials, and the creation of savings in waste disposal costs, is invoked as one of the key reasons to promote recycling programmes. However, the lack of a standard approach has resulted in incomplete or inaccurate cost data being reported, with the risk that this could lead to inappropriate or sub-optimal recycling systems being implemented.

According to Waite (1995, p. 111), a cost of recycling can be defined as any cost incurred which is in addition to the costs that would have been incurred for the standard collection and disposal of household waste. This definition of a cost of recycling automatically takes into account any collection and disposal savings that could arise as a result of recycling.

Next, as it is expected that the collected and processed materials are to be sold on the market and an income received from such sales, to estimate the net costs of recycling, this income must be set-off against the gross costs of collection and processing of recyclable materials.

The application of this method is straightforward when applied to a recycling plan that collects, processes and reprocesses only one material (e.g. glass). However, when the collection is of commingled materials which have to be separated in subsequent processing operations, the dilemma arises of how to allocate the costs of the collection and processing activities to the different materials involved. This difficulty in determining the net income from recycling is important, because this informs the rationale for further expanding the strategy on purely economic grounds, whether this be in terms of reducing the costs of waste disposal or the promotion of recycling to make profit (Gandy, 1994, p. 33).

However, as underlined by the majority of the literature (see e.g. Diamadopoulos et al., 1995), within the contemporary and administrative framework for municipal waste management, comprehensive recycling programmes are in general more expensive than waste disposal by landfill or incineration. Nevertheless, the cost of recycling is just one additional measure of the performance of a recycling scheme. While it is very important, it is not the only measure of performance.

7.3.2.4 Environmental impacts of recycling

Among solid waste management alternatives, recycling is implicitly considered to be environmentally beneficial (Craighill and Powell, 1996, p. 76). There is a variety of environmental justifications supporting recycling strategies (Gandy, 1994, p. 14; Daskalapoulos et al., 1997, p. 244). Recycling mitigates resource scarcity, decreases demand for landfill space, and generally involves savings in energy consumption and a reduction in greenhouse gas emissions. Some authors also underline potential environmental-education benefits of public participation in recycling (Daskalapoulos et al., 1997, p. 244). Nevertheless, recycling has its own environmental costs as well, namely the energy used in collection and sorting, and impacts arising from converting the recovered materials into new products (Craighill and Powell, 1996, p. 76). The relative importance of these environmental considerations differs according to the characteristics of each recycling scheme. For example, the recycling of different components of the waste stream generates a particular environmental impact, depending on which materials form the focus of recycling policy (Gandy, 1994, p. 15).

To sum up, the recycling of waste makes environmental sense, provided that the process does not itself create more environmental damage than that which is avoided. But while we should seek to maximise beneficial recycling, there will always be a need for the disposal of some household waste that cannot be recycled, due either to technical constraints, excessive financial costs or environmental reasons.

Given that the need for waste disposal will continue, it is important to ensure the compatibility of recycling with other waste management methods. Indeed, under the right circumstances, far from being mutually exclusive, the recycling activities can encourage a change in individual attitudes which leads to actions of waste minimisation, such as refusing unnecessary plastic bags, reusing or repairing products, or simply reducing the consumption levels (Waite, 1995, p. 36). Material recovery and energy recovery also can be compatible methods of waste treatment, if not mutually beneficial. The most obvious example of compatibility is the magnetic extraction of steel (predominantly steel cans) from mixed refuse, prior to waste incineration. Obviously, the successful combination of material recycling and energy recovery is dependent upon which materials are recycled and in what proportion. The decision as to whether it is better to recycle or to recover energy is dependent on local circumstances, such as proximity to an incinerator, and proximity to recyclable material markets (Waite, 1995, p. 40). Finally, recycling can contribute significantly to extending the lifetime of a landfill, as well as simplifying the landfill operations (e.g. by removing part of its organic content, the resulting waste will be more stable and produce less landfill gas and leachate).

7.3.3 Incineration and Other Thermal Processes

In the context of municipal waste management, the systematic use of fire as a strategy to treat waste dates from the nineteenth century, as part of the drive to improve sanitary conditions in emerging industrial cities. The option of incinerating waste was initially developed as an hygienic alternative to open dumping.

The amount of waste, and its potential to be incinerated, increased dramatically in the boom years following the World War II, with the growth of consumerism and increased use of plastics and paper in packaging. This, coupled with the fact that waste avoidance and recycling were then of no real concern, led to a major wave of construction of waste incinerators in the 1960s and 1970s. In addition, in those countries where land constraints make it difficult to find suitable sites for landfills, such as the Netherlands and Japan, waste combustion was encouraged even more, due to its potential to reduce the volume and the weight of material requiring disposal (Williams, 1998, p. 90).

However, the increase in waste incineration during this period was not accompanied by improvements in operating standards and most incinerators had no, or only minimal, control of emissions. Public concerns about incineration were initially focused on the smoke and unpleasant odours. However, the discovery in 1977 of dioxins in fly ash from waste incinerators (Hartenstein and Horvay, 1996, p. 22), indicated that waste incinerators could be a major source of other harmful substances. This motivated public concerted reactions and pressed policy makers to raise incineration operating standards.

As recently as 30 years ago, beyond being a waste disposal alternative, municipal solid waste combustion practices started to be considered as a potential source of energy[7] (Berenyi, 1996, p. 1; Williams, 1998, p. 89). Due to soaring prices of oil and fuel shortages in the 1970s, burning refuse to produce steam or electricity was promoted as a method to manage waste and reduce dependence on foreign oil. Later, with the easing of the energy crisis, the attractiveness of municipal waste combustion as a means of conserving energy was reduced and the emphasis was placed on reducing risks, through pollution control technology and monitoring (Berenyi, 1996, p. 3).

7.3.3.1 Technology description

Today, thermal treatment of municipal waste through incineration is a well-established and proven method of processing the combustible fraction of the waste stream (Daskalopoulos et al., 1997, p. 224). The majority of the existing facilities make use of two main technologies, both of which can operate in a way whereby energy is recovered from the combustion process: moving grate and fluidised bed. There is also interest in the development of gasification and 'pyrolysis' technologies, for smaller scale operations.

Moving grate technology

The moving grate is the most widely used waste incineration technology throughout the world (Whiting, 1998, p. 31; Berenyi, 1996, p. 10). The design of the grate and its movement seeks to transport the combusting mass of solids from the feed end to the ash discharge, in a controlled time period. Typically, the grate is divided into three sections which perform different functions within the combustion process: drying and preheating of the solid waste; gasification of the waste with ignition and combustion of the volatiles[8]; and carbon burnout and ash removal for subsequent disposal. Usually, moving grate technologies are associated with 'mass burning' processes, i.e. raw municipal solid waste is taken 'as is' with little or no shredding or separation prior to combustion (Berenyi, 1996, p. 7).

Fluidised bed technology

The technology of fluidised bed combustion was originally developed for power generation from the combustion of coal, and its application to a much wider range of fuels (including refuse derived fuel and municipal solid waste) has taken place only over recent years, in Japan and Europe (Whiting, 1998, p. 31). This technology is based on a system whereby, instead of the refuse being burned on a grate, the fire bed is composed of a granular inert material (usually sand and limestone). In many respects this 'fluidised bed' resembles a boiling liquid. The large thermal mass of the bed acts to stabilise the temperature of combustion and minimises any changes due to variations in the calorific value or the moisture content of the waste. However, fluidised bed furnaces have difficulties in handling non-homogeneous waste. In addition, this technology requires that glass and low melting-point metals (such as aluminium) be removed from the waste feedstock. Consequently, its application to municipal waste incineration usually requires some pre-treatment, which constitutes a major disadvantage in comparison to 'mass burn of waste' options (Hartenstein and Horvay, 1996, p. 22). Conversely, fluidised bed systems guarantee a high level of combustion due to both the preparation of the waste and the method of combustion.

Gasification and pyrolysis

Gasification is the conversion of a solid or liquid feedstock into fuel rich gases by partial oxidation, under the application of heat (around 900°-1400°C). Partial oxidation is achieved by restricting the supply of the oxidant, which can be air, oxygen enriched air or oxygen (IEA, 1998, p. 4). Gasification with air is the most widely used technology, producing a low heating-value gas. Gasification with oxygen produces a better quality gas.

Pyrolysis involves the thermal degradation of a material in anaerobic conditions, at temperatures in the range of 400°-800°C. The molecular structure of the waste is broken down by heat, but no combustion occurs (Whiting, 1998, p. 31). The process yields gaseous, liquid and solid fuels, the relative proportions of each depending on the method of pyrolysis and the reaction parameters, such as temperature and pressure.

Both technologies, gasification and pyrolysis, have primarily been used for specific and generally unmixed waste materials (e.g. plastics) or to process refuse derived fuel. However, further applications are currently in transition between research and demonstration phases. The promotion of advanced thermal conversion technologies can be an attractive addition to the range of waste management options. In certain situations they can be most appropriate, for example where a local-scale waste management solution is required. Other potential benefits relative to traditional municipal solid waste combustion include: lower environmental impacts, higher electricity conversion efficiencies, and greater compatibility with recycling and 'combined heat and power' generation (IEA, 1998, p. 29).

7.3.3.2 The economics of municipal waste incineration

Economic and financial factors play a primary role in the municipal solid waste decision making process. Municipal solid waste incineration is an expensive option, which involves very capital intensive investment (Daskalapoulos et al., 1997, p. 231) and requires highly skilled operators and careful maintenance (Rand et al., 2000, p. 1). Furthermore, developing a waste incineration project tends to be a complex and lengthy process that requires making decisions which have long-term consequences.

From a strictly financial point of view, the net cost of municipal solid waste incineration is frequently estimated as significantly higher than for other waste management options, especially landfilling (Rand et al., 2000, p. 9). Typically, municipal solid waste incineration does not appear to be a cost-effective option in regions where suitable landfilling space is easily available.

For a municipal waste incineration plant to be economically feasible, all costs need to be minimised and the possibility of generating some revenues through the sale of energy recovered, or at least some form of materials recycling, is a crucial element to be considered.

Economic assessment of costs and benefits is a major issue in the success of a municipal waste incineration project. However, it is extremely difficult to compare the net costs on a direct basis. When comparing economic data, special attention should be given to the fact that capital and operating costs are application and country specific. Furthermore, costs are dependent on the level of engineering, requirements imposed by technological options, regulations, architectural considerations and local financial and commercial conditions. As such, comparisons should be made relative to the relevant case-specific conditions (Whiting, 1998, p. 32).

In general, the cost assessment of an incineration plant should consider several main components, such as land acquisition costs, assessment costs, development and capital costs, operating costs and decommissioning costs. Typically, incineration plants require a relatively small amount of land and its acquisition is expected to represent a modest percentage of the total costs. However, several restrictions should be noted; where energy or heat distribution is involved, proximity to the relevant customers will be a determining factor. It will also be important to have ready access to landfill to accept the residues from incineration (Daskalopoulos et al., 1997, p. 232; Houghton et al., 1993, p. 128) and a location close to the 'centre of gravity' of waste generation will significantly reduce the cost of waste transportation (Rand et al., 2000, p. 1).

Assessment costs include such management-related issues as the choice of technology and all the aspects concerning the plant's operation (Houghton et al., 1993, p. 129). These are crucial issues, but the assessment costs represent only a small fraction of the total costs.

The development (or capital) costs, in spite of being assumed as incurred prior to the operation stage, may be spread out over a longer timeframe according to some predetermined financing schedules (Daskalopoulos et al., 1997, p. 232).

The operating costs are mainly related to the monitoring and disposal of the residues from the facility. Nowadays, investments in pollution abatement systems (e.g. the flue gas cleaning and residual handling systems) are large and expensive, and may well represent one third or more of the total investment costs of a fully equipped municipal waste incineration plant (Harstenstein and Horvay, 1996, p. 30; Houghton et al., 1993, p. 29).

Finally, the decommissioning costs are usually expressed as a proportion of the capital costs for all main engineering works, not exceeding the range of 5-10 per cent (Houghton et al., 1993, p. 130). It is important to point out that, unlike landfills, there is no after-care period required, and combustion plants typically have an economic life which corresponds closely to their operational life. In the case of recovering energy for electricity or steam generation purposes, additional capital and operating costs would be required (Daskalopoulos et al., 1997, p. 232).

Other important elements to consider relate to the scale of the project. Economies of scale in municipal solid waste incineration are strong with respect to investment and net treatment costs (Rand et al., 2000, p. 8). Furthermore, the eventual addition of power generation reinforces these potential economies (Houghton et al., 1993, p. 134).

There are significant economies of scale with incinerators, i.e. the operation and maintenance costs per tonne decrease as the plant size increases, favouring the option of higher handling capacity plants. Because of this, it is often suggested that establishing regional or intermunicipal waste management co-operations may be the solution to provide the indispensable scale that such capital intensive facilities require (Rand et al., 2000, p. 9). However, these economies of scale should be carefully compared against the associated increased costs of transport.

To conclude, it is important to stress that any forecast of the economic costs or benefits of these activities should be cautious and accompanied by a sensitivity/risk analysis. For example, the net treatment costs of a municipal solid waste incineration plant are rather dependent on fluctuations in the quantity and quality of waste treated. If the waste has a reduced calorific value, or if the supply of waste falls short of the design load (as a result, e.g. of a shortage of waste or extended periods of maintenance), the treatment costs could increase significantly (Rand et al., 2000, p. 8).

7.3.3.3 Environmental impacts of waste incineration

Potential forms of environmental impacts derived from waste incineration processes can include a multiplicity of considerations. These include concerns about visual intrusion (the visual impact of an incineration plant can be significant depending on its bulk and design), the level of traffic generated by vehicle movements handling the waste, and noise from the use of mechanical equipment (Houghton et al., 1993, Chapter 7).

However, traditionally the environmental impacts of waste incineration are primarily associated with the generation of: solid residues, mainly contaminated ash and other particulate emissions; contaminated wastewater; and pollutant emissions to the atmosphere.

Incineration of municipal solid waste substantially reduces its volume by up to 90 per cent, although it leaves solid residues, respectively bottom ash and fly ash, which will need to be disposed of. Fly ash corresponds to the bulk of the fine particulate matter trapped by the gas cleaning equipment in the exhaust gases, which rises from the furnace during burning; such fly ash comprises about 10-15 per cent of the whole ash residue. These residues are environmentally the most hazardous portion of the incineration solid residues. Consequently, their disposal is a highly complex task, due to the serious health and environmental risks involved (e.g. by groundwater contamination).

Bottom (or grate) ash consists mainly of slag and cinders, i.e. that portion of the unburned waste that passes through or is discharged from the grate (Berenyi, 1996, p. 8). These residues are biologically inert, and typically contain no more than three per cent unburned carbon. Bottom ash can be processed in order to remove valuable, useful or harmful materials, to facilitate disposal, or prepare portions of the ash for beneficial use, e.g. as secondary aggregates or as a cover material in landfill sites.

Pollution control systems are also responsible for the generation of liquid effluents (e.g. 'wet systems', where pollutants are removed in scrubbers incorporating liquid cleaners, usually slaked lime). At some facilities, wastewater can also comes from the quench tank, used to cool hot ashes from the grate, but these effluents are normally less heavily contaminated. Water pollution from incinerators is not generally considered to be a major problem because of the limited amount of wastewater generated (Daskalopoulos et al., 1997, p. 229). However, the liquid effluents from waste incineration plants are potentially contaminated with heavy metals and inorganic salts. These can be discharged at high temperatures and have a high acidity or alkalinity, which requires great care in order to minimise potentially negative environmental impacts.

Finally, the pollutants traditionally associated with the highest damage per unit of waste incinerated are those that are emitted to the atmosphere. Air pollution during waste incineration may occur in various ways (Daskalopulos et al., 1997, p. 226). However there is special concern about the following potential emissions:

- Waste incineration leads to the emission of large amounts of carbon dioxide, which directly contributes to the greenhouse effect;
- Metals and metal compounds may evaporate in the furnace to condense eventually in the colder parts of the flues and generate an aerosol of extremely fine particles;
- Waste may include compounds containing acidic gases (hydrogen chloride, hydrogen fluoride, nitrogen oxides, sulphur dioxide) and other elements which could result in the generation of toxic or corrosive gases;
- Some of the combustion products arising in volatile form during the waste thermal decomposition may be combusted incompletely, so result-

ing in the emission of tar and soot particles, carbon monoxide, and volatile organic compounds.

The volatile organic compounds that cause most concern are commonly known as dioxins and furans[9]. These are of particular concern because of their extremely high toxicity, persistence in the environment and ability to concentrate through the food chain. The effects that organic compounds can have on human health vary from causing skin disease and liver disorders to cancer (Daskalopulos et al., 1997, p. 226).

In assessing the impact of greenhouse gas emissions from municipal waste incineration activities, several factors have to be taken into account. For example, it is important to examine whether the carbon dioxide emissions released as a result of waste incineration represent a net addition to these emissions. As such, consideration should be given to the opportunity cost associated with carbon dioxide and methane emissions[10] produced by the alternative waste management methods (i.e. landfilling). Furthermore, if energy is recovered from the incineration process, it can be used as a substitute for fossil fuels in energy production, helping to reduce even more the greenhouse gas emissions.

Pipatti and Savolainen (1996) present the results of a study on the greenhouse impact of eight different waste treatment alternatives for municipal waste (combinations of landfilling, landfill gas recovery and energy use, biological treatment and incineration), and conclude that while waste incineration produces emissions of carbon dioxide, methane and nitrous oxide, these are less than those from corresponding landfilling. The net greenhouse impact can in fact be negative for alternatives that include incineration and energy recovery.

To sum up, assessing the acceptability of waste incineration in terms of environmental impacts is a highly complex task. Numerous pollutants and effects need to be considered in an integrated way. For example, several technologies are available to achieve an effective control and minimisation of pollution, but it is critical to ensure that the benefit from a reduction in releases to one medium is not outweighed by an increase in another form of pollution. It is generally considered that achieving highly efficient combustion and minimising the formation of pollutants within the process is always preferable to removing pollutants from the diversity of solid, liquid or gaseous effluents subsequently.

7.3.3.4 Examples of successful waste incineration practices
Incineration processes are capital-intensive and require high operating and maintenance costs. Additionally, skilled manpower is essential for operation and maintenance. Mainly as a result of these circumstances, up-to-date, full-

scale incinerators are currently in service only in large communities of more industrialized regions, such as North America, Australia, Japan, and Northern European countries[11]. In countries such as Japan, Denmark, Sweden, Switzerland and the region of Brussels, incineration is the most important route for the municipal solid waste generated (Eurostat, 2000, p. 54).

The energy generated by European waste-to-energy plants, mainly in the form of steam to supply district-heating loops, is an important factor underlying the public approval of incineration in Europe (UNEP, 1996, p. 272). Additionally, European countries tend to be well advanced in the utilisation of by-products of incineration. The use of bottom ash and slag as an aggregate in road construction, or in the production of brick materials, is quite common in some of these countries. However, while accepting waste incineration as a viable disposal and energy recovery strategy, many European governments, such as the United Kingdom, are phasing out an older generation of non-energy-generating incinerators, as these do not comply with emissions limitations in national and European Community law.

7.3.4 Landfilling

Landfill is the term used to describe the physical facilities used for the disposal of solid wastes and solid waste residuals in the surface soils of the earth (Tchobanoglous and O'Leary, 1994, p. 12.1).

Modern landfilling can be defined as the process of controlled deposit of waste in, on or above the land, in such a way that both short-term and long-term environmental risks are reduced to an acceptable level (Westlake, 1997, p. 453). This definition importantly distinguishes modern controlled landfilling activities from the 'illegal practice of waste dumps'. Additionally, it recognises that the complete prevention of environmental landfill pollution can never be guaranteed.

Landfilling has served humans for much longer than any other alternative disposal option (Clarke et al., 1999, p. 127). Currently, landfills are still a vital and major component of any waste management system, as they constitute the ultimate repository of the waste that society produces, after all other waste management options have been exercised. Indeed, it is not possible to foresee a time when the need for landfill disposal can be completely avoided, as typical alternatives to landfilling are regarded as merely volume reduction processes, because they produce waste fractions (e.g. ash and slag from combustion) which ultimately must be landfilled (El-Fadel et al., 1997, p. 1).

Landfilling is the most widely used waste management method to dispose of the municipal solid waste generated. Depending on location, up to 97 per cent of solid waste generated worldwide is currently disposed of in landfills

(El-Fadel et al., 1997, p. 1; Clarke et al., 1999, p. 130). Data is not available for less developed countries, but according to UNEP (1996), in those countries landfilling is clearly the cheapest and most prevalent method of municipal solid waste disposal. In many cases, it is the only solid waste management option after the municipal waste is collected (UNEP, 1996, p. 91).

Numerous landfill classifications have been proposed over the years (Tchobanoglous and O'Leary, 1994, p. 12.4). A commonly used classification, according to waste type only (adopted, e.g. in the European Union Landfill Directive) distinguishes between hazardous waste landfills, municipal waste landfills and designated waste landfills (concerning specific waste materials such as combustion ash, asbestos, or other similar inert wastes). In practice, these categories are not clear-cut, and variants are recognised, such as joint-disposal, where municipal and hazardous type wastes may be co-deposited in order to gain benefit from municipal waste decomposition processes. Alternatively, landfills can be categorised according to their management strategy. Hjelmar et al. (1995) use this criterion to distinguish between total containment landfills, landfills with containment and collection of leachate, landfills with controlled contaminant release, and landfills with unrestricted contaminant release. More simply, in UNEP (1996, p. 93) landfills are grouped into three general categories: open dumps, controlled dumps and sanitary landfills.

Due to the low initial private costs of landfills with unrestricted contaminant release (or open dumps), and lack of expertise and equipment to follow other alternatives, this type of site is common in developing countries, which causes significant risks to human health and the environment. In developed countries, currently the most common strategy for municipal solid waste landfilling is sanitary landfills, where appropriate technology and techniques are used to minimise the pollution potential and health effects associated with the release of hazardous substances to the environment (Tchobanoglous and O'Leary, 1994, p. 12.2; UNEP, 1996, p. 98). Those measures will vary according to the composition of the waste landfilled and the different site characteristics, such as soil conditions and topography, climatological conditions, surface-water hydrology, geologic and hydrogeologic conditions, existing land use patterns and local environmental conditions (Westlake, 1997, p. 454; Tchobanoglous and O'Leary, 1994, p. 12.8). Ideally, all of these elements should be carefully considered when planning a new landfill site.

Good landfill practice starts with the selection of a suitable site (DoE, 1986, p. 1), taking into account the planned capacity, the risks to ground and surface water, the risks from gaseous emissions, the impact of traffic, vermin, litter and noise on the area, and the potential for recovery of the land after the site has completed the post-closure phase. Ideally, the final decision on the location of a landfill site should be based on the results of a detailed site survey, considering engineering design aspects and cost studies, as well as the outcomes of comprehensive environmental impact assessments and local public hearings (Tchobanoglous and O'Leary, 1994, p. 12.8).

7.3.4.1 Environmental impacts of landfilling

The environmental impacts of municipal solid waste landfilling basically relate to emissions of leachate and landfill gas, as well as the construction and operation of the landfill itself.

Leachate

Leachate is a liquid product resulting from the non-uniform and intermittent percolation of water through the refuse mass, which may include potentially toxic contaminants, such as ions (e.g. calcium, magnesium, iron, sodium, ammonium, carbonate, sulphate and chloride), trace metals (e.g. manganese, chromium, nickel, lead and cadmium) and a wide variety of organic compounds. The sources of percolating water are primarily external, such as precipitation, uncontrolled runoff, and surface drainage. However, leachate will also include liquids initially present in the refuse moisture content and, to a lesser extent, resulting from the natural waste decomposition processes. It should be noted that the chemical composition of leachate is highly dependent upon the stage of waste digestion within the site, the initial waste composition and landfilling operational procedures (El-Fadel et al., 1997, p. 9). This high variability in the characteristics of the leachate significantly increases the technical problems in the design and management of leachate treatment systems (Tchobanoglous and O'Leary, 1994, p. 12.35).

Leachate management is a key factor in safe landfill design and operation. Natural or synthetic materials (e.g. clay or polymeric flexible membrane liners, such as high density polyethylene) are often used to line the bottom and sides of landfills to minimise the leachate generation and its migration into nearby groundwater and surface water (UNEP, 1996, pp. 98-99). Leachate retained by the liner will accumulate and possibly leak through the liner unless it is removed by a leachate collection system. After collection, a number of alternatives have been used to treat the leachate, including aerobic biological treatments, leachate recirculation, or on-site treatment followed by spray disposal, or discharge to sewerage or surface water (depending on the quality of treated leachate)[12].

Landfill gas

The production of landfill gas is an inevitable consequence of the disposal and subsequent anaerobic biological decomposition of the biodegradable organic materials included in the municipal solid waste stream. Methane and carbon dioxide are the two principal components of landfill gas and form more than 90 per cent of the total gas generated. Other gases are also present in small percentages (the trace gases), such as nitrogen and oxygen, and over 100 different types of volatile organic compounds have been identified, such as benzene and vinyl chloride (El-Fadel et al., 1997, p. 4).

Emissions of methane and carbon dioxide from landfill sites represent an important contribution to the anthropogenic greenhouse gas emissions, which are responsible for the global warming phenomenon. Indeed, it is estimated that methane contributes about 18 per cent towards total global warming (500 million tons per year approximately), of which 10 to 15 percentage points (40 to 75 million tons per year) are attributed to emissions from landfills (Westlake, 1997, p. 457; El-Fadel et al., 1997, p. 14). On the other hand, emissions of volatile organic compounds may be toxic and/or carcinogenic, raising special apprehension concerning their health effects. Finally, some of the minor constituents present in landfill gas composition (e.g. esters, hydrogen sulphide, organsulphurs, alkylbenzenes, limonene and other hydrocarbons) are responsible for the typical unpleasant odour associated with landfill gas (El-Fadel et al., 1997, p. 11).

It should be noted that considerable variations in landfill gas generation and composition are likely, mainly depending on the rate at which the organic material landfilled is decomposed biologically, through the distribution of the organic components in landfill, the moisture content of waste, temperature (ambient and source), pH, the availability of nutrients, and the degree of initial compaction (DoE, 1986, p. 133; El-Fadel et al., 1997, p. 7). For a brief description, based on the reported literature of the general influence of these variables, see El-Fadel et al. (1997, pp. 7-8).

Landfill gas is highly flammable and poses a risk of fire or explosion if not properly managed. Gas monitoring is therefore a major concern for landfill operators. In some circumstances, landfill gas may be produced in such quantities that its extraction as a fuel becomes worthwhile. From an environmental perspective, collecting and using landfill gas as a fuel is ideal, because it captures the energy value in the gas and prevents the release of a potent greenhouse gas (methane) to the atmosphere (UNEP, 1996, p. 101). Furthermore, the net energy recovered displaces environmental impacts associated with the production of energy from conventional sources.

Other environmental impacts
Other environmental impacts related to landfill disposal of municipal solid waste include the occurrence of landfill settlement, land use, and disamenity impacts resulting from the construction and operation of the landfill itself (such as traffic congestion, noise, dust, the presence of vermin, etc.).

Landfill disposal is associated with the use of land, which is generally considered to be a negative externality, which can affect the market value of the nearby properties and represents an important restriction to the potential for the land use of the site.

Landfill settlement is caused primarily by waste decomposition, which increases the void ratio and reduces the structural strength of the refuse within the landfill, leading to a substantial loss of volume and settlement.

7.3.4.2 The economics of landfilling

Municipal solid waste disposal to landfill is a complex and inherently long-term operation, with corresponding difficulties in fully assessing the financial implications of a proposed development. Furthermore, increasingly stringent regulations governing landfill construction, operation and maintenance are forcing up the costs of land disposal (Renkow and Keeler, 1996, p. 67). At the same time, in the foreseeable future no community will be able efficiently to manage its waste without the land disposal option. Consequently, economic efficiency is a high priority to engineers and economists when implementing municipal solid waste landfilling projects.

Costs are associated with all stages of the landfill, from the initial selection and acquisition of the land, through design, operation and final closure and post-closure of the site. These costs may be broken down into capital costs and operation costs (UNEP, 1996, p. 110).

Capital costs include land acquisition, assessment costs (e.g. professional services for design and the procurement of permits), development costs (e.g. machinery and equipment purchases, site preparation and construction), and allocations for closure and post-closure operations (proper site development and operation are crucial to minimise the aftercare costs). Capital costs can range from 25 to 50 per cent of the total lifetime cost of a landfill (UNEP, 1996, p. 110).

Operation costs are associated with the landfill day-to-day operational expenditures, and are the most important unit cost over the lifetime of a landfill (Daskalopoulos et al., 1997, p. 222). As the operational costs are dependent on variations in the expected waste input, or changes in working practice, a sensitivity/risk analysis may be important for the economic assessment of a municipal solid waste landfill site (DoE, 1986, p. 167).

7.4 CONCLUSIONS

Given the wide range of available technical options, the central question is of how an appropriate municipal solid waste management system can be defined and implemented. The process of formulating a municipal solid waste strategy is complex. There is no single prescription. Each situation must be analysed individually, and a sensible combination of technologies, which fits the situation best, should be carefully planned. Ultimately, the system must be holistic, i.e. where each of the respective components, in spite of having its own purpose, is configured to work in tandem will all of the other pieces. As such, special attention should be given to potential trade-offs between the different waste management decisions.

However, arriving at successful municipal solid waste management solutions requires more than just good planning. The best technical solution may fail if politicians and government officials do not consider a series of other important elements. Aspects concerning the problems of public acceptance, public participation in planning and implementation, consumer behaviour and changing value systems are no less fundamental than the technical, economic and environmental aspects. The potentially best technical solution is unlikely to work unless the public is active in helping to reach the final choice of options. Indeed, a key aspect of strategic solutions to the actual municipal waste management dilemmas is getting the public to accept responsibility for the ownership of the waste problem and its resolution.

In the last decade, and in global terms, we have witnessed a positive shift in municipal solid waste management practices. The world's relative dependence on landfilling and incineration has been reducing. At the same time, recycling rates in many countries have significantly risen, and diversion from landfills is still on the rise as recycling increases for organic materials. But even with these notable achievements, a major drawback is evident in the waste management framework: the strategies implemented have clearly failed to advance effective policies on waste prevention. This is in large part due to waste management's focus on reactive measures, i.e. on the best way of handling and managing solid waste after it has been generated. A different paradigm will not be possible until all environmental costs and benefits are made transparent to the generators and users of materials flowing through the economic system. As such, efforts should be concentrated on the development of 'fuller-cost' accounting systems that incorporate positive and negative externalities.

REFERENCES

Berenyi, E. (1996), 'The status of municipal waste combustion in the United States', *Journal of Hazardous Materials*, **47**, 1-17.
Clarke, M., A. Read, and P. Phillips, (1999), 'Integrated waste management planning and decision-making in New York City', *Resources, Conservation and Recycling*, **26**, 125-41.

Craighill, A., and J. Powell (1996), 'Lifecycle assessment and economic evaluation of recycling: a case study', *Resources, Conservation and Recycling*, **17** (2), 75-96.

Daskalapoulos, E., O. Badr and S. Probert (1997), 'Economic and environmental evaluations of waste treatment and disposal technologies for municipal solid waste', *Applied Energy*, **58** (4), 209-55.

Diamadopoulos, E., Y. Koutsantonakis, and V. Zaglara (1995), 'Optimal design of municipal solid waste recycling systems', *Resources, Conservation and Recycling*, **14** (1), 21-34.

Diaz, L., G. Savage and C. Golueke (1994), 'Composting of municipal solid wastes' in *Handbook of Solid Waste Management*, F. Kreith (ed.), New York: McGraw Hill.

DoE (UK Department of the Environment) (1986), *Landfilling Wastes: A Technical Memorandum for the Disposal of Wastes on Landfill Sites*, Waste Management Paper N° 26, London: HMSO.

EEA (European Environment Agency) (2000), *Household and Municipal Waste: Comparability of Data in EEA Member Countries*, Copenhagen: EEA.

El-Fadel, M., A. Findikakis and J. Leckie (1997), 'Environmental impacts of solid waste landfilling', *Journal of Environmental Management*, **50**, 1-25.

Eurostat (2000), *Waste Generated in Europe: Data 1985-1997*, Theme 8 Energy and the Environment, Luxembourg: Eurostat.

Finnveden, G. (1999), 'Methodological aspects of life cycle assessment of integrated solid waste management systems', *Resources, Conservation and Recycling*, **26**, 173-87.

Fishbein, B., K. Geiser and C. Gelb (1994), 'Source reduction' in *Handbook of Solid Waste Management*, F. Kreith (ed.), New York: McGraw Hill.

Gandy, M. (1994), *Recycling and the Politics of Urban Waste*, London: Earthscan Publications.

Goddard, H. (1995), 'The benefits and costs of alternative solid waste management policies', *Resources, Conservation and Recycling*, **13**, 183-213.

Hartenstein, H.-U. and M. Horvay (1996), 'Overview of municipal waste incineration industry in west Europe (based on German experience)', *Journal of Hazardous Materials*, **47**, 19-30.

Hjelmar, O., L. Johannessen, K. Knox and H. Ehrig (1995), 'Composition and management of leachate from landfills within the EU', in *Proceedings Sardinia 95: Fifth International Landfill Symposium, Vol. 1*, T. Christensen, R. Cossu and R. Stegmann (eds.), Cagliari: Centro di Ingegneria Sanitaria Ambientale.

Horrigan, A. and J. Motavali (1997), 'The roots of recycling', *The Environmental Magazine*, **8** (2), 28-36.

Houghton, J. (Chairman), G. Allen, B. Clayton, H. Charnock, H. Fell, P. Jacques, J. Lawton, R. Macrory, J. Morris, D. Reeve, E. Rothschild and A. Silberston (1993), *Incineration of Waste, Seventeenth Report of the Royal Commission on Environmental Pollution*, London: HMSO.

IEA (International Energy Agency) (1998), *Advanced Thermal Conversion Technologies for Energy from Solid Waste*, IEA Bioenergy Programme and the IEA CADDET Renewable Energy Programme, http://www.caddet-re.org/assets/EFW.pdf.

Lober, D. (1996), 'Municipal solid waste policy and public participation in household source reduction', *Waste Management and Research*, **14**, 125-43.

Mata-Alvarez, J., S. Macé and P. Llabrés (2000), 'Anaerobic digestion of organic solid wastes: an overview of research achievements and perspectives', *Bioresource Technology*, **74**, 3-16.

144   *Waste in Ecological Economics*

Pipatti, R. and I. Savoilainen (1996), 'Role of energy production in the control of greenhouse gas emissions from waste management', *Energy Conversion Management*, 6 (8), 1105-10.

Powell, J., A. Craighill, J. Parfitt and R. Turner (1996), 'A lifecycle assessment and economic valuation of recycling', *Journal of Environmental Planning and Management*, 39 (1), 97-112.

Rand, T., J. Haukohl and U. Marxen (2000), *Municipal Waste Incineration. A Decisions Makers' Guide*, Washington: The International Bank for Reconstruction and Development and The World Bank.

Read, A., P. Phillips and G. Robinson (1997), 'Landfill as a future waste management option in England: the view of landfill operators', *Resources, Conservation and Recycling*, 20, 183-205.

Renkow, M. and A. Keeler (1996), 'Determining the optimal landfill size: is bigger always better?', *Journal of Environmental Management*, 46, 67-75.

Renkow, M. and A. Rubin (1998), 'Does municipal solid waste composting make economic sense?', *Journal of Environmental Management*, 53, 339-47.

Tchobanoglous, G. and P. O'Leary (1994), 'Landfilling', in *Handbook of Solid Waste Management*, F. Kreith (ed.), New York: McGraw Hill.

UNEP (United Nations Environmental Programme) (1996), *International Source Book on Environmentally Sound Technologies for Municipal Solid Waste Management*, Osaka: International Environmental Technology Centre, Technical Publication Series 6.

USEPA (United States Environmental Protection Agency) (1993), *Waste Prevention: It Makes Good Business Sense*, Washington: EPA 530-F-93-008.

USEPA (United States Environmental Protection Agency) (1995) *Decision Maker's Guide to Solid Waste Management*, Washington: EPA 530-R-95-023.

USEPA (United States Environmental Protection Agency) (2000) *Municipal Solid Waste Generation, Recycling and Disposal in the United States: Figures for 1998*. Facts and Environmental Fact Sheet, www.epa.gov/osw.

van Beukering, P., M. Sehker, R. Gerlagh and V. Kumar (1999), *Analyzing Urban Solid Waste in Developing Countries: A Perspective on Bangalore, India*, CREED Working Paper N° 24, Amsterdam, http://www.waste.nl.

Waite, R. (1995) *Household Waste Recycling*, London: Earthscan Publications.

Westlake, K. (1997) 'Sustainable landfill - possibility or pipe-dream?', *Waste Management and Research*, 15, 453-61.

Whiting, K. (1998) 'Special report: waste to energy and Incineration. Gasification: a viable energy from waste option in the UK?', *Wastes Management*, March, 31-32.

Williams, P. (1998) *Waste Treatment and Disposal*, Chichester: John Wiley and Sons.

NOTES

1   According to Fishbein et al. (1994, section 8.6) source reduction is, in fact, resource management rather than material or waste management.
2   For an analysis of the mechanics and engineering aspects of composting see Diaz et al. (1994). A broad discussion of environmental impacts of waste composting and economics of municipal composting operations can be found on Daskalopoulos et al. (1997) or Renkow and Rubin (1998).
3   For a comprehensive overview of research achievements and perspectives on anaerobic digestion of organic solid wastes, see Mata-Alvarez et al. (2000).

4   The literature offers a number of other alternatives that can be understood as variants within each of these two broad approaches.

5   It is generally accepted that bring systems are unlikely to collect more than 15 per cent of the total waste stream (Waite, 1995, p. 48). Consequently, to achieve high levels of recycling other methods of collection for recycling need to be considered.

6   In a comparative analysis of the two recycling schemes, Powell et al. (1996) demonstrate that the method of collection has a significant effect on the overall economic impacts of recycling. However, the authors indicate that when considering the external costs and benefits from recycling, the bring scheme has potentially a higher external cost than the kerbside collection scheme. This result shows the importance of a comprehensive analysis of the external costs and benefits, in addition to private financial costs, to provide a complete assessment of recycling.

7   Evaluating municipal solid waste as a fuel, Daskalopoulos et al. (1997, p. 224) stress that it has approximately 30-40 per cent of the calorific value of an industrial bituminous coal, and a density, as fired, of 20 per cent.

8   The essential conditions for an effective gas-phase incineration are that the volatised elements must remain in the combustion chamber for an adequate time (retention time), at a high enough temperature, and in the presence of a sufficient supply of air.

9   Dioxin is used as the shorthand descriptor of the family of polychlorinated dibenzo-para-dioxins and the related compounds dibenzofurans. As a class, dioxins are organic chemicals that exhibit varying degrees of chlorine content and varying degrees of toxicity. They are formed by the presence of carbon, oxygen, hydrogen and chlorine; in most cases, heat is also a contributor. To take account of the extensive range of congeners, dioxin emissions are usually expressed in terms of 'Toxicity Equivalents'. This allows the total mass of dioxin congeners to be expressed in terms of the mass of the most toxic form (the 2,3,7,8-tetrachlorodibenzo-para-dioxin), which has a toxic equivalence of unity (Commission of the European Communities, 1997, section 1-1).

10 Methane is a particularly powerful greenhouse gas. According to Pipatti and Savolainen (1996, p. 1105) the warming impact of methane is tenfold compared with carbon dioxide.

11 Currently, incineration does not play a significant role in municipal solid waste management in less developed regions. High costs relative to other waste management options, a limited infrastructure of human, mechanical and institutional resources, and the composition of the waste stream itself, suggest that incineration is an inappropriate technology for these countries now and for the foreseeable future (UNEP, 1996, p. 125).

12 For a review of the methods that have been used for the removal of leachate that accumulates within a landfill, see Tchobanoglous and O'Leary (1994).

8. Toxic Waste

Francis O. Adeola

8.1 INTRODUCTION

There has been an enormous acceleration in the production and distribution of toxic chemicals and hazardous wastes over the past two centuries. Industrial revolution, scientific and technological breakthroughs in the synthesis and production of chemical compounds, and the rise of consumerism culture, are directly linked to the growth of hazardous wastes. In the most part, hazardous and toxic wastes are the by-products of a highly technological society. From agricultural to industrial activities, from private households to the public arena, and from commercial to military operations, hazardous wastes are ubiquitous in society. Toxic wastes and their deleterious effects on human health and the environment are now of growing concern. As noted by Lichtveld and Johnson (1993), concerns about toxic and hazardous wastes continue to increase globally. Generally, people are concerned about hazardous waste sites, accidental releases of toxic substances, expensive clean-up costs, property values depreciation, stigma and other social and psychological costs, adverse ecological effects, and human health diminution (Adeola, 2000a; Blackman, 1996; Lave and Upton, 1987; Thornton, 2000; Brown, 2001).

Public consciousness, knowledge, and concerns about the danger of toxic contamination have increased in the United States, Europe, and other parts of the world in the post-World War II era (Carson, 1962; Freudenberg, 1984; Erikson, 1994; Setterberg and Shavelson, 1993; Edelstein, 1988). Yet, policies and programmes aimed at curbing toxic waste production, release and dispersion remain grossly inadequate. The problem of toxic wastes control is exacerbated by the lack of a universally acceptable system of waste classification. Grouping and characterisation of wastes vary by region, country, and industry. Even government agencies differ in their schemes of classification of hazardous substances.

Through their properties of corrosiveness, ignitability, irritability, reactivity and toxicity (as established under the US Resource Conservation and Recovery Act (RCRA)), hazardous wastes pose significant danger to human and non-human species in the environment. In recognition of how widespread are technologically induced risks and environmental hazards, Ulrich Beck (1990) has coined the term 'risk society' to describe the contemporary advanced industrial societies, where the social production of wealth is inextricably coupled with the social production of hazards and associated risks. Thus, 'risk society' connotes an epoch in which the 'dark sides' of modernity are increasingly dominant in social discourse; self-endangerment and the ruination of nature or massive environmental degradation have become prominent among the major concerns (Beck, 1995). Toxic releases and psycho-physiological problems associated with modernity and its technological accoutrement have been referred to as 'a new species of trouble' (Erikson, 1994). Acknowledging the ubiquity of toxins in the environment, Brown and Mikkelson (1994) concluded there is no safe place. As noted by Epstein et al. (1982, p. 37), the materials and functions that are generally taken for granted as basic aspects of everyday life in modern society depend upon a geometric increase, proliferation and distribution of an array of heterogeneous toxic chemicals.

The post-World War II era in particular has witnessed an unparalleled acceleration of the production and distribution of synthetic toxic organic chemicals, including pesticides (e.g. dichlorodiphenyl-trichloroethane (DDT)), dioxin, polychlorinated biphenyls (PCBs), synthetic fibres, and other chlorine products, all with significant adverse impacts (Carson, 1962; Epstein et al., 1982; Brown, 2001; LaGrega et al., 2001; Field and Field, 2002). From the 1930s to the present, the production of synthetic organic chemicals in the United States has increased more than thirty-fold. Currently, there are more than 70,000 industrial chemicals being sold in the market (Thornton, 2000; Cohen and O'Connor, 1990). Brown (2001, p. 131) contends that the exact number of manufactured chemicals presently in society is unknown; however, with the introduction of synthetic chemicals, the number of chemicals in use is estimated at 100,000.

Today's toxic pollution problem consists of many interrelated aspects that can be summed up as the 'toxics cycle' or 'treadmill of toxics.' O'Connor (1990) defines the 'toxics cycle' as the production, use, and disposal of toxic chemical products considered essential in modern society. The 'treadmill of toxics', on the other hand, refers to societal inclination towards ever increasing demand and supply of toxic materials as a major aspect of industrial capitalism (see Schnaiberg and Gould, 1994). The petrochemical industry has created both the 'toxics cycle' and 'treadmill of toxics' by shaping public demand through the production and advertisement of large volumes of synthetic chemicals offered as substitutes for naturally occurring products. Consistent with Schnaiberg and Gould's (1994) treadmill of production, the treadmill of toxics is rooted in a network of regional, national and transnational corporations which place profits above human health and environmental protection. Increased toxic waste generation is a major aspect of the planned obsolescence scheme on the treadmill of production and consumption now pervasive in advanced industrial societies.

Recent data from the US Environmental Protection Agency (EPA) show that industries in the US produced and released 7.8 billion pounds of toxic wastes in 1999 (EPA, 2001, pp. E-2-3). The metal mining industry, which started reporting in 1998, accounted for 51.2 per cent; the original chemical manufacturing industries accounted for 29.9 per cent; electric generating facilities for 15 per cent; RCRA subtitle C TSD and Solvent Recovery Facilities for 3.7 per cent, and others including coal mining, chemical wholesale distributors and petroleum terminals and bulk storage facilities for the remaining small percentage of total toxic releases. Thus, the US is the world's largest generator of hazardous wastes. According to Epstein et al. (1982), the majority (if not all) of Americans carry substantial burdens of lead, pesticides, PCBs, and other harmful chemicals in their bodies as a result of exposure to polluted air, soil, and water, food chain contaminants, and direct use of toxic consumer products. In some cases, the source of exposure to toxic elements are the homes and work environment, where thousands of people across the US are directly exposed to lead, asbestos, radon, and other xenobiotics (Edelstein and Makofske, 1998). Thus, toxic chemicals are present in the air we breathe, the land we tread upon, and the water we drink. Toxic wastes are present in our work places, on our farms and gardens, and lawns in our neighbourhoods, and in our bodies (Brown, 2001; O'Connor, 1990; Thornton, 2000).

The central focus of this chapter is on the different categories of toxic wastes and their etiology in the environment. First, the concepts of 'hazardous waste' and 'toxic waste' are defined. Second, to facilitate our understanding of the nature of toxic waste vis-à-vis other hazards, a distinction between toxic/technological hazards and natural disasters will be presented and how toxic wastes have become prominent as a major social problem that evolved through social construction will be discussed. Subsequently, attention is focused on different types of toxic wastes, their sources and adverse health effects. The cases of community toxic contamination at the Love Canal, Woburn, and Agriculture Street, New Orleans, are summarised. Pertinent environmental legislation that form the legal frameworks addressing the problems of toxic wastes in society will also be summarised.

8.2 WHAT IS TOXIC WASTE?

Generally, a waste is defined as any unwanted materials either in solid, liquid or contained gaseous form discarded by being disposed of, buried, burned or incinerated, or recycled (EPA, 1996). Although the terms 'hazardous' and 'toxic' are frequently used interchangeably in the literature, these terms, however, are not quite the same. In simple terms, 'hazardous' connotes harmful or dangerous materials while 'toxic' implies lethal or poisonous substances (Cunningham and Saigo, 1999). Hazardous waste represents a broad category of wastes in solid, liquid, or containerised gaseous form known to be harmful to humans and other species due to their ignitable, corrosive, explosive, toxic, carcinogenic, mutagenic or teratogenic characteristics (Miller, 2001; EPA, 1996; Epstein et al., 1982; Nebel and Wright, 2000). Nebel and Wright (2000) define hazardous material as anything that can cause injury, disease or death; damage to property; or significant destruction of the biophysical environment. Toxic waste represents a subcategory of hazardous waste which may cause death, permanent (irreversible) or severe (reversible) impairment to human and non-human species upon contact (LaGrega et al., 2001; Tammemagi, 1999; Asante-Duah, 1993).

Another attribute of toxic wastes involves their degree of toxicity. Acute toxicity and chronic toxicity may occur upon exposure to toxic wastes by humans and other living organisms. The former results as either sudden death or illness shortly after a single exposure to a toxic substance, while the latter may take a long latency period to manifest as found in Woburn, Massachusetts, Love Canal, New York, and numerous other contaminated communities across the US. (See Levine, 1982; Brown and Mikkelsen, 1990; Edelstein, 1988). Most of this type of waste now represents the dark side of modern science and technology. As noted by Field and Field (2002, p. 333), hazardous and toxic substances possess traits that pose unique difficulties for monitoring and control, both at the national and cross-national levels including:

- the fact that hundreds of new chemicals are developed and introduced into the market annually;
- more than 300 million tons of chemicals are produced;
- tracking what substances are being used and in what quantity remains extremely difficult.

Given the fact that thousands of chemicals are in use, each with different chemical and physical properties, it becomes virtually impossible to be completely informed about their toxicity and adverse effects on humans and other species in the ecosystem.

Monitoring and tracking small quantity generators of heterogenous toxic chemicals is especially difficult. Most small quantity generators are extremely difficult to police in their surreptitious disposal practices often known as 'midnight dumping'.

Health problems and other damages due to exposure to hazardous/toxic materials generally take many years to manifest; thus, the time lag and chronic nature of damages often blur the direct 'cause' and 'effect' connection.

8.3 TECHNOLOGICAL HAZARDS VS. NATURAL HAZARDS

Social scientists have distinguished toxic disasters from natural calamities. Unlike natural disasters, toxic waste contamination and the consequent health and socio-psychological problems are anthropogenic in origin (Picou, 2000; Erikson, 1994; Edelstein, 1988; Baum, 1987). A number of studies have shown that human-induced toxic disasters are technological in origin and often yield greater chronic (long-term) physical, biological, and psychosocial problems of epic proportions (see Edelstein, 1988, p. 6; Baum, 1987; Baum and Fleming, 1993; Picou, 2000). Technological disasters such as toxic releases, oil spills, and any other suddenly imposed technological disruptions tend to create a social condition of uncertainty, anger, anxiety, frustration, blame, depression, isolation, a loss of control, and distrust of governmental authority and other related agencies (Edelstein, 1988; Tucker, 1995; Picou, 2000; Adeola, 2001; Levine, 1982; Hallman and Wandersman, 1992). Chronic environmental disasters are more difficult for people to cope with compared to acute environmental problems, due to systemic natural forces. As noted by Erikson (1994, p. 144):

> Toxic poisons provoke a special dread because they contaminate rather than merely damage; they are stealthy (silent killers) and deceive the body's alarm systems; they pollute, taint, and befoul rather than just create a wreckage; and because they can be absorbed into the very tissues of the body and crouch there for years, even generations, before doing their deadly work.

In an expert panel workshop on the psychological responses to hazardous substances, convened by the Agency for Toxic Substances and Disease Registry (ATSDR) in 1995, the unique psychosocial aspects of exposure to man-made toxic substances were summarised (Tucker, 1995, p. 2) as:

> Unlike the damage and injuries inflicted by natural disasters, many toxic substances are invisible to the senses; this invisibility results in feelings of

uncertainty. People cannot be sure without instrumentation if they have been exposed to a toxin and how much they have been exposed. Furthermore, due to significant time lag between exposure and manifestation of a chronic illness related to exposure, it is extremely difficult to establish a direct cause and effect relationship between past exposure and subsequent illness.

Social conflict is endemic in cases of toxic disasters while cases of natural disasters are less contentious or litigious (Adeola, 2000a). The chronic toxic effects often entail significant biological dysfunctions including the destruction of vital body organs, central nervous system, gastro-intestinal tract, and genetic materials. Different types of cancers, birth defects, embryo toxicity, mutations, and other dreadful diseases are associated with long term exposure to toxic elements in the environment. Unfortunately, tracing the specific environmental etiology of these health problems over time is often difficult. For natural disasters, however, the impacts are typically of short duration, identifiable, and recovery generally occurs within a reasonable time span.

8.4 TOXIC WASTE AS A SOCIAL PROBLEM

A social problem implies any existing undesirable condition adversely affecting a substantial segment of the society, viewed apprehensively and distastefully by an influential group who believes this condition can be mitigated or eliminated through concerted collective efforts (Zastrow, 2000). A social problem generally evolves through the process of social construction involving claims making, counter-claims and a resolution (see Hannigan, 1995; Greider and Garkovich, 1994; Albrecht and Amey, 1998). The major factors essential for a successful construction of an environmental issue as a social problem are (Hannigan, 1995; Faupel et al., 1991):

- An influential group or claims promoter organising and making a claim or pursuing a cause concerning a putative condition;
- community consensus regarding the existence and nature of the problem upon which a claim is centred;
- scientific endorsement of the claim;
- significant media attention and coverage;
- dramatisation of the problem in symbolic and visual terms;
- economic and socio-political incentives; and
- an institutional sponsor that can ensure legitimacy and continuity of the claim(s).

These factors have played important roles in the process of naming and framing toxic waste as a major social problem.

The issues of toxic wastes have been galvanised by extensive media coverage of toxic waste-related disasters in recent years (Gill and Picou, 1998; Faupel et al., 1991). A number of toxic chemical disasters that have made national and international headlines are:

- the Union Carbide chemical releases in Bhopal, India;
- nuclear meltdown at Chernobyl, Soviet Union (now Ukraine);
- massive oil spill by Exxon Valdez in Prince William Sounds, Alaska, USA;
- severe and chronic toxic chemical contamination at the Love Canal, New York, USA;
- mercury poisoning in Minamata Bay, Japan;
- dioxin contamination in Seveso, Italy;
- exposure of thousands of migrant farm-workers to pesticides in the US; and
- toxic chemical contamination in Koko, Nigeria, and several others.

The proliferation of anti-toxic movements, Not-in-My-Backyard (NIMBY) syndrome, and powerful environmental organisations, have been instrumental in framing toxic or hazardous waste issues as a social problem at the local grassroots, national, and international levels. The new social movement for environmental justice has played vital roles in raising people's consciousness and activism concerning toxic waste problems at the local, national and global levels. Mass media exposure, coupled with increased knowledge about acute and chronic health effects of toxic wastes in the environment, have contributed to the conception of toxic waste as a major social problem in today's society. This is particularly so because most toxic waste contamination episodes are attributed to humans' reckless activities rather than natural forces as mentioned earlier (Gill and Picou, 1998; Edelstein, 1988; Baum et al., 1983). Most toxic wastes are externalities of industrial production in which the costs of production are shifted to innocent by-standers – mostly powerless and disenfranchised groups in society (see Adeola, 2000b; 2001).

Several cases of community contamination, such as those mentioned above, have served as eye-openers concerning the deleterious consequences of technological disasters and toxic wastes on humans and the environment (see Adeola, 2000a; Edelstein, 1988; Picou, 2000; Brown and Mikkelsen, 1990). These catastrophes have convinced the general public about the significant dangers associated with the production, distribution, use and improper disposal of toxic substances. Most of these cases elicit powerful images of toxic chemicals causing severe ecological destruction, community disruptions or disorganisation, acute and chronic toxicity affecting human and non-human species (Edelstein, 1988; Levine, 1982; Picou and Gill,

1996). Most importantly, these cases have exposed the frailty of modern science and technology, leading to a substantial erosion of public trust in the system and in government.

There is a growing consensus among experts, scientists, government, industry and the lay public, that toxic waste releases in the environment constitute a significant social problem. Available data indicate that the spread of toxic chemicals in the environment is causing a public health crisis of huge proportions, e.g. different types of cancers, respiratory problems, chemical hypersensitivity syndrome, sterility, birth defects, embryo toxicity, nervous system dysfunctions, vital organs dysfunctions, mutations and retardation, are among the litany of health problems associated with toxic waste pollution (Adeola, 1994; Acury and Quandt, 1998; Brown, 2001; Thomas et al., 1998; Tsoukala, 1998). Annually, Americans spend billions of dollars to address these adverse health conditions. With our understanding that toxic wastes and associated health issues constitute a serious social problem affecting a large segment of the society, it is crucial to gain familiarity with toxic waste classification. The next section is devoted to the issue of classification of toxic waste with emphasis on the US.

8.5 CLASSIFICATION OF TOXIC WASTES

In order to develop effective strategies to manage and control wastes, and at the same time protect human health and the environment, it is imperative to identify and classify toxic wastes properly. There have been numerous attempts at the classification of hazardous wastes. Toxic wastes are usually treated as a sub-category of hazardous wastes (Asante-Duah, 1993; Epstein et als., 1982; LaGrega et al., 2001). One crude approach is to group wastes according to the degree of risks they pose to humans and the environment. Thus, wastes are put into high, intermediate, and low risk categories. High risk wastes have the properties of being highly toxic, persistent, mobile, ignitable, and bioaccumulative. Examples of this type of wastes include chlorinated solvents, persistent organic pollutants (POPs), heavy metals such as lead and cyanide wastes, and PCB wastes. Intermediate risk wastes are mostly insoluble and have low mobility, e.g. metal hydroxide sludges. Low risk wastes generally include high volume, non-toxic, and malodorous wastes, e.g. municipal solid waste (see Asante-Duah, 1993). A waste is considered hazardous or toxic if it meets any of the four properties set by the EPA under the provisions of the RCRA, i.e. ignitability, corrosiveness, reactivity, and toxicity.

Any liquid with a flash point of less than 60°C or a solid that is capable of causing fire either through friction or absorption of atmospheric moisture, or can undergo spontaneous chemical change resulting in fire, is defined as ignitable or flammable waste. Ignitable wastes are given EPA hazardous waste number of D001. Corrosiveness is determined by using a pH scale. Thus, any waste with a pH of less than or equal to 2, or equal to or greater than 12.5, is considered a corrosive waste. The EPA number D002 classifies corrosive wastes.

Table 8.1 Department of Transportation hazardous materials classification system

Classification	Typical Hazardous Substance(s)
Flammable liquid	Gasoline, alcohol
Combustible liquid	Fuel oil
Flammable solid	Nitrocellulose (film), phosphorus
Oxidizer	Hydrogen peroxide, chromic acid
Organic peroxide	Urea peroxide
Corrosive	Bromine, hydrochloric acid
Flammable gas	Hydrogen, liquified petroleum gas
Nonflammable gas	Chlorine, anhydrous ammonia
Irritants	Tear gas, monochloroacetone
Poison A	Hydroorganic acid, phosgene
Poison B	Cyanide, disinfectants
Etrologic agents	Polio virus, salmonella
Radioactive material	Uranium hexafluoride
Explosives:	
Class A	Jet thrust unit
Class B	Torpedo
Class C	Signal flare, fireworks
Blasting agent	Blasting cap
Other Regulated Materials (ORM)	
ORM A	Trichloroethylene, chloroform
ORM B	Calcium oxide, potassium fluoride
ORM C	Cotton, inflatable life rafts
ORM D	Small arms ammunition
ORM E	Ketone polychlorinated biphenyls

Source: US Office of Technology Assessment (1986).

Reactive wastes are materials that are unstable and can undergo violent chemical change without detonating, and can react violently with water to form possible explosive mixtures, or that may generate poisonous gases. They are coded as D003 waste by the EPA. Acute toxicity is defined as a lethal dose of a chemical that takes less than 50 mg per kilogram of body weight to kill 50 per cent of the population exposed (<LD50), e.g. hydrogen cyanide or hydrogen sulfide. Other toxicity thresholds have been established by the EPA based on oral, dermal, and inhalation toxicity (see Tammemagi,

1999, p. 80). Thus, any waste that may cause death or severe injuries to the exposed victims is considered a toxic waste.

Hazardous wastes are produced and transported across the nation and in some cases cross-nationally. Within the country, the US Department of Transportation (DOT) has developed a system of classification of hazardous and toxic substances transported within the interstate commerce. Table 8.1 presents the DOT classification scheme and representative hazardous substances the agency regulates. Flammable and combustible substances are involved in most cases of accidents. Hazardous materials that are explosive, poisonous, corrosive and radioactive are of greatest concern.

Toxic wastes have also been classified by source, industry, chemical composition and degree of toxicity, persistence in the environment, radioactivity and public health threats (see Epstein et al., 1982; Tammemagi, 1999; Asante-Duah, 1993; McGinn, 2000; LaGrega, et al., 2001). For the present purpose, toxic wastes are classified by type, i.e. inorganic and organic compounds, industry, and sources. The EPA has developed a classification of hazardous wastes by industry. The typical industry and the types of toxic and hazardous wastes generated are shown in Table 8.2.

Table 8.2 Sources and types of toxic waste by industry or generators

Industrial Waste Source(s)	Type of Waste
Agriculture and Lawn Care	Pesticides, toxic fertilisers, ignitable wastes.
Chemical Industry	Strong acids and bases, solvents and reactive wastes, and Persistent Organic Pollutants (POPs).
Automobile, Aerospace, Automotive Repair and Body Shops	Heavy metals, paint wastes (petroleum products), used lead acid batteries, remnant solvents.
Printing Industry	Heavy metal solutions, waste inks, spent solvents, electroplating wastes inks, sludges with heavy metal.
Metal Smelting and Refinery Wastes	Heavy metal.
Leather Products Manufacturing	Waste Toluene and Benzene.
Paper Industry	Paint wastes, heavy metals, ignitable solvents, strong acids and bases.
Construction Industry	Ignitable paint wastes, spent solvents, strong acids and bases.
Hospitals, Clinics, and Laboratories	Biohazards, biological, medical, and pharmaceutical wastes.
Military	Munitions and radioactive wastes.

Source: Adapted from the US Environmental Protection Agency (1996).

Most hazardous and toxic wastes are produced by chemical manufacturing, paper and construction, automotive, and printing and leather products industries. Although not required to report toxic releases by the EPA, agriculture and lawn care industries are responsible for the release of toxic substances such as pesticides, toxic fertilisers, and some ignitable wastes. Biomedical and pharmaceutical wastes from hospitals, clinics, and laboratories also pose significant threats to humans and the environment if not managed properly. The military is a major culprit releasing significant amounts of highly toxic and radioactive substances into the environment.

It is a common practice to distinguish between inorganic and organic compounds. The former, mostly consisting of heavy metals and trace minerals, are examined first and the organic compounds are discussed thereafter.

8.5.1 Inorganic Compounds: Heavy Metals

The major inorganic elements including aluminum, arsenic, cadmium, chromium, copper, cyanide, iron, lead, mercury, nickel, silicates, tin, zinc and their compounds, are abundant in nature. The most dangerous inorganic elements include arsenic, cadmium, chromium, copper, lead, mercury, and zinc (Nebel and Wright, 2000; ATSDR, 1999). Some of these heavy metals have been relied upon as raw materials for industrial production for centuries. Advances in science and technology and industrialisation, have contributed to a wide range of uses of these heavy metals and their trace elements. The mining and industrial use of inorganic compounds have grown exponentially over the past two centuries (Nriagu, 1996; US Department of the Interior (DOI)/Bureau of Mines (BOM), 1993).

Table 8.3 Metal ore and metal waste production in the US, 1960-1990 (billion short tons and per cent)

Selected Year	Crude Ore	(%)	Waste	(%)	Total
1960	0.421	45.0	0.516	55.0	0.938
1970	0.586	37.5	0.975	62.5	1.560
1980	0.597	33.4	1.190	66.5	1.790
1991	0.892	38.0	1.450	62.0	2.340

Source: Adapted from the US Department of the Interior, Bureau of Mines. (1993). Metals include bauxite, copper, gold, iron ore, lead, silver, titanium, zinc, etc.

Since the industrial revolution, human releases of heavy metals have surpassed the systemic releases of these metals into the environment by nature. For instance, worldwide production and consumption of heavy metals such as mercury, lead, cadmium, beryllium, iron and copper, have increased substantially since World War II. As shown in Table 8.3, the production of heavy metals has more than doubled and the generation of metal ore wastes has multiplied threefold in the US since 1960. The advanced industrial societies consume the lion's share of the world's heavy metals, as well as generating the most wastes. Finding safe and sound mechanisms of disposing toxic wastes containing heavy metals remains a serious challenge in the US. With the growing 'Not in My Backyard' (NIMBY) opposition to new facility siting, the transfer of scrap metals and other types of toxic waste to less developed countries has increased significantly from the 1980s to the 1990s (see Greenpeace, 1994; Adeola, 2000b; Moyers, 1990). However, Third World NIMBY is growing strong as increasing numbers of underdeveloped countries are resisting or putting a complete ban on hazardous wastes importation.

Table 8.4 Top 20 hazardous substances and substances most frequently found in completed exposure pathways (CEPs)

Substances	Hazard Rank	No. of NPL Sites	CEP Order
	1	147	3
Lead*	2	206	1
Mercury*	3	74	12
Vinyl Chloride	4	75	21
Benzene	5	116	5
Polycholorinated Biphenyls (PCBs)	6	96	8
Cadmium*	7	105	6
Benzo(a)pyrene	8	46	23
Benzo(b)fluoranthene	10	28	36
Chloroform	11	81	15
DDT, P'P'	12	28	44
Aroclor 1260	13	13	83
Aroclor 1254	14	17	76
Trichloroethylene	15	239	2
Chromium (+6)*	16	102	7
Dibenz[a,h]anthracene	17	25	42
Dieldrine	18	19	56
Hexachlorobutadiene	19	-	-
DDE P,P'	20	37	44

Sources: ATSDR/EPA (1999).
* toxic heavy metals commonly found in waste streams.

Heavy metals are not biodegradable; they remain toxic for as long as they exist. Most of these compounds also bioaccumulate as they work their ways through the food chain or trophic levels. They are used for an array of industrial, commercial, agricultural, and household purposes. Serious illnesses have been linked to both acute and chronic exposure to these elements and their compounds. For example, mercury is a known neurotoxin, arsenic may cause skin and other types of cancer, and lead is associated with neurological disorder and mental retardation, especially among children (Rice and Silbergeld, 1996). The National Academy of Science has reported that the neurological effects of methyl-mercury toxicity are most pronounced and damaging to children under 12 years of age and those contaminated in the womb (Raines, 2001). Cadmium is linked to high blood pressure, heart disease, and lungs and prostrate cancers (Tsoukalas, 1998; Waalkes and Misra, 1996; Nogawa and Kido, 1996; WRI et al., 1998). Selected toxic heavy metals including their sources, properties, possible pathways, and health effects are discussed in the following sections. As shown in Table 8.4, these elements are among the top 20 toxic substances commonly found in waste streams and especially in hazardous waste sites across the country.

8.5.1.1 Arsenic
Arsenic is ranked number one among the top 20 most hazardous substances commonly found in waste streams in the US (see Table 8.4). It is a naturally occurring heavy metal, present in soils, rocks, water and plants. Given the fact that arsenic is a naturally occurring element in the earth's crust, some level of exposure to this metal is inevitable. Civilisations have found a wide variety of uses for this heavy metal. Ancient Greek, Roman, Arabic, Peruvian and Egyptian societies used the compounds of arsenic therapeutically, as poisons, and for other purposes. In contemporary society, arsenic compounds are employed in the production of insecticides, herbicides, fungicides and rodenticides, desiccants and defoliants used to facilitate the mechanical harvesting of cotton, and wood treatments. Arsenic is also used in the glass industry and other metal smelting operations. These industrial processes represent the sources of arsenic waste releases into the environment. Of course, arsenic is also released into the environment through the systemic process of weathering of the rocks and surface run-offs. As noted by Wang and Rossman (1996, p. 221) and Berman (1980), arsenic may be released from soil or rocks into hot spring waters. Thus, this heavy metal is commonly found in drinking water, seawater, and food such as vegetables, grains, fruits and seafood.

Clear scientific evidence has established the toxicity of arsenic. In higher concentration, this metal is poisonous. It is a known carcinogen associated with various types of cancer including bladder, kidney, liver and lung cancers. Exposure to higher concentrations of arsenic (>400 micrograms/day) may cause death while exposure to lower levels (100 to 400 micrograms/day) may induce morbidity conditions such as abnormal heart functions, liver and kidney dysfunctions, gastro-intestinal tract, nerves and skin disorders (Wang and Rossman, 1996; ATSDR, 1998). Furthermore, non-allergic contact dermatitis and conjunctivitis have been found among workers exposed to arsenic-containing dusts. Other serious health problems associated with arsenic poisoning include birth defects, mental and physical impairments especially in children, loss of memory, and suppression of immune systems (Berman, 1980; Crawford, 1997).

8.5.1.2 Asbestos
Asbestos is a naturally occurring fibrous minerals of six different forms: (1) amosite, (2) chrysolite, (3) crocidolite, (4) termolite, (5) actinolite, and (6) anthophyllite. The most popular mineral type is white (chrysolite), however, other varieties may be blue (crocidolite), gray (anthophyllite) or brown (amosite). Asbestos fibres do not possess any typical odour or taste. They are resistant to heat and chemicals and as such, asbestos fibers have been used in a wide range of products including heat-resistant fabrics, insulation of electrical wiring, hot pipes and furnaces, building materials, and friction products. Asbestos is commonly used as insulation and flame retarding materials, roofing materials, floor coverings, and automobile brake shoes (ATSDR, 1995; Chapman, 1998). Incidentally, these diverse applications represent the major sources of asbestos waste generation and release into the environment. Approximately nine million metric tons of asbestos wastes are generated annually in the US.

In its natural form, asbestos is generally not harmful. However, it becomes hazardous when improperly disposed of as waste and through the breakdown of its fibres over time. The wearing down of products made with asbestos releases ultra-fine asbestos fibres, which become airborne and quite toxic upon exposure. Asbestos wastes generally comes from mining, construction, automotive repair, and older building structures. Asbestos is very dangerous because of its fibrous nature and non-biodegradable property. Exposure to asbestos fibres has been linked to serious health problem known as asbestosis, a non-cancerous lung disease. Epidemiological studies have identified the health hazards of asbestos exposure as: leukaemia, lung cancer and mesothelioma, cancers of the pleura, peritoneum, larynx, pharynx, and oral cavity, oesophagus, stomach, colon and rectum, and kidney respectively (see Epstein et al., 1982; EPA, 1985; Chapman, 1998; ATSDR, 1995).

The Federal Government in the US has taken several measures to protect citizens from exposure to asbestos. The EPA banned new uses of asbestos as of July 1989 and the agency has established regulations that require schools to inspect their buildings and remove asbestos. The agency has promulgated a National Emission Standard for asbestos under section 112 of the Clean Air

Act, which established asbestos disposal requirements for active and inactive waste sites. This regulation requires owners and operators of demolition and renovation projects to follow specific guidelines and procedures to prevent asbestos releases to the outside air, and further requires that demolition and renovation materials be controlled if the materials contain more than one per cent asbestos by weight in a form that hand pressure can crumble, pulverise, or reduce to powder when dry (EPA, 1985, pp. 4-34). These initiatives notwithstanding, thousands of homes across America still contain asbestos materials, posing substantial health risks to the residents.

8.5.1.3 Lead

Similar to asbestos, lead is ubiquitous in the environment and it is especially a serious problem in working class to lower income homes in central cities in the US. Lead is considered as one of the metals of antiquity that has been used by all known human civilisations. For example, ancient Greek and Romans used lead for a wide variety of purposes and lead toxicity was recognised in antiquity (Berman, 1980). Some scholars have speculated that lead toxicity might have contributed to the fall of the Roman Empire (see Berman, 1980; Drotman, 1985). It is a highly toxic metal that poses major health risks to exposed populations. It is a naturally occurring element in the earth's crust, that does not display any characteristic taste or smell and will not burn or dissolve in water. However, lead can bind with other chemicals to form lead salts or compounds. Some man-made lead compounds can burn, e.g. organic lead compounds in gasolines. With mounting epidemiological evidence based on studies carried out in the past three decades, many public health authorities in the US have concluded that there may be no acceptable level of lead exposure (CDC, 1991).

Annually, more than nine million metric tons of lead wastes are generated in the US. The EPA has found lead in at least 1,026 out of the 1,467 waste sites currently placed on the National Priority List (NPL). This finding reflects the fact that lead is widely dispersed in the environment. In contemporary society, lead has been used for several purposes including the manufacture of batteries, glass, ammunition, a wide variety of metal products (e.g. sheet lead, solder, pipes, brass and bronze products), medical equipment, paints, ceramics, scientific equipment and military equipment. In the past, lead compounds such as tetraethyl lead and tetramethyl lead have been used in the US as gasoline additives to increase octane rating. The use of these chemicals was discontinued in the 1980s, and lead was banned for use in gasoline effective January 1996.

According to the ATSDR (1997), most lead used by industry derives from mined ores or from recycled scrap metals or batteries. Human activities, such as the use of leaded gasoline and lead-based paints, have released lead and substances containing lead throughout the environment. Substantial amounts of lead can be encountered in air, soil, drinking water, rivers and lakes, and most building structures. As a result of the ban on leaded gasoline, the release of lead to air through automobile exhaust pipes has declined significantly in recent years. The majority of the lead in inner city soils is from older homes with lead-based paints.

There are many sources of exposure to lead and lead products including residential proximity to hazardous waste sites, living in older homes, consumption of foods contaminated by lead, drinking water from lead pipe, and using health-care products that contain lead. Substances such as folk remedies, certain health foods, cosmetics, and 'moonshine whiskey' are sources of lead exposure that are difficult to monitor or control. Occupational exposure is common among people employed in mines, soldering shops, plumbing and pipe fitting, lead smelting and refining industries, brass/bronze foundries, battery manufacturing plants, and lead compound manufacturing facilities. Construction workers and employees of municipal waste incinerators are also prone to exposure to lead (Drotman, 1985).

Exposure to lead poses a variety of health hazards. Even in small doses, neurotoxicity, IQ deficits, learning disorders, attention span disorder and hyperactivity, especially among children, are possible health effects of lead exposure (Rice and Silbergeld, 1996; ATSDR, 1997; Drotman, 1985). At high concentrations (i.e. >15 mcg/dL), lead may also cause significant damage to the brain and kidneys in adults and children. Other health problems include cancer, hearing loss, and chronic neurobehavioral dysfunctions. It has been associated with miscarriage among pregnant women. Lead poisoning may also result in anaemia, increased blood pressure, hypertension, and associated cardiovascular disease (ATSDR, 1997; Epstein et al., 1982; Drotman, 1985; Chapman, 1998; WRI et al., 1998). Although there is no subgroup immune to lead toxicity, either by race or socioeconomic status, minority groups such as African Americans, Mexican Americans, Puerto-Rican Americans, and American Indians and their children, are at higher risk of lead exposure and associated health diminution. According to the ATSDR, approximately 17 per cent of children in the US are at risk of lead poisoning; for minority groups, about 46 per cent of African American children were estimated to be at risk of lead toxicity (ATSDR, 1998). African Americans are disproportionately at risk of occupational and residential exposure to lead and other xenobiotics, as a result of combination of factors including poverty, historical housing and occupational discrimination, and the patterns of hazardous facilities' siting in low-income, powerless neighbourhoods (Adeola, 1994).

8.5.1.4 Mercury
Similar to lead, mercury is a naturally occurring heavy metal which exists in many forms. The three basic chemical forms are elemental or metallic mercury, inorganic mercury and organic mercury (such as alkylmercury, phenylmercury, methylmercury, and methoxyethylmercury) (Hamada and Osame, 1996; ATSDR, 1999). As a pure form of mercury, elemental mercury is the common liquid used in thermometers, barometers, and some electrical switches. Inorganic mercury compounds are produced when elements such as oxygen, chlorine, sulfur, etc. combine with elemental mercury. Interaction of metallic mercury with carbon also yields organic mercury compounds (see ATSDR, 1999; Allchin, 1999; Smith and Smith, 1975). As noted by Hamada and Osame (1996), each form of mercury produces toxic effects in humans and each form can be transformed to other form. For instance, some micro-organisms and other natural factors can transform each form of mercury to another form becoming more lethal to humans and other life forms. Methyl-mercury produced by these agents generally bioaccumulates within the food chain, especially becoming more concentrated in fish and marine mammals as found in the case of Minamata, Japan (see Smith and Smith, 1975).

Inorganic mercury compounds have been used as fungicides and mercuric chloride and iodide are major ingredients of some cosmetics, such as skin bleaching creams. Mercuric chloride has also been used as a topical antiseptic agent in some medicated soaps in the past, and it has been used in medicinal products such as laxatives, warming remedy, and teething powders for children. Thus, mercury wastes are generated in numerous ways, including private household, industrial, commercial, medical and laboratory sources. In most part, human activities such as mining, smelting, industrial processes, and burning of fossil fuels, have substantially elevated the amount of mercury released into the environment. According to the ATSDR (1999), about 80 per cent of the mercury released into the environment through human activities is metallic mercury. The principal sources of metallic mercury emission include solid waste incineration, mining, smelting, and burning of fossil fuels. Approximately 15 per cent of the total mercury in the environment is released to soil via fertilisers, fungicides, and municipal solid wastes, especially containing discarded batteries, thermometers, fluorescent light bulbs, and electrical switches. Industrial waste water accounts for about five per cent of mercury in the environment. In the US, mercury has been found in most hazardous waste sites, especially those placed on the National Priority List (NPL), a list of the most dangerous hazardous waste sites in the US compiled by the EPA, through the use of its Hazards Ranking System (HRS).

The problems of bioaccumulation, the biomagnification of methylmercury within the food chain, have been studied extensively. For instance, several cases of mercury poisoning disasters include: Minamata, Japan;

Ontario, Canada; Pakistan; Guatemala; and Iraq (where organomercury-treated seed grains were consumed by humans (see Hamada and Osame, 1996; Allchin, 1999; Smith and Smith, 1975). The etiology of methylmercury poisoning in Japan was the reckless discharge of methylmercury compounds into the sea and rivers of fishing communities in Minamata, Japan. This episode was described by Smith and Smith (1975:26):

> Undoubtedly, the chemical company called Chisso contaminated the resource dependent communities in Minamata Bay area by poisoning the fishing waters, aquatic food chain, and a large number of the inhabitants. The company discharged methylmercury through waste pipes into Minamata Bay and turned the fishing waters into a sludge dump which destroyed the entire habitat, killing thousands of people including their culture and heritage.

Among the symptoms of methylmercury poisoning (also known as Minamata disease) are: cerebellar ataxia, dysarthria, concentric constriction of the visual field, sensory impairment and hearing impairment. Other symptoms include involuntary movements, nerve dysfunctions, impaired brain development and other abnormalities. Elemental mercury toxicity manifestations include mental changes (including irritability, excitability, insomnia, and problems of concentrations and hallucinations), salivation, gingivitis, stomach upset, and contact dermatitis in cases of skin exposure to mercury (see Hamada and Osame, 1996, pp. 341-2; Smith and Smith, 1975; ATSDR, 1999).While elemental mercury will produce acute toxic effects, methylmercury or organic mercury will bioaccumulate and cause chronic (long-term) effects.

8.5.2 The Organic Compounds

Organic compounds are produced in nature through the combination of carbon, hydrogen, and nitrogen molecules. The bonds of natural hydrocarbons are easily broken through decomposition as they are recycled. Advances in organic chemistry, however, have led to artificial production of synthetic organic compounds which are more durable, lipophilic, versatile, and toxic than their natural counterparts. Synthetic organic compounds are derived from a petroleum base. These petrochemical organic compounds are used in the manufacture of a wide array of modern products, including plastics, cooking utensils, synthetic fabrics, synthetic rubber, paint-like coatings, solvents, pesticides, toxic wood preservatives, and numerous other products. As mentioned earlier, synthetic organic chemicals are in most part, the products of the twentieth century chemical revolution. Two broad categories of organic compounds that pose serious health risks to humans and the environment are Persistent Organic Pollutants (POPs) including organochlorine products and non-Persistent Organic Pollutants (non-POPs). In general, synthetic organic compounds are toxic to humans, decomposer organisms, and the environment. POPs are not bio-degradable and generally bioaccumulate in the environment as compared with natural organic compounds (Nebel and Wright, 2000, p. 478; Thornton, 2000; Epstein, et. al., 1982).

Table 8.5 presents a list of anthropogenic organic compounds commonly found in waste streams across the US and their established adverse health effects. The twelve POPs asterisked are of the most concern to the international community (UNEP, 2000, 1996). Some countries have restricted or completely banned these chemicals. Even though the use of POPs is restricted or banned in developed nations, the US and other advanced industrial nations continue to manufacture them for export to Third World countries.

POPs are defined as a group of synthetic organic compounds that, to a varying extent, are resistant to degradation, soluble in lipids but not in water, semi-volatile, toxic, bioaccumulative, and capable of migrating long distances from the point of original release. These chemical compounds have been found in remote regions of the world where they have never been manufactured or used. Two basic groups of POPs are polycyclic aromatic hydrocarbons and some halogenated hydrocarbons, which include several organochlorines. The organochlorines are the most persistent with wide production, use and toxic releases.

As McGinn (2000, p. 80) points out, some of these synthetic organic compounds were in fact considered modern miracles that have helped humans gained substantial control over nature, especially by increasing the levels of food production and health standards through the control of pests, insect-borne diseases and soil fertility. Paul Muller received a Nobel Prize for developing DDT in 1948. However, numerous previously unknown adverse health effects of DDT and other POPs have been identified since the 1960s. As a legacy of the anthropogenic organic chemical revolution of the twentieth century, a toxic brew of thousands of chemicals are now ubiquitous in every biome on the planet. The outcome is a litany of environmental problems that have permeated the mass media since the 1960s including: DDT and the decline of bald eagles; toxic waste at Love Canal and numerous other communities; cancers; PCBs in polar bear tissue; groundwater contamination; dioxin contamination and fish-kills; embryo toxicity; hormone dysfunctions; breast-milk contamination; vital organs dysfunctions, and many new adverse health conditions (see Thornton, 2000, p. 2; Thomas et al., 2001).

The POPs that are well-recognised for their persistence, bioaccumulation, and biomagnification within the food web are organochlorines or organohalogens.

Table 8.5 Toxic synthetic organic compounds commonly present in chemical wastes and their health effects

Toxic Chemical	Established Adverse Health Effects
1-1'-(2,2,2-Trichloroethylid-ene) bis (4-chlorobenzene) (DDT)*	Cancer of liver, immune system suppression.
Aldrin*	Dizziness, nausea, malaise, liver and biliary cancers.
Benzene+	Mutations, cancers, birth defects, still-births.
Carbon tetrachloride+	Cancers, birth defects, stillbirths, neurotoxicity, hepatoxicity, and kidney diseases.
Chlordane*	Cancers (tests remain inconclusive).
Chloroethylene (vinyl chloride)+	Mutations, cancers, nervous disorders, liver disease, and lungs disorders.
Chloroform+	Cancers, birth defects, embryo toxicity, and hepatoxicity.
Chlorotoluene+	Mutations, cancers.
Dichlorobenzene+	Mutations, nervous disorders, liver disease, and kidney disease.
Dichloroethylene+	Mutations, cancers, birth defects, stillbirths, nervous disorders, and liver and kidney disorders.
Dieldrin*	Liver and biliary cancers.
Endrin*	Cancers.
Furfural+	Mutations, nervous disorders.
Heptachlor*+	Mutations, cancers, stillbirths, birth defects, and liver disease.
Hexachlorobenzene (HBC)*	Mutations, cancers, birth defects, foetal and embryo toxicity, nervous disorders, liver disease, photosensitive skin lesions, and hyperpigmentation.
Mirex*	Acute toxicity, possible cancers.
Polychlorinated Biphenyls*+	Mutations, cancers, birth defects, foetal and embryo toxicity, neurological disorders, and liver disease.
Polychlorinated Dibenzo-p-Dioxins* and Furans*	Peripheral neuropathis, fatigue, depression, hepatitis, liver disease, abnormal enzyme levels, chloracne, embryo toxicity, and gastric lesions.
Tetrachloroethylene+	Cancers, nervous disorders, liver disease, and kidney dysfunctions
Toluene+	Mutations, birth defects, stillbirths, and nervous disorders.
Toxaphene*	Cancers, chromosome aberrations, liver and kidney dysfunctions.
Trichloroethylene+	Mutations, cancers, nervous disorders, and liver disease.
Xylene+	Birth defects, stillbirths, and nervous disorders.

Sources: Adapted from Epstein et al. (1982, pp. 415-27) and UNEP (1996, 2000).
+ compounds commonly present in hazardous waste; * POPs.

This group includes dioxins and furans (produced and released through the incineration of industrial wastes, combustion and industrial processes), Polychlorinated Biphenyls (PCBs), hexaclorobenzene (HCB), mirex, toxaphene, heptachlor, chlordane, and DDT (see Table 8.5 for a complete list).

PCBs, dioxins and furans are among the several modern industrial products or byproducts that have been found to be extremely harmful to humans and the environment. Halogenated compounds, especially organochlorines, are used by the chemical industry in the manufacture of a wide variety of products, including polyvinyl chloride (PVC), solvents, pesticides (used in agriculture and municipalities), and specialty chemical and pharmaceutical products. Table 8.5 also presents other synthetic organic chemicals most commonly found in hazardous waste sites across the US and their known health hazards.

Non-POPs are non-chlorinated hydrocarbons which are generally soluble, volatile, poorly adsorbed but rapidly degradable. They are mostly used as solvents (e.g. xylene, acetone, ethyl benzene and methyl isobutyl ketone), used as paint and varnish solvents, engine and machinery cleaners, in the manufacture of rubber, for fuels and gasoline, and several other industrial applications (Tammemagi, 1999, p. 71). Even with their relative non-persistence, these synthetic chemicals pose a number of serious health concerns ranging from birth defects, cancers, to still births and liver and kidney problems. Industries are largely responsible for the production and improper releases of synthetic organic compounds including the POPs and non-POPs. The cases of Love Canal, New York, Woburn, Massachusetts, and Agriculture Street, New Orleans reveal the economic, environmental, health, and psychosocial dimensions of community toxic contamination. Most of the chemicals buried at the Love Canal in particular are of the POPs group.

8.6 SELECTED CASES OF TOXIC CONTAMINATION: LOVE CANAL, WOBURN, AND AGRICULTURE STREET

The cases of Love Canal, New York, and Woburn, Massachusetts are particularly instructive relative to hundreds of other community contamination cases across the US. Levine (1982) provides a detailed account of the contamination episode at Love Canal, New York. The history of Love Canal began in 1892 when William T. Love proposed to build an eight-mile long power-generating canal along the Niagara River in New York. The canal was dug half-way when the project was abandoned. In the 1940s, the Hooker Chemical Company bought the canal and used it as a dump site for toxic chemical wastes. The canal was about 10 feet deep, 60 feet wide and 3,000 feet long, embedded in an area of orchards and farms. It was considered to be an excellent waste disposal site, accommodating about 20,000 metric tons of heterogeneous toxic chemical wastes in metal drums, which was later covered up with clay soil (Levine, 1982, p. 9). In 1953, the Hooker Chemical Company (later acquired by OxyChem in 1968), sold the land including the land-filled canal to the Niagara Board of Education for one dollar ($1), with a declaration that the canal was filled with chemical waste products and a disclaimer of any future liabilities. However, there was no public health warning about potential adverse health effects of the wastes. Shortly after the acquisition of the land, a school was built and the rest of the land was sold for development, involving the construction of single family homes.

The first sign of health problems occurred in 1958, when school children received serious chemical burns while playing around the road construction operations. The leaking drums were covered up as a quick fix. In 1976, residents of homes adjacent to the Canal started to complain about chemical odours and seepage of wastes from the Love Canal property. By 1978, Love Canal has gained national prominence as a case of a contaminated community. Over 400 toxic chemicals, most of which are carcinogenic, teratogenic, and mutagenic, have been identified at the site. Residents began to understand the roots of their ill-health or somatic conditions ranging from untimely deaths of relatives, cancers, miscarriages, birth defects, skin rashes and irritations to major organ dysfunctions (see Levine, 1982; Miller and Miller, 1991). Of course there were social and psychological dimensions to the contamination episode at Love Canal, as homes became the major source of dread and anxiety about the future. Love Canal was declared a Federal Disaster Area in 1978; the Federal Government assumed the responsibility of buying-out about 800 homes in addition to cleaning up the toxic wastes. Thus, there was major community destruction and loss of social capital in addition to different levels of conflict caused by the Love Canal toxic contamination. By 1990, the EPA has issued its Record of Decision (ROD) indicating that the danger of toxic chemicals was no longer a threat in most of the Love Canal area. However, for many environmental and community activists, the EPA's ROD remains controversial.

As aforementioned, conflict is endemic in cases of toxic contamination of communities. After a protracted court battle, OxyChem (identified as the Potentially Responsible Party (PRP) under CERCLA), agreed on a $98 million settlement to be paid to the state of New York. In 1999, OxyChem also agreed to repay the Federal Government and the state of New York the sum of $7.1 million for the cleanup of the Love Canal. Furthermore, the company assumed the responsibility for future treatment of wastes at the site.

In Woburn, Massachusetts, chemical companies, tanneries, and a glue-manufacturing plant dumped toxic wastes into empty lots for over a century, creating approximately 60 acres of a toxic brew of arsenic, lead, chromium and synthetic organic compounds. Through 'midnight dumping' operations, 184 drums (55 gallons each) of toxic chemicals were deposited in a vacant lot near the east bank of the Aberjona River. Residents obtain their water supply from several wells in the area. Although the state environmental agency found the drums had not leached toxic chemicals into the wells, tests revealed that wells G and H from which most residents obtained their water, were highly contaminated with chlorinated organic compounds including trichloroethylene (TCE) and tetrachloroethylene (also known as perchloroethylene (PCE)). The unpleasant results were acute and chronic toxicity upon exposure, leading to death, leukaemia, and various other debilitating health problems, especially among the children (see Brown and Mikkelsen, 1990; Freudenberg, 1984, p. 31).

Other health problems associated with the contamination of wells G and H include cardiac arrhythmias, and liver, nervous system, and immune system disorders (Kennedy, 1997).

This contamination episode led to the formation of a grassroots group and a subsequent long legal battle against W.R. Grace and Company, Beatrice Foods Company and UniFirst Corporation, alleged to be the potentially responsible parties for the toxic contamination in Woburn (see Brown and Mikkelsen, 1990; Kennedy, 1999). UniFirst settled for $1.05 million without admitting fault; Grace and Company settled out of court for an estimated sum of $8 million; and the case against Beatrice Foods, Inc. was dismissed. Recently, the EPA has indicated its intention to clean the groundwater in East Woburn and restore it to drinking water quality. The cleanup cost is estimated at about $70 million (to be paid by the PRP) and would take 30 to 50 years to complete.

Agriculture Street is 95 acres of land in Eastern New Orleans, housing a community of predominantly African Americans. The history of Agriculture Street dates back to 1910, when the area was designated as the city dump. It operated as a municipal landfill from 1910 to 1966. A wide variety of wastes were dumped at the site without specific standards, regulations, or guidelines about the type of wastes to be accepted. In addition to municipal solid wastes, pesticides, petrochemical wastes, tires, old lead-based paints, and solvents were deposited and buried at the site. Similar to Love Canal, redevelopment of the site was undertaken in 1969 with the construction of low-to-middle income homes, condominiums, apartment complexes, and an elementary school directly on top of the old Agriculture Landfill. Between 1986 and 1993, there were conflicting claims about the extent of contamination and associated health problems in the community.

Scientific tests conducted revealed the presence of about 100 toxic chemicals in the soil of the community, some of which are known carcinogens, including PCBs, polynuclear aromatic hydrocarbons (PAH), lead, arsenic, chlordane and DDT. In 1994, Agriculture Street was declared a NPL site by the EPA. Unlike the Love Canal, however, despite media coverage and grassroots mobilisation efforts, relocation of residents and buyout of contaminated houses were not favoured by the federal government. The preferred remedial action for the entire community was the removal and replacement of the top soil. Most residents feel strongly that they are victims of environmental injustice and environmental racism (Adeola, 2000a). Nevertheless, the EPA has issued its ROD not to implement any remedial measure for the elementary school and ground water beneath the site. It was acknowledged that the 'no action' remedies will result in hazardous substances remaining within the site; however, a review will be conducted every five years consistent with the CERCLA provisions. Many Agriculture Street homeowners, community activists, and environmental justice advocates remain sceptical about the efficacy of the remedial measure undertaken by the EPA. Numerous adverse health conditions, economic, social and psychological problems have been reported by Agriculture Street residents (Adeola, 2000a).

8.7 THE LEGAL FRAMEWORK

The systems of environmental legislation specifically addressing hazardous and toxic waste problems are recent development in the US. Most of the legislative responses to toxic substances and hazardous wastes occurred in the post-World War II era, especially from the mid 1960s to the 1990s. The publication of *Silent Spring* in 1962 by Rachel Carson, a marine biologist, was a major catalyst to the subsequent legislation aimed at protecting the environment and human health. A series of technological disasters causing massive ecological destruction in both the built and natural environments also led to public outcry and support for governmental regulation. Environmental laws and their provisions are initiated, implemented, and enforced at the Federal level. The EPA is the arm of the Federal Government charged with the task of enforcing environmental laws and regulations. However, state environmental protection agencies often act as proxies in the implementation and enforcement process. In fact, some states enact their own environmental legislation to protect unique environments under their jurisdiction. In general, however, state laws and regulation are patterned after the Federal statutes. Thus, both the Federal and state government environmental agencies are charged with the tasks of implementing and enforcing applicable environmental laws.

8.7.1 Legislative Responses to Toxic Waste Problems

Table 8.6 Selected Federal statutes regulating hazardous and toxic
substances in the US, 1965-2001

Statute	Year Passed	Enforcement Agency	Target of Statutes Regulation
Solid Waste Disposal Act	1965	EPA	Municipal wastes
Clean Air Act	1965 1970 1977	EPA	Air pollution; air emission from area, stationary and mobile sources
Clean Water Act (Water Pollution Control Act)	1972 1977	EPA	Water pollution; restoration of water quality
Hazardous Materials Transportation Act	1975 1994	DOT	Interstate transportation of hazardous materials in commerce
Toxic Substances Control Act	1976	EPA	Existing and impending new toxic chemical hazards, hazardous substances including asbestos, radon, lead, PCBs, etc.
Resource Conservation and Recovery Act (RCRA)	1976	EPA	Cradle to grave management of wastes and recovery of resources
Comprehensive Environmental Response, Compensation, and Liability Act (CERCLA)	1980	EPA	Hazardous waste sites; compensation for and restoration of contaminated sites
Hazardous and Solid Waste Amendments	1984	EPA	Underground storage tanks and land-based hazardous waste treatment, storage, and disposal facilities.
Asbestos Hazard Emergency Response Act (AHERA)	1986	EPA	Asbestos abatement in schools and commercial buildings.
Lead Exposure Reduction Act	1992	EPA	Reduction of lead contamination and toxicity
Emergency Planning and Community Right to Know Act	1986	EPA	Emergency preparedness, minimisation of chemical accidents and dissemination of information to the community
Pollution Prevention Act	1990	EPA	Waste reduction, pollution prevention education, training and information exchange

Sources: Adapted from various sources including Plater et al. (1992); Jain et al. (1993); Kubasek and Silverman, (2000); Chapman (1998); and EPA (1976).

From 1965 to the present, several laws and legislative amendments specifi-cally addressing toxic and hazardous waste releases, ecological disruptions, human habitat destruction, and numerous environmentally-induced health risks across the US were established.

Prominent among the environmental statutes designed to regulate hazard-ous and toxic substances in the environment are the Toxic Substances Control Act, Clean Air Act, Clean Water Act, Resource Conservation and Recovery Act (RCRA), the Comprehensive Emergency Response, Compen-sation and Liability Act (CERCLA), and the Pollution Prevention Act. These statutes are briefly discussed in this section. A brief summary of selected Federal statutes regulating hazardous/toxic substances is presented in Table 8.6.

8.8 SUMMARY AND CONCLUSIONS

In this chapter, several aspects of toxic wastes were considered, including the definition and social construction of toxic wastes as a social problem; the classification and identification of wastes and their deleterious health effects on humans and the environment; and the major environmental laws regulat-ing toxic waste management. The nature of risks associated with toxic wastes and technological hazards in general, calls for our immediate concerns. While natural disasters involve a loss of control over processes perceived to be uncontrollable in the first place, toxic disasters involve a loss of control over conditions or processes perceived to be controllable (Baum et al., 1983). Thus, parties to blame are often identified in cases of toxic contamination and other technological accidents. With increasing knowledge and public aware-ness of the problem of toxic waste releases, scientists, environmental activists, lay persons and the media are among the key players in the social construction of toxic waste as a serious problem. In some cases, people directly affected by toxic waste contamination employed popular epidemio-logy approach to understand the roots of their somatic conditions as found in Woburn. Ontological security becomes questionable when people are con-fronted with exposure to toxic materials. Erosion of trust in established social institutions is among the symptoms of psychological syndromes commonly found among the victims of toxic contamination (see Erikson, 1994; Edel-stein, 1988). Therefore, conflicts among experts, lay people and scientists, scientists and government agencies are quite common in cases of community toxic contamination.

It is essential to understand wastes by sources, types, chemical composi-tion, and associated risks. Several classification schemes, by industry, chemical composition, inorganic and organic types, and persistence in the environment, have been discussed in this chapter. Furthermore, specific types of toxic and hazardous wastes and their adverse health effects on humans and the ecosystem were presented. While quite extensive, the classification presented in this chapter is by no means exhaustive. In addition, a number of selected cases of community toxic contamination were discussed; the cases of the Love Canal and Woburn, Massachusetts were particularly instrumental to the subsequent Superfund legislation.

Although significant progress has been made in legislative responses to environmental pollution in general and toxic waste problems in particular since the publication of *Silent Spring* by Rachel Carson, there is still a long way to go to protect human health from heterogeneous toxic chemicals being produced and released at such an alarming rate in the US and other advanced industrial countries. These toxic elements are being produced and released at such a faster pace than the enactment of laws that are supposed to regulate them. Many new chemicals are persistent, deadly, and trans-boundary in nature that international laws and co-operation are required to regulate them. The precautionary principle is now being advocated both in the US and across the globe (Goklany, 2001). This principle suggests that whenever there is scientific uncertainty about the safety or potentially serious harm from chemicals or technologies, manufacturers or decision makers shall do everything possible to prevent harm to humans and the environment. In other words, 'it is better safe than sorry', and manufacturers of toxic chemicals should be held accountable for any latent or manifest serious adverse health effects of these chemicals to humans and the environment.

REFERENCES

Adeola, F.O. (1994), 'Environmental hazards, health, and racial inequity in hazardous waste distribution', *Environment and Behavior*, **26**, 99-126.

Adeola, F.O. (2000a), 'Endangered community, enduring people: toxic contamination, health, and adaptive responses in a local context', *Environment and Behavior*, **32** (2), 207-47.

Adeola, F.O. (2000b), Cross-national environmental injustice and human rights issues: a review of evidence in the developing world', *American Behavioral Scientist*, **43** (4), 686-705.

Adeola, F.O. (2001), 'Environmental injustice and human rights abuse: the states, MNCs, and repression of minority groups in the world system', *Human Ecology Review*, **8** (1), 39-59.

Albrecht, S.L. and R.G. Amey (1999), 'Myth-making, moral communities, and policy failure in solving the radioactive waste problem', *Society and Natural Resources*, **12** (8), 741-61.

Allchin, D. (1999), *The Poisoning of Minamata*, Ships Teachers' Network, http://www2.utep.edu/;allchin/ships/ethics/minamata.htm

Arcury, T.A. and S.A. Quandt (1998), 'Chronic agricultural chemical exposure among migrant and seasonal farmworkers', *Society and Natural Resources*, **11** (8), 829-43.

Asante-Duah, K.D. (1993), *Hazardous Waste Risk Assessment*, Boca Raton, FL: Lewis Publishers.

ATSDR (Agency for Toxic Substances and Disease Registry) (1995), Public Statement for Asbestos, Atlanta, GA: ATSDR.

ATSDR (1997), *Public Health Statement for Lead*. Atlanta, GA: ATSDR, http//www.atsdr.cdc.gov/toxprofiles/ phs13.html.

ATSDR (1998), *Case Studies in Environmental Medicine: Lead Toxicity*. Atlanta, GA: ATSDR/US Department of Health and Human Services, http://www.atsdr. cdc.gov/HEC/caselead.html

ATSDR (1999), *Public Statement for Mercury*. Atlanta, GA: ATSDR, http://www. atsdr.cdc.gov/ToxProfiles/phs8916.html

Baum, A. (1987), 'Toxins, technology and natural disaster', in G. Van de Bos (ed.), *Cataclysms, Crises, and Catastrophes*, Washington, DC: American Psychological Association, pp. 5-54.

Baum, A., R. Fleming and J.E. Singer (1983), 'Coping with victimization by technological disaster', *Journal of Social Issues*, **39** (2), 117-38.

Baum, A. and I. Fleming (1993), 'Implications of psychological research on stress and technological accidents', *American Psychologist*, **48** (6), 665-72.

Beck, U. (1992), *Risk Society: Towards a New Modernity*, Newbury Park, CA: Sage Publications.

Beck, U. (1995), *Ecological Enlightenment: Essays on the Politics of the Risk Society*, Atlantic Highlands, NJ: Humanities Press.

Berman, E. (1980), *Toxic Metals and Their Analysis*, Philadelphia: Hayden and Son.

Blackman, W.C. Jr. (1996), *Basic Hazardous Waste Management*, New York: Lewis Publishers.

Brown, L. (2001), *Eco-Economy: Building and Economy for the Earth*, New York: W.W. Norton and Co.

Brown, P. and E.J. Mikkelsen (1990), *No Safe Place: Toxic Waste, Leukemia and Community Action*, Berkeley: University of California Press.

Carson, R. (1962), *Silent Spring*, Boston: Houghton and Mifflin.

CDC (1991), Preventing Lead Poisoning in Young Children: A Statement by the Centers for Disease Control, Atlanta, GA: US Department of Health and Human Services.

Chapman, S.R. (1998), *Environmental Law and Policy*, Upper Saddle River, NJ: Prentice Hall.

Cohen, G. and J. O'Connor (1990), *Fighting Toxins: A Manual for Protecting Your Family, Community, and Workplace*, Washington, DC: Island Press.

Crawford, M. (1997), *Toxic Waste Sites: An Encyclopedia of Endangered America*, Santa Barbara, CA: ABC-CLIO, Inc.

Cunningham, W.P. and B.W. Saigo (1999), *Environmental Science: A Global Concern*, New York: McGraw-Hill.

Drotman, P.D. (1985), 'Chemicals, health, and the environment', in D.S. Blumenthal (ed.), *Introduction to Environmental Health*, New York: Springer Publishing Company, pp. 47-77.

Edelstein, M.R. (1988), *Contaminated Communities: The Social and Psychological Impacts of Residential Toxic Exposure*, Boulder, CO: Westview Press.

Edelstein, M.R. and W.J. Makofske (1998), *Radon's Deadly Daughers: Science, Environmental Policy, and the Politics of Risk,* New York: Rowman and Littlefield.

Epstein, S.S., L.O. Brown and C. Pope (1982), *Hazardous Waste in America,* San Francisco: Sierra Club Books.

Erikson, K. (1994), *A New Species of Trouble: Explorations in Disaster, Trauma, and Community,* New York: W.W. Norton.

Faupel, C.E., C. Bailey and G. Griffin (1991), 'Local media roles in defining hazardous waste as a social problem: the case of Sumter County, Alabama', *Sociological Spectrum,* **11** (4), 293-319.

Field, B.C. and M.K. Field (2002), *Environmental Economics: An Introduction,* New York: McGraw-Hill.

Freudenberg, N. (1984), *Not in Our Backyards: Community Action for Health and the Environment,* New York: Monthly Review Press.

Gill, D.A. and J.S. Picou (1998), 'Technological disaster and chronic community stress', *Society and Natural Resources,* **11** (8), 795-815.

Goklany, I.M. (2001), *The Precautionary Principle: A Critical Appraisal of Environmental Risk Assessment.* Washington, D.C.: CATO Institute.

Greenpeace (1994), *The Database of Known Hazardous Waste Exports from OECD to Non-OECD Countries, 1989-1994,* Washington, DC: Greenpeace.

Greider, T. and L. Garkovich (1994), 'Landscapes: the social construction of nature and the environment', *Rural Sociology,* **59,** 1-24.

Hallman, W.K. and A. Wandersman (1992), 'Attribution of responsibility and individual and collective coping with environmental threats', *Journal of Social Issues,* **48** (4), 101-18.

Hamada, R. and M. Osame (1996), 'Minamata Disease and other mercury syndromes', in L.W. Chang (ed.), *Toxicology of Metals,* New York: CRC Lewis Publishers, pp. 337-51

Hannigan, J.A. (1995), *Environmental Sociology: A Social Constructionist Perspective,* New York: Routledge.

Jain, R.K., L.V. Urban and H.E. Balbach (1993), *Environmental Assessment,* New York: McGraw-Hill.

Kennedy, D.D. (1997), *Stalking Woburn's Mystery Killer,* http://www2.shore.net/~dkennedy/woburn_mit.html

Kennedy, D.D. (1999), *Death and Justice: Environmental Tragedy and the Limits of Science,* http://www2.shore.net/~dkennedy/woburn_trial.html

Kubasek, N.K. and G.S. Silverman (2000), *Environmental Law,* Upper Saddle, NJ: Prentice Hall.

LaGrega, M.D., P.L. Buckingham, J.C. Evans and Environmental Resources Management (ERM) (2001), *Hazardous Waste Management,* New York: McGraw-Hill.

Lave, L.B. and A.C. Upton (eds) (1987), *Toxic Chemicals, Health, and the Environment,* Baltimore, MD: Johns Hopkins University Press.

Levine, A.G. (1982), *Love Canal: Science, Politics and People,* Lexington, MA: Lexington Books.

Lichtveld, M.Y. and B.L. Johnson (1993), 'Public health implications of hazardous waste sites in the United States', Paper Presented at the ATSDR Hazardous Waste Conference, http://www.atsdr.cdc.gov/cxic.html

Litmanan, T. (1996), 'Environmental conflict as a social construction: nuclear waste conflicts in Finland', *Society and Natural Resources,* **9,** 523-35.

McGinn, A.P. (2000), 'Phasing out persistent organic pollutants', in L.R. Brown et al. (eds), *State of the World*. New York: W.W. Norton, pp. 79-100.

Miller, G.T. Jr. (2001), *Environmental Science*, Belmont, CA: Wadsworth.

Miller, E.W. and R.M. Miller (1991), *Environmental Hazards: Toxic Waste and Hazardous Materials, A Reference Handbook*, Denver, CO: ABC-CLIO, Inc.

Moyers, B. (1990), *Global Dumping Ground: The International Traffic in Hazardous Waste*, Washington, DC: Seven Locks Press.

Nebel, B.J. and R.T. Wright (2000), *Environmental Science: The Way the World Works*, Upper Saddle River, NJ: Prentice Hall.

Nogawa, K. and T. Kido (1996), 'Itai-Itai Disease and health effects of cadmium', in L.W. Chang (ed.), *Toxicology of Metals*, New York: CRC-Lewis Publishers, pp. 353-69.

Nriagu, J.O. (1996), 'History of global metal production', *Science*, **22** (April 12): 223-24.

O'Connor, J. (1990), 'The toxic crisis', in G. Cohen and J. O'Connor (eds), *Fighting Toxics: A Manual for Protecting Your Family, Community, and Workplace*, Washington, DC: Island Press, pp. 11-24

Piasecki, B.W. and G.A. Davis (1987), 'Restructuring toxic waste controls: intrinsic difficulties and historical trends', in B.W. Piasecki and G.A. Davis (eds), *America's Future in Toxic Waste Management: Lessons from Europe*, New York: Quorum Books, pp. 1-13

Picou, J.S. (2000), 'The talking circle as sociological practice: cultural transformation of chronic disaster impacts', *Sociological Practice: A Journal of Clinical and Applied Sociology*, **2** (2), 77-97.

Picou, J.S. and D.A. Gill (1996), 'The Exxon Valdez oil spill and chronic psychological stress', *American Fisheries Symposium*, **18**, 879-93.

Picou, J.S. and D.A. Gill (1998), 'Technological disaster and chronic community stress', *Society and Natural Resources*, **11** (8), 795-815.

Plater, Z.J.B., R.H. Abrams and W. Goldfarb (1992), *Environmental Law and Policy: A Coursebook on Nature, Law, and Society*, St. Paul, MN: West Publishing Co.

Raines, B. (2001), 'Tests reveal high mercury in some Gulf fish', *The Times Picayune*, July 28: A-13.

Rice, D. and E. Silbergeld (1996), 'Lead neurotoxicity: concordance of human and animal research', in L.W. Chang (ed.), *Toxicology of Metals*, New York: CRC-Lewis Publishers, pp. 659-75

Schnaiberg, A. and K.A. Gould (1994), *Environment and Society: The Enduring Conflict*, New York: St. Martin's Press.

Setterberg, F. and L. Shavelson (1993), *Toxic Nation: The Fight to Save Our Communities from Chemical Contamination*, New York: John Wiley and Sons.

Smith, E.W. and A.M. Smith (1975), *Minamata*, New York: Holt Rinehart and Winston.

Tammemagi, H. (1999), *The Waste Crisis: Landfills, Incinerators, and the Search for a Sustainable Future*, New York: Oxford University Press.

Thomas, J.K., J.S. Kodamanchaly and P.M. Harveson (1998), 'Toxic chemical wastes and the coincidence of carcinogenic mortality in Texas', *Society and Natural Resources*, **11**, 845-65.

Thomas, J.K., B. Qin, D.A. Howell and B.E. Richardson (2001), 'Environmental hazards and rates of female breast cancer mortality in Texas', *Sociological Spectrum*, **21** (3), 237-45.

Thornton, J. (2000), *Pandora's Poison: Chlorine, Health, and a New Environmental Strategy*, Cambridge, MA: MIT Press.

Tsoukala, T.H. (1998), 'Science, socioenvironmental inequality, and childhood lead poisoning', *Society and Natural Resources*, **11**, 743-54.

Tucker, P. (1995), *Report of the Expert Panel Workshop on the Psychological Responses to Hazardous Substances*, Atlanta, GA: ATSDR.

United Nations Environmental Program (UNEP) (1996), 'UNEP survey on sources of POPs', Prepared for International Forum on Chemical Safety Experts Meeting on POPs, Manila, The Philippines, June 17-19. http://irptc.unep.ch/pops/indxhtms/manexp3.html.

United Nations Environmental Program (UNEP) (2000), 'Report of the intergovernmental negotiating committee for an international legally binding instrument for implementing international action on certain persistent organic pollutants on the work of Its fifth session', Geneva: UNEP/POPS/INC.5/7, 26 December.

U.S. Department of Interior (DOT), Bureau of Mines (BOM) (1993), *Mining and Quarrying Trends in the Metals and Industrial Minerals Industries, 1991*, Washington, DC: DOT/BOM.

US Environmental Protection Agency (EPA) (1976), *Toxic Substances Control Act* (TSCA), http://tis.eh.doe.gov/oepa/law-sum/TSCA.HTM.

U.S. Environmental Protection Agency (EPA) (1985), *Wastes From the Extraction and Beneficiation of Metallic Ores, Phosphate Rock, Asbestos, Overburden from Uranium Mining, and Oil Shale*, Washington, DC: EPA.

U.S. Environmental Protection Agency (EPA) (1996), *Understanding the Hazardous Waste Rules: A Handbook for Small Business*, Washington, DC: EPA.

U.S. Environmental Protection Agency (EPA) (1997), *The Preliminary Biennial RCRA Hazardous Waste Report*, Washington, DC: EPA.

U.S. Environmental Protection Agency (EPA) (1999), *Toxic Release Inventory Public Data Release*, Washington, DC: EPA.

U.S. Environmental Protection Agency (EPA) (2000), *Toxic Release Inventory Public Data Release, 1999*, Washington, DC: EPA.

U.S. Office of Technology Assessment (1986), *Transportation of Hazardous Materials*, Washington, DC: Government Printing Office.

Waalkes, M.P. and R.R. Misra (1996), 'Cadmium carcinogenicity and genotoxicity', in L.W. Chang (ed.), *Toxicology of Metals*, New York: CRC-Lewis Publishers, pp. 231-43

Wang, Z. and T.G. Rossman (1996), 'The carcinogenicity of arsenic', in L.W. Chang (ed.), *Toxicology of Metals*, New York: CRC-Lewis Publishers, pp. 221-29

World Resources Institute (WRI), United Nations Environmental Program (UNEP), United Nations Development Program (UNDP) and World Bank (1998), *World Resources: Environmental Change and Human Health*, New York: Oxford University Press.

Zastrow, C. (2000), *Social Problems: Issues and Solutions*, Belmont, CA: Wadsworth.

APPENDIX

Table A8.1 Industrial toxic chemical releases by states in the USA, 1999 (million pounds)

State	Release	State	Release
Alabama	138.13	Montana	127.62
Alaska	433.02	Nebraska	27.27
American Samoa	0.01	Nevada	1,168.41
Arizona	963.33	New Hampshire	5.87
Arkansas	41.53	New Jersey	31.28
California	69.05	New Mexico	262.28
Colorado	26.09	New York	71.81
Connecticut	7.84	North Carolina	158.35
Delaware	11.38	North Dakota	23.66
District of Columbia	0.98	Northern Marianas	0.00
Florida	149.41	Ohio	303.23
Georgia	126.92	Oklahoma	37.07
Guam	0.50	Oregon	67.70
Hawaii	2.58	Pennsylvania	252.78
Idaho	85.98	Puerto Rico	18.17
Illinois	165.06	Rhode Island	1.39
Indiana	198.87	South Carolina	12.13
Iowa	48.79	Tennessee	144.31
Kansas	42.57	Texas	313.87
Kentucky	106.21	Utah	1,161.79
Louisiana	150.15	Vermont	0.65
Maine	7.85	Virgin Islands	0.77
Maryland	43.98	Virginia	80.57
Massachusetts	11.88	Washington	28.48
Michigan	142.29	West Virginia	100.49
Minnesota	31.28	Wisconsin	58.38
Mississippi	75.80	Wyoming	19.43
Missouri	129.74	Total	7,688.92

Source: EPA (1999).

9. Nuclear Waste

John Proops

9.1 INTRODUCTION

For the purposes of this chapter, 'nuclear waste' will mean that material which exhibits radioactivity at potentially damaging levels, and which is being produced as part of some economic activity. The great bulk of such waste arises from the fission reactions in nuclear power plants, though a very small amount can be generated by the concentration of naturally radioactive material (e.g. radium), for research or medical purposes (Lenssen, 1991).

The radioactive waste generated at nuclear facilities can take several forms. Most is produced within the reactors, by fission or neutron irradiation (see Section 9.3). However, some may result from the contamination of non-radioactive material with radioactive waste (e.g. protective clothing). Such low radioactive contamination usually constitutes 'low-level waste', and it is mostly disposed of by burial in landfill sites, much like other forms of waste (see Section 9.5.2).

While low-level waste is dealt with relatively easily, highly radioactive waste from reactors and reprocessing plants presents quite different hazards and disposal problems, and it is on this highly dangerous material that we shall focus.

A fortunate property of nuclear waste it that the radioactivity naturally decays over time. Indeed, the most dangerous nuclear wastes are precisely the highly radioactive materials, which are decaying very rapidly (see Section 9.3.2). Consequently, simply storing nuclear waste for a few years allows much of the radioactivity to disappear. However, unlike other sorts of waste, there are no feasible means of speeding-up this process of radioactive decay. While chemically toxic materials can often be treated to render them less noxious, radioactive material is be rendered less dangerous only by the passage of time.

The structure of the rest of this chapter will be as follows. In Section 9.2, the nuclear fuel cycle is described. This is the process by which uranium ore is converted into useful power, simultaneously generating radioactive waste as a joint product. Section 9.3 looks at the physics of nuclear reactors, to give an insight into the nature of the processes of nuclear fission and radioactive decay. The nature and dangers of radioactive waste are discussed in Section 9.4, and strategies for disposing of radioactive waste are outlined in Section 9.5. Some historical and social reflections on nuclear waste are offered in Section 9.6; there are some conclusions in Section 9.7.

9.2 THE NUCLEAR FUEL CYCLE

To understand how nuclear waste can arise, we need to understand the nuclear fuel cycle. Generating nuclear power involves a 'fuel cycle' not unlike that of the generation of power from fossil fuels. (The standard work on the nuclear fuel cycle is the volume edited by Wilson (1996a), and this will be referred to extensively in the rest of this chapter.) The nuclear fuel cycle can be represented as follows:

- Uranium mining and concentration of the ore;
- Enrichment of the Uranium-235 proportion;
- Extraction of power by fission in a nuclear reactor;
- Extraction of some remaining fissile material (i.e. plutonium);
- Disposal of remaining radioactive material.

Each of these steps deals with material which is radioactive to some degree, and is potentially hazardous. However, the final three stages produce and deal with by far the most hazardous material, so in this chapter we shall concentrate on the 'end' of the fuel cycle.

In particular, as with other forms of waste, nuclear waste is dangerous when it is released into the environment. While it is contained in nuclear reactors or storage facilities, its danger is much reduced.

Release of radioactive waste into the environment can take two forms; by accident or by design. We are familiar with the accidental release of radioactive material from the UK Windscale fire in 1957, from the nuclear waste catastrophe at Chelyabinsk in the USSR, also in 1957, and from the Chernobyl accident in 1986. (For a listing of nuclear US accidents, see Lutins, 1999.) The deliberate release of radioactive material is usually less recognised, but it takes place all of the time from both nuclear reactors and reprocessing plants, usually into the air or bodies of water. Indeed, such deliberate releases of radioactive material from the UK reprocessing site at Sellafield, on the Irish Sea, is a long-standing source of complaint by the Irish government.

Because nuclear waste is not susceptible to treatment to reduce its radio-activity, to reduce the emissions of nuclear waste into the environment, the only possibility (for a given level of nuclear power generation) is to increase nuclear storage.

From this necessity a potential conflict can be detected between the urge to make use of nuclear waste and the desire to reduce emissions. Extracting plutonium from spent nuclear fuel generates further fuel that can be used in nuclear reactors. However, the process of extraction may cause the release of radioactive material that otherwise could be contained. For example, a fission product is Krypton-85. Now krypton is a 'noble' gas, which is extremely chemically unreactive and difficult to immobilise. The reprocessing of spent nuclear fuel releases Krypton-85 into the atmosphere and increases the general radiation dose on the biosphere, including on humans. In contrast, not reprocessing the spent fuel leaves the krypton immobilised within the fuel rods, which can then be stored with a relatively slight release of radioactivity.

9.3 THE PHYSICS OF NUCLEAR REACTORS

Before we look at the process of induced nuclear fission in reactors, a brief review of the physics of the atom and modes of nuclear decay is necessary. This then allows a brief discussion of the processes that take place inside nuclear reactors. (For a useful history of uranium, see Goldschmidt (1989). A good general introductions to this area are IEER, 2000 and Wilson, 1996b.)

9.3.1 Atoms, Nuclei and Isotopes

An atom consists of a positively charged nucleus surrounded by negatively charged electrons. The nucleus of an atom is itself composed of more basic components; i.e. positively charged protons and (neutral) neutrons. The various elements (e.g. hydrogen, helium, etc.) have specific chemical characteristics, largely determined by the number of protons in the nucleus (as this 'atomic number' determines the number of orbiting electrons, which in turn determines chemical behaviour).

For any particular element, the nuclear protons may be accompanied by various numbers of neutrons. For example, carbon has six protons, and most commonly six neutrons. As protons and neutrons have very nearly the same mass, this gives it an atomic weight of (6+6=) 12; i.e. Carbon-12, or ^{12}C. (NB The mass of atomic electrons is negligible in comparison with the nucleus.) However, another possibility is carbon nuclei with eight neutrons, giving an atomic weight of 14 (i.e. Carbon-14, or ^{14}C). These various nuclear configurations for an element all have the same chemical properties, and so they all lie in the same place in the Periodic Table of the elements. In recognition of this, they are called 'isotopes' (Greek – 'same place'). So we speak of ^{12}C and ^{14}C as both being isotopes of carbon.

9.3.2 Nuclear Decay

All nuclei decay, although some decay so slowly as to be regarded as 'stable'. Conversely, all of the isotopes of the element Technetium (atomic number 43) have short half-lives on a geological scale, so this element does not occur naturally on Earth. The rate of nuclear decay is characterised by the time it takes for half of the nuclei to decay; i.e. the 'half-life' of that isotope. The spontaneous decay of nuclei generally takes one of two forms:

- Alpha decay – this involves the emission of a helium nucleus (two neutrons plus two protons), know as an 'alpha ray'. This may be accompanied by the emission of short-wavelength electromagnetic radiation, known as 'gamma rays'. The effect of alpha decay is to reduce the atomic weight by 4 and reduce the atomic number by two. The outcome is an isotope of a different element, two places to the left in the Periodic Table; (e.g. Uranium-238 [atomic no. 92] alpha decays with a half-life of 4.47 billion years, to Thorium-234 [atomic no. 90]).
- Beta decay – this involves the emission of an electron (a 'beta ray'), through the conversion of a neutron to a proton, with the emission of an electron; this is also often accompanied by the emission of gamma rays. Beta decay leaves the atomic weight unchanged, but increases the atomic number by one. Again, a different element is produced, though this time it is one place to the right in the Periodic Table; (e.g. Thorium-234 [90] beta decays with a half-life of 1.06 days, to Palladium-234 [91]).

Both alpha and beta decay are usually accompanied by the release of energy, which causes the decaying material to become warmer. (The terminology of alpha, beta and gamma rays stems from the early days of research on spontaneously decaying nuclei. For a detailed discussion of pathways of decay, see Wilson (1996a, pp. 310-313).)

The health risk of such spontaneous nuclear decay lies in the effects of these rays on matter. They are sufficiently energetic to affect molecules in living matter, stripping off one or more electrons to generate positively charged ions. These ions can be disruptive to cells, potentially causing cancers and genetic mutations in the germ cells (thus affecting subsequently conceived children). Nuclear waste is mostly composed of such unstable isotopes, with their consequent biological dangers (Bertell, 2000)

9.3.3 Nuclear Fission

Uranium exists in two common isotopes; Uranium-238 constitutes 99.3 per cent of the naturally occurring form, while Uranium-235 accounts for the remaining 0.7 per cent. For nuclear reactors, ^{235}U is the key material.

^{235}U is unstable, with a half-life of 704 million years (exhibiting alpha decay to Thorium-231). As well as being unstable, ^{235}U is unique among the naturally occurring elemental isotopes in exhibiting 'nuclear fission' (i.e. it is 'fissile'). Nuclear fission occurs when a free neutron encounters and is absorbed by a ^{235}U nucleus. The resulting ^{236}U is extremely unstable, and does not exhibit the usual alpha or beta decay. Instead, it shatters into a number of fragments, which comprise a range of unstable (and hence highly radioactive) isotopes. Also emitted are further neutrons.

The emission of these extra neutrons means that further induced fission of ^{235}U can be stimulated, so there is the potential for a self-maintaining 'chain reaction'. If the ^{235}U is highly concentrated, then the resulting chain reaction may be almost instantaneous, releasing large amounts of energy and radioactive material (i.e. it constitutes a fission or 'atom' bomb; 'hydrogen' bombs work on the quite different principle of 'fusion'). The first detonation of a nuclear weapon took place in 1945 in the Nevada desert.

If ^{235}U is used in a less concentrated form, the nuclear fission chain reaction can be controlled. Then the reaction takes place at a rate which allows it to deliver useful but limited amounts of energy, for use in electricity generation (as in nuclear power plants). The first controlled nuclear reaction took place in 1942 in Chicago. (For the history of the development of nuclear technology see Rhodes, 1986)

9.3.4 Nuclear Power Plants

Within a nuclear power plant's core, the induced fission of ^{235}U releases large quantities of heat; this is used, via steam generation, to produce electricity. Also produced is an intense flux of free neutrons. While some of these neutrons are absorbed by ^{235}U, to continue the chain reaction, many are absorbed by the structural material within the core, and convert the originally stable isotopes into unstable ones, which are therefore radioactive. (For a clear introduction to his area, see Hesketh, 1996.)

Many of the neutrons are also absorbed by the other form of uranium, ^{238}U, which in all commercial and most military reactors is the predominant form of uranium in the reactor core. When ^{238}U absorbs a neutron it becomes ^{239}U, which is unstable and successively beta decays to Neptunium-239 and then to Plutonium-239. This ^{239}Pu has a half-life of 24 thousand years, and like ^{235}U it is fissile and can be used to make bombs or power nuclear reactors. Because of its relatively short half-life ^{239}Pu does not occur naturally, so it is spoken of as an 'artificial element'. (As ^{238}U allows the generation of fissile material, but is not itself fissile, it said to be 'fertile'.)

Further neutrons can be absorbed by ^{239}Pu, to give ^{240}Pu, ^{241}Pu and ^{242}Pu. Through successive beta decay and further neutron absorption, these can give rise to the artificial elements Americium and Curium, as the isotopes ^{241}Am, ^{242}Am, ^{243}Am, ^{242}Cm, ^{244}Cm, ^{245}Cm, ^{246}Cm and ^{247}Cm. From these isotopes, successive chains of alpha and beta decay generate a further and extensive range of radioactive isotopes.

9.3.5 Waste from Nuclear Reactors

From the above discussion, one can identify three sorts of nuclear waste arising from the operation of nuclear reactors:

- Fission waste – the radioactive nuclei resulting from the fission of ^{235}U;
- Irradiation waste – this is either the irradiated fabric of the core, or the radioactive isotopes derived from the transmutation and decay of ^{239}Pu;
- Fissile material – this is the ^{239}Pu derived from the ^{238}U.

The first two categories of material clearly constitute waste, as this has no (or very little) economic or social value, and is extremely hazardous to humans and the biosphere.

The third category, the ^{239}Pu, may be regarded as waste *or* a useful resource, depending on whether or not it is considered to be socially beneficial to use it for making bombs (national defence) or as nuclear reactor fuel.

9.4 THE NATURE AND DANGERS OF NUCLEAR WASTE

The negative effects of nuclear waste, as mentioned in Section 9.3.2, are that if it is not contained, but released into the environment, the alpha, beta and gamma radiation are both carcinogenic and mutagenic. However, it must be stressed that nuclear waste is extremely heterogeneous, and the various isotopes it comprises:

- change over time, through alpha and beta decay,
- emit different mixes and energies of alpha, beta and gamma radiation, and
- have different chemical properties and affinities with various environmental media.

Clearly, the most short-lived isotopes are also exhibiting the highest rates of radiation. As such, highly radioactive and dangerous isotopes have short half-lives, and tend to disappear most rapidly. However, the isotopes resulting from the decay may also be highly radioactive (and short-lived).

9.4.1 Gamma Rays

The most penetrating and damaging of the emissions are gamma rays (i.e. very short-wave electromagnetic radiation), though not all alpha and gamma emissions are accompanied by significant gamma radiation. The shorter the wavelength of the gamma rays, the more penetrating (or 'harder') it is.

For example, cobalt is a common additive to structural steel, in the form of the stable isotope ^{59}Co. If such cobalt-rich steel is used for structural members in a nuclear reactor core, neutron irradiation produces the unstable isotope ^{60}Co, which beta decays with a half-life of 5.3 years. This decay is accompanied by the emission of very hard (i.e. penetrating) gamma rays.

9.4.2 Fission Products

The isotopes produced by ^{235}U fission range in atomic mass from about 70 to 160, with the greatest yields lying in two ranges, 80-105 and 130-150.

These isotopes almost all have too many neutrons to be stable, and exhibit successive beta decay to isotopes of the same atomic mass but higher atomic number. The half-lives of these isotopes range from a few milliseconds to millennia. As noted in Section 9.3.4, the elements deriving from ^{239}Pu exhibit both alpha and beta decay, and the daughter isotopes here also have a great variety of half-lives.

The isotopes offering the greatest long-run environmental threat are those that are long-lived and which chemically bind with elements of the food chain.

9.4.3 Examples of Dangerous Fission Products

An example of a dangerous fission product is radioactive iodine. This is particularly hazardous, as iodine is very environmentally mobile and easily taken into the food chain. It is concentrated in the thyroid gland, especially in young children, so the presence of radioactive iodine in the environment can be a cause of thyroid cancer.

Iodine is a fission product in the form of isotopes ^{127}I through to ^{136}I. Of these, only ^{127}I is stable; all of the others exhibit beta decay. The two most commonly emitted isotopes are ^{129}I and ^{131}I, with half-lives of 15.7 million years and eight days, respectively. If fresh nuclear material is released accidentally then ^{131}I is the more immediately dangerous, while ^{129}I poses the greater long-term threat to health.

Technetium is also an environmentally mobile element, and like iodine it too concentrates in the thyroid gland. With a half-life of 213 thousand years, ^{99}Te is a major fission product.

Caesium is chemically similar to potassium, and can be taken-up by organisms in place of that element. Caesium is a fission product as the isotopes ^{134}Cs, ^{135}Cs and ^{137}Cs, with half-lives of two years, 2.3 million years and 30 years, respectively. Caesium binds well with soils (especially clays), so its entry into the food chain is mainly in solution in water. However, in acid soil (e.g. granitic uplands), caesium is available for uptake by plants and thence by animals. (This was particularly important in some areas of Europe after the Chernobyl accident.) Caesium tends to be concentrated in muscle tissue; this, combined with its availability in water, means that fish can be potent modes of its entry into the human food system.

With a half-life of 29 years, ^{90}St is an important fission product. Strontium is chemically similar to calcium, and is concentrated in bones. It is also concentrated in arctic lichens, and so it can enter the human food system by lichen-grazing reindeer.

9.5 THE STORAGE AND DISPOSAL OPTIONS FOR NUCLEAR WASTE

Having outlined the origin and nature of nuclear waste, we can now begin to examine storage and disposal options. However, before we look at these in detail, it is first necessary to discuss the measurement of radioactivity. Without an understanding of how radioactivity is measured, it will not be possible to offer judgements on the various options available for nuclear waste.

9.5.1 Measuring Radioactivity

The measurement of radioactivity is a potential source of confusion, as there are four distinct approaches (Health Physics Society, 2000). There is further scope for confusion, as each approach has two distinct sets of units: the so-called 'common units' (generally used in the USA) and the SI (Système International – generally used in Europe). The four approaches, and corresponding units, are:

- *Activity* This is a purely physical measure of how many radioactive disintegrations take place in a certain amount of material per second. It does not distinguish between more energetic and less energetic decays, and takes no account of whether it is alpha or beta decay, or of the level or type of any accompanying gamma radiation (i.e. hard or soft). This is, therefore, a rather general and often not very useful measure of radioactivity. The units used are:

SI – Becquerel (Bq), defined as that quantity of material giving rise to 1 radioactive transformation per second. This is a tiny unit, and more commonly used are thousands (kBq), millions (MBq) and billions (GBq) of becquerels

Common Units – Curie (Ci), which equals 3.7×10^{10} Bq. This is a very large unit, and more commonly used are thousandths (mCi), millionths (µCi) or billionths (nCi) of a curie.

- *Exposure to Gamma Rays and X-Rays* The principal ionising agent that causes carcinogenic and mutagenic effects is gamma rays (and x-rays, which have a longer wavelength), so it is useful to measure the ionising potential of this electromagnetic radiation that results from radioactivity. The units used are:
  Common Units – Roentgen (R), which is the amount of electromagnetic radiation which deposits in dry air 2.58×10^{-4} coulombs per kilogram.

- *Dose* This reflects the amount of energy absorbed by some material, and can be used for any type of radiation and any material. This is clearly an improvement on simple measures of activity or ionising potential, as it is only absorbed radiation that is damaging. This has units:
  SI – Gray (Gy), defined as the one joule of energy deposited in one kg of material.
  Common Units – Rad (Radiation absorbed dose), defined as the absorption of 100 ergs per gramme (i.e. 1 Rad = 10^{-2}Gy).

- *Dose Equivalent* This is the final move towards a measure which represents tissue damage. As not all radiation has equal biological effects per unit of energy deposited, to measure actual damage, the absorbed dose must be multiplied by a 'quality factor' (Q) that is unique to the type of incident radiation. The units used are:
  SI – Sievert (Sv)
  Common Units – Rem (Roentgen equivalent man) 1 Rem = 10^{-2}Sv.

Building on the definition of dose equivalent, a range of related concepts has been developed, such as:

- 'dose limit' (defining what is regarded as acceptable exposure to radiation),

- 'dose per unit of intake' (relating to radioactivity from food),
- 'collective effective dose' for populations rather than individuals),
- 'organ dose' (for specific bodily organs), etc.

So we see that the measurement of radioactivity is itself a complex task. In particular, we need to distinguish between:

- the amount of radioactivity that occurs in a mass of material,
- the ionising effect this material has,
- the energy absorbed from radioactive emissions, and
- the damage done by this absorbed radiation.

As the intention of radioactive waste storage and disposal is to ensure that physical radioactivity does not translate into tissue damage, the units used for discussing quantities of radioactive material will generally be Becquerels. The intensity of this ionising radiation will be Roentgens. If the waste is not properly treated, and escapes into the environment, the potential damage it causes is measured in Sieverts.

Concerning the damage caused by adsorbed radiation, experience has suggested the following impacts upon humans.

- 40 Grays – Extensive tissue damage, including cerebral oedema. Death occurs within 48 hours.
- 10 to 40 Grays – Extensive tissue damage, including to the vascular system. Death generally occurs within 10 days.
- 1.5 to 10 Grays – Tissue damage including probable destruction of the bone marrow. This dose is often fatal.

The experience of the effects of such doses has led to the general acceptance of a dose limit from anthropogenic radioactive material of 10^{-3} Gray per year. This is approximately half of the typical background radiation dose received from natural radioactive decay of materials in the earth's crust, and from cosmic rays arriving from outer space.

9.5.1 Classifying Nuclear Waste

In the West, two quite different methods of classifying nuclear waste are in use, which can lead to confusion, and even to different regulatory regimes for similar material. In Europe, radioactive waste materials are generally classified in terms of their degree of radioactivity, while in the US they are classified in terms of sources. The UK classification system makes the following distinctions (Hutson, 1996, p.162):

- High level waste (HLW) – material which is so radioactive that it emits significant amounts of heat, entailing storage conditions which allow this heat to dissipate.
- Intermediate level waste (ILW) – more radioactive than Low level waste, but with levels of heat emission which do not require special storage conditions.
- Low level waste (LLW) – radioactive enough not be permissible for disposal with other types of waste (e.g. household refuse), but not exceeding 4 GBq/tonne alpha radiation, or 12 GBq/tonne beta/gamma radiation.
- Very low level waste (VLLW) – waste which can be safely disposed of with household refuse. Each 0.1 m^3 contains less than 400kBq/tonne alpha activity, or any single item less than 40kBq beta/gamma activity.

In the US the classification of nuclear waste is rather more complex, deriving from an accumulation of legal and administrative definitions (Lowenthal, 1997). Broadly, the definition of radioactive waste reflects both the source of the waste and its nature. For example, in the US the definition of high level waste mentions 'the highly radioactive material resulting from the reprocessing of spent nuclear fuel' (Lowenthal, 1997, Table 1).

However, the US classifications are broadly in line with those used elsewhere, which generally focus on the nature of the radioactive waste, and take little account of its source.

9.5.2 Low Level Waste Disposal

Low level waste (LLW) includes materials such as rubble from decommissioning of nuclear power plants, and protective clothing and packaging from the nuclear industry.

Disposal of LLW is by landfill, usually in specially prepared sites. However, the level of preparation of such sites differs only in degree from that for sites for the disposal of household rubbish (Richardson et al., 1996, pp. 186-190). In both cases, steps are taken to reduce the inflow of water into the waste, and the flow of contaminated water out of the site. This is through careful choice of geology; the use of lining materials; and by covering with impermeable materials. However, unlike household rubbish, LLW may also be housed in impermeable containers before burial.

Disposal of LLW waste is generally not seen as problematic, and its burial has gone on during the whole of the nuclear age, with little associated controversy.

9.5.3 Intermediate Level Waste

Intermediate level waste (ILW) involves material that definitely needs to be kept away from biological systems. It includes material from nuclear fuel reprocessing, as well as some elements from plant operation and decommissioning.

So far, relatively little of the ILW produced has been disposed of. An exception is in Sweden, where an underground repository is in operation (Uranium Information Centre, 1998). It is the deep repository approach that is generally being pursued, with the long-run aim of reducing the risk of human exposure to this potentially very damaging material.

If deep repositories are to be used, as ILW remains dangerous for many generations, the principle of risk reduction implies an 'engineering in depth' approach. In particular, as for LLW, the repository must be engineered so that water cannot enter or leave the site. If this cannot be maintained, then water will inevitably corrode the protective material and the waste itself, and some of the radio-nuclides will be transported by water out of the repository. To an extent, this transport by water can be reduced by siting the repository in geological strata which tend to bind chemically with the principal radioactive elements likely to escape.

As most countries do not yet have long-term repositories for ILW, the great bulk of that so far generated is stored on the surface, most of it at nuclear reactor or reprocessing sites.

9.5.4 High Level Waste

High level waste (HLW) has many of the same characteristics as ILW, but more so. It too is long-lived and highly damaging to organisms; however, it is even more strongly radioactive. Therefore, the principal method of disposal under consideration is, as for ILW, underground storage. However, active consideration has been given to other possibilities, such as disposal in space, or nuclear transmutation into less damaging isotopes. The former was rapidly rejected, given the cost of sending material into solar orbit, and the failure rate of space launches. The latter is still being mooted, but the necessary technology is at least several decades away from being even tested on a significant scale. Other possibilities discussed but since dismissed were deposition under the sea bed, and in Antarctica; both would have violated international treaties.

One source of HLW is the reprocessing of spent nuclear fuel, and a significant proportion of such waste arises in liquid form. Thus before indefinite underground disposal can be contemplated, this must be transformed into solid form. Even solid HLW must be further treated, to reduce the chances of its transport by any intruding water, and one method being developed is embedding the HLW in a glassy matrix. Also under discussion is the use of ceramics as the containing medium.

The actual nature and location of HLW repositories has yet to be decided upon, though the Yucca Mountain site in Nevada is that nearest to decision and implementation (Yucca Mountain Project, 2000). As intruding groundwater is potentially so undermining of the principles of isolation required for HLW, one major reason for the selection of Yucca Mountain is its aridity, with the water table being far below the proposed level for the repository. However, it has been pointed out that, on a geological time scale, this fortunate feature is relatively new in that locale, and cannot be depended on to last for the necessary several millennia (Dublyansky, 2000). Another HLW disposal site under active consideration is in northern Australia, (Uranium Information Centre, 2000)

However, as no HLW waste repositories have yet been developed, all of the several thousand tonnes of such material so far accumulated is in surface storage. Indeed, many opponents of the further development of commercial nuclear power urge that surface storage be maintained indefinitely. They argue that as nuclear power must be abandoned, the generation of HLW must cease in the foreseeable future, at a large but given quantity. Given the uncertainties associated with long-term storage repositories, they argue that a safer option is continued surface storage, under conditions of the highest security and monitoring.

9.5.5 Reprocessing as a Disposal Route

As plutonium is such a potentially dangerous material, the reprocessing of used fuel elements to allow the extraction of their ^{239}Pu, can be considered a type of waste disposal. The extracted plutonium can be combined with non-enriched uranium to form a hybrid fuel for nuclear reactors. As this material is usually in oxide form, it is known as 'mixed oxide' or MOX fuel (Pam et al., 1997).

As well as being a means of reducing the need to dispose of unwanted plutonium, this route also potentially extends the amount of available fissile fuel, by substituting for ^{235}U. Therefore reprocessing acts as both a form of waste disposal and of resource-stretching (Denniss and Jeapes, 1996).

While many European counties, and Japan, reprocess spent fuel to extract plutonium, the US has explicitly rejected this approach, on the grounds of limiting the potential for weapons proliferation. This is because pure ^{239}Pu is excellent material for bomb manufacture. As well as being suitable for the production of bombs by states, it could be diverted for use by terrorist groups. Hence the notion prevalent in the US that plutonium is best left in the highly radioactive spent fuel containers, from which it is difficult to extract in pure form. The converse argument put forward is that plutonium is most safely stored inside nuclear reactors, as recycled fuel.

9.5.5 Intermediate Storage and Transportation of HLW

While long-term repositories for HLW are being awaited, this material is currently stored in 'temporary' storage facilities. These may be at the nuclear power stations themselves, or at reprocessing sites (where these are operated), or at other nuclear facilities. This need for interim storage also raises the requirement for the transport of HLW between sites (Haslett, 1996).

Current intermediate storage technologies can be termed 'wet' and 'dry'. The wet technology stores the used fuel under water, which acts as both shielding and coolant. Usually, normal convection is sufficient to allow the decay heat to be transported out of the water. The dry technology stores the spent fuel in air, which has the benefit of reducing the scale of the construction and also removes the danger of water leaks, which may carry radioactive material with it. However, dry storage often needs forced cooling, which cannot be guaranteed as 'fail-safe'. For either type of storage, remote access to the HLW is necessary, to avoid injury to operators. Also, as these sites are on the surface, they need to be guarded and kept under continual surveillance.

Transporting HLW requires massive containment vessels, which satisfy three requirements:

- Immense strength, to prevent leakage in the case of any reasonably foreseeable accident;
- Sufficiently thick walls, to act as radiation barriers;
- Reasonably high conductivity, to allow the escape of decay heat.

So far, the current designs of these vessels seem to be satisfactory, as there have been no recorded incidents of significant leaks of radiation during the transport of HLW.

9.6 HISTORICAL AND SOCIAL REFLECTIONS ON NUCLEAR WASTE

When nuclear waste is compared with other sources of waste, certain similarities and differences emerge. In some ways, nuclear waste is similar to toxic waste. Both need careful segregation from society, both are produced in relatively small quantities, and both need expensive capital facilities to deal with them. However, while toxic waste is amenable to treatment to reduce its danger to humans, nuclear waste is not. Instead, the only way that nuclear waste can be treated is either by reprocessing the plutonium, and/or simply by storage and waiting.

It is this temporal aspect of nuclear waste that is so distinctive from other forms of waste. While much domestic waste is put into indefinite storage in landfill sites, this is not because it is the only option, simply the cheapest (often). Nuclear waste, however, is being put into indefinite storage because it is the *only* option. Indeed, one can imagine circumstances where in future, societies may see present domestic landfill sites as suitable for mining, to obtain recyclable material. (This would be similar to the UK experience, where some nineteenth century coal slag heaps are being reworked to win more coal with modern sorting technologies). This recycling possibility is hard to imagine for nuclear waste, and the proposed technology of its long-term containment is precisely aimed to make it inaccessible to future generations.

Another intriguing aspect of nuclear waste is the way its problems were given so little attention for so long. The very earliest theory and experiments on nuclear fission showed that relatively large quantities of highly dangerous material would, necessarily and unavoidably be produced. Each nuclear reactor over its life time would generate many tonnes of radioactive spent fuel, and at the end of its life would constitute several thousand tonnes of more or less radioactive material. This was known from 1942. However, serious study of the way this waste could be disposed of was initially dilatory to the extent of wilful negligence. What was seen as 'sexy' engineering was building bigger and better power stations, using newer, more advanced and safer methods of control. It seems that the implicit assumption was that 'we' would eventually find a means of dealing with this waste. In the meantime, we could put the waste into interim storage, perhaps reprocessing the plutonium, and wait for a solution to 'emerge'.

This negligent approach to nuclear waste also has a temporal aspect. It seems that what economic capital theorists call the 'time horizon' of the relevant decision makers was just too short to look to the end of the nuclear fuel cycle; i.e. to nuclear waste disposal. I have argued elsewhere (Proops, 2001) that this rather surprising myopia of decision-making can be understood with reference to discourse analysis. The problem with nuclear electricity generation is that it is:

• dangerous (cf. Chernobyl);
• expensive (it has never been economically competitive with fossil fuel plants, if subsidies are excluded); and
• produces hazardous, long-lived and untreatable waste.

So why was there a commercial nuclear power programme? I argue that it is because the 'discourse' of nuclear power was similar to that of the modernising, centralising state of the post-World War II era. Both stressed control, modernity and technological solutions to social problems. As such, the nuclear power industry was a good 'fit' for political decision makers eager to forge societies in the 'white heat of technology' (to use the term of UK Prime Minister Harold Wilson's).

Finally, we should recall that the roots of nuclear science were strictly military. The initial research was funded from military budgets, with the aim of producing bombs. Indeed, one might posit that if ^{235}U and ^{239}Pu did not exhibit the 'fast criticality' which make them suitable as bomb-making material, there may have been *no* commercial nuclear industry, and no nuclear waste. To that extent, unlike other forms of waste, nuclear waste may be an unnecessary social product. Societies could generate electricity by other much less hazardous means, and probably at a lower economic cost.

9.7 CONCLUSIONS

Nuclear waste is a strictly modern phenomenon, and all that we know of its causes, avoidance and disposal has come about through study over just the past 60 years. Now that the mid-to-late twentieth century phase of building civil nuclear reactors is probably almost complete, the human race has to attempt to deal with the legacy of this period of construction. The process of dismantling the old nuclear power plants will take decades, while the disposal of the high level waste in secure repositories is still far from even begun, and will continue for centuries.

A further feature distinguishing nuclear waste from other forms of waste is the fact that it was almost certainly avoidable, at least in large part. The nuclear weapons programmes in various countries almost all involve the generation of plutonium in breeder reactors, with their corresponding generation of waste. However, much more nuclear waste has been generated by the civil nuclear programmes, and this certainly was not necessary. There has never been a very strong case for civil nuclear reactors, and once the costs of accident insurance, nuclear decommissioning and waste disposal are included, then nuclear power is not competitive with fossil fuels. It seems that a modicum of economic rationality could have avoided the largest part of nuclear waste production, by not investing in civil nuclear power systems.

Finally, the nature of some nuclear waste is itself a debatable topic; here this issue is the social attitude towards plutonium. Is this a valuable by-product of nuclear power generation, or is it a highly toxic and potentially destabilising bomb-making material? Clearly, the way we view plutonium is intimately connected to our attitudes towards the nuclear power debate more broadly, and to the way society views its own future. After the events of 11 September 2001, the technologically optimistic view from the mid-twentieth century may have been destroyed, and with it the hope that the plutonium economy can be mastered. Conversely, though, fears of fuel security could lead to a (perhaps reluctant) return to the nuclear fuel cycle to provide reliable power for the twenty-first century, and with it the generation of yet larger quantities of this most problematic form of waste.

REFERENCES

Bertell, R. (2000), 'The problem', http://www.ratical.org/radiation/NRBE/NradBio EffectsP.html.

Dublyansky, Y.V. (2000), 'Yucca Mountain, Nevada: geologically young hydrothermal activity and its implication to the problem of high-level nuclear waste repository', http://geology.uiggm.nsc.ru/uiggm/mineralogy/lab436/dubl/yucca/yuccad.htm

Denniss, I.S. and A.P. Jeapes (1996) 'Reprocessing irradiated fuel', in Wilson (1996a), pp. 116-37.

Goldschmidt, B. (1989), 'Uranium's scientific history 1789-1939', Paper presented to the Fourteenth International Symposium of the Uranium Institute: London, http://www.uilondon.org/ushist.html.

Haslett, D.E. (1996), 'Transport and storage of irradiated fuel', in Wilson (1996a), pp. 102-15.

Health Physics Society (2000), 'Radiation fact sheets', http://www.hps.org/publicinformation/radfactsheets.

Hesketh, K.W. (1996), 'Power reactors', in Wilson (1996a), pp. 78-101.

Hutson, G.V. (1996), 'Waste treatment', in Wilson (1996a), pp. 161-83.

IEER (2000), 'Basics of nuclear physics and fission', http://www.ieer.org/ieer/reports/m-basics.html.

Lenssen, N. (1991), *Nuclear Waste: The Problem That Won't Go Away*, Worldwatch Paper 106, Washington, DC: Worldwatch Institute.

Lowenthal, M.D. (1997) 'Radioactive-waste classification in the United States: history and current predicament', Lawrence Livermore National Laboratory Report URCL-CR-128127, Berkeley, CA: University of California, http://cnwm.berkeley.edu/cnwm/reports/RE97-0001/.

Lutins, A.H. (1999), *U.S. Nuclear Accidents*, http://www.nitehawk.com/alleycat/nukes.html.

Pam, L., J. Boer and D. Bannink (1997), 'The MOX myth: the dangers and risks of the use of mixed oxide fuel', http://www.antenna.nl/~wise/mox0.html.

Proops, J. (2001), 'The (non-)economics of the nuclear fuel cycle: an historical and discourse analysis', *Ecological Economics*, **39** (1), 13-19.

Rhodes, R. (1986), *The Making of the Atomic Bomb*, New York: Simon and Schuster.

Richardson, S., P. Curd and E.J. Kelly (1996), 'Disposal of fuel or solid wastes', in Wilson (1996a), pp. 184-206.

Uranium Information Centre (1998), 'Nuclear energy in Sweden', http://www.uic.com.au/nip39/htm.

Uranium Information Centre (2000), 'International nuclear waste disposal concept', http://www.uic.com.au/nip49/htm.
Wilson, P.D. (ed.) (1996a), *The Nuclear Fuel Cycle*, Oxford: Oxford University Press.
Wilson, P.D. (1996b) 'Basic principles', in Wilson (1996a), pp. 1-17.
Yucca Mountain Project (2000) 'The Yucca Mountain Project', http://ymp.gov/.

Index

Abrams, R.H., 175
Acury, T.A., 153, 173
Addams, H., 68, 70
Adeola, F.O., 146, 150-53, 157, 161,
 169, 172
Agency for Toxic Substances and
 Disease Registry (ATSDR), 150,
 157, 159, 160-62, 173
Agenda 21, 120
Agriculture Street, New Orleans, 148,
 166, 168, 169
Albrecht, S.L., 151, 172
Allchin, D., 162-63, 172
Allen, G., 143
alpha decay, 181
Amey, R.G., 151, 172
anaerobic digestion, 126
Arbuthnot, J., 64, 70
Arco, case, 106
Arcury, T.A., 173
Armour, A., 61, 71
Arora, S., 77, 98
arsenic, 158, 159
 toxicity, 158
 uses, 158
Asante-Duah, K.D., 149, 153, 155,
 173
asbestos, 159, 160
 forms, 159
 toxicity, 159
 uses, 159
atom bomb, 182
attitudes to waste, 8, 57-70
 investigating, 66-69
 negative, 58-60
 positive, 62-65
available energy, 20
available work, 20
Ayres, L.W., 32, 33, 35
Ayres, R.U., 16, 20-22, 30, 32-35

Bacot, H., 61, 70
bacteriological paradigm, 48
Badr, O., 143
Bailey, C., 174
Balbach, H.E., 174
Balian, R., 29, 33, 36
Bannink, D., 194
Basel Convention, 103, 104
Bateman, I.J., 75, 98, 99
Bateman, S.D., 98
Bates, M.P., 99
Baum, A., 150, 171, 173
Baumgärtner, S., 10, 20, 22-24,
 32-34, 36, 37
Baumol, W.J., 98
Bayerl, G., 54
Beard, T.R., 33, 36
Beck, U., 147, 173
Becquerel, 186
Beder, S., 59, 60, 70
behavioural change, 66
Bejan, A., 25, 28, 33
Berenyi, E., 130, 131, 135, 142
Berliner Geschichtswerkstatt, 54
Berman, E., 158-60, 173
Bernhardt, C., 54
Berry, R.S., 33, 37
Bertell, R., 181, 194
Best Environmental Option, 88
Best Practicable Environmental
 Option, 92, 101, 109
 definition, 109, 110
 superiority to the waste
  management hierarchy, 110
beta decay, 181
Bhopal, India, 152
biogasification, 88, 91
Blackman, W.C. Jr., 146, 173
Blumenthal, D.S., 173
Boer, J., 194

Boltzmann, L., 18, 19, 33
Boulding, K.E., 21, 33
Bowen, T., 70
Brisson, I., 94, 95, 98
Brodyansky, V.M, 25, 33
Bromley, D., 76, 77, 100
Brown, L., 146-48, 173
Brown, L.O., 174
Brown, L.R., 175
Brown, P., 147, 149, 152, 168, 173
Brown, S.R., 70, 72
Bruggink, J.J.C., 34
Buckingham, P.L., 174
Burn, E.H., 101, 112
Burness, H.S., 21, 33

Callen, H.B., 33, 36
Calließ, J., 53
carbon dioxide from waste
  incineration, 135
Carson, R., 146, 147, 169, 172, 173
Cason, T.N., 77, 98
Cavaliere, A., 77, 98
Center for Disease Control (CDC),
  173
Centre for the Exploitation of Science
  and Technology (CEST), 83, 98
Chadwick, E., 48, 53
Chang, L.W., 174, 175, 176
Chapman, S.R., 159, 161, 170, 173
Charnock, H., 143
Chelyabinsk, USSR,
  nuclear accident, 179
Chernobyl, Ukraine, 152
  nuclear accident, 179, 185
chlorine products, 147
cholera, 50
Christensen, T., 143
Chung, S.S., 64, 70
citizen, Sagoff's, 4
Clark, G.L., 99
Clarke, M., 118-20, 137, 142
Clausius, R., 18, 19, 33
Clayton, B., 143
clean, meanings, 43
clinker, 51
closed thermodynamic system, 16
Coase theorem, 8, 82
Coasean school, 76
Coggins, P.C., 83, 98
Cohen, G., 147, 173, 175

combined heat and power, 132
command and control, 80
  instruments, 81
Commission of the European
  Communities (CEC), 108, 112, 145
compliance plus, 77
compostable organic material, 49
composting, 88, 126
concept of waste,
  non-substantive, 105
  value, 107
concerned egalitarian, 52
conflict,
  displaced, 62
  false, 62
Conservation of Mass Law, 17
consumer, Sagoff's, 4
consumption, and economic systems,
  14
Cossu, R., 143
cost-benefit analysis, 75
  social, 75
Council of the European
  Communities, 110, 112
Craighill, A., 99, 129, 143, 144
Crawford, M., 159, 173
Creyts, J.C., 25, 33
CSERGE, 94, 98
cultural anthropology, 38
cultural theory, 38, 46
culture, and waste, 5
Cumbler, J.T., 48, 52
Cummings, R.G., 33
Cunningham, W.P., 149, 173
Curd, P., 194
Curie, 186

d'Arge, R.C., 34
Daly, H.E., 21, 33
Dasgupta, P.S., 34, 37
Daskalapoulos, E., 125, 129,
  131-36, 141, 143-45
Davis, G.A., 175
DDT, 164
de Swaan Arons, J., 31, 34
De Young, R., 64, 65, 70
definitions of waste, 2, 39
  legal, 102-7
Denniss, I.S., 190, 194
Department of Environment Food and
  Rural Affairs (USA), 113

Department of the Environment, UK
  (DoE), 138, 140, 141, 143
Department of the Environment,
  Transport and the Regions UK
  (DETR), 57, 70, 96, 98
Department of Trade and Industry,
  UK (DTI), 83, 84, 98
desired goods,
  joint production with waste, 22-30
Dewulf, J., 25, 34
Diamadopoulos, E., 129, 143
Diaz, L., 143, 144
Dickens, Charles, 6
Dietz, T., 71
dioxin, 51, 130, 136, 166
Dirlmeier, U., 47, 53
dirt, 43
  definitions, 43
discard into nature,
  principle, 4
discard,
  meaning, 105
discourses on waste, 67
displaced conflict, 62
disposal awareness, 58
disposal of hazardous waste, 104
district heating systems, 93
Dittman, R.H., 35, 36
doctrine of waste, 101
domestic heating and waste, 49
dose equivalent, 186
dose measures, 186, 187
Douglas, M., 43, 44, 53
Drotman, P.D., 160, 161, 173
Dryzek, J., 67, 70
Dublyansky, Y.V., 190, 194
dung in European agriculture, 42
dung-heap valuation, 41
Dunlap, R.E., 63, 72
Dupuy, G., 40, 53, 54
Dyckhoff, H., 33
dynamics of waste, 38

Earle, T.C., 60, 71
early mover advantage, 80
Earth Summit, 120
Ebreo, A., 63, 64, 72
ecoefficiency, 80
eco-labeling, 46
economic damage approach, 75
economic history and waste, 40, 41

economic incentive instruments, 81
economic metabolism,
  and thermodynamics, 14
economic systems,
  consumption 14, 15
  production, 14, 15
  reduction, 14, 15
economic valuation, 91
economics and waste, 3
economics of,
  landfilling, 141
  nuclear power, 191
  recycling, 128, 129
  source reduction, 123
  waste, 8, 73-98
economising individualist, 52
economy-environment interactions,
  15-16
Edelstein, M.R., 146, 148-50, 152,
  171, 173, 174
Edley, M., 84, 98
Edwards, T.C., 71
EEA (European Environment
  Agency), 143
EFTEC, 98
egalitarians, 46
  concerned, 52
Ehrig, H., 143
El-Fadel, M., 137, 140, 143
Elias, N., 43, 53
end of pipe,
  control, 79
  disposal, 120
energy from waste, 67, 93
engineering thermodynamics, 28
entropy, 2, 18, 19
  law, 18, 21
environmental
  attitudes survey, 85
  benefits, 74
  costs, 74
  externalities, 76
  history, 40
  justice, 152
  racism, 169
Environmental Protection Act (UK),
  93
Environmental Protection Agency,
  USA, (EPA), 123, 124, 144, 148,
  149, 155, 157, 159, 160, 170, 176,
  177

Environmental Resources
  Management (ERM), 174
Environmental Services Association
  Research Trust (ESART), 59, 70
environmentalism,
  private sphere, 62
environmentally significant
  behaviour, 62, 63
Epstein, S.S., 147-49, 153, 155, 159,
  161, 164, 165, 174
equilibrium, thermodynamic, 16
Erikson, K., 146, 147, 150, 171, 174
Erkman, S., 34, 35
estovers, 102
European Court of Justice, 105
European Environment Agency
  (EEA), 118
European Waste Catalogue, 104
Eurostat, 137, 143
Evans, J.C., 174
exergy, 25, 27, 29, 31
  entropy, 20
  definition, 20
  values, 26
expert monopolies of information, 59
extensive,
  quantities, 22
  variables, 16
externality,
  dealing with, 80, 81
  definition, 76
  environmental, 76
extrinsic motivations, 64, 65
Exxon Valdez, 152

Faber, M., 2, 10, 22, 30, 32, 33, 34
faeces, as waste, 3
fairness, perceptions of, 61
Falk, G., 20, 34
false conflict, 62
fast criticality, 193
fatalist, 46, 52
Faucheux, S., 10, 34
Faupel, C.E., 151, 152, 174
Federal Disaster Area, 167
Feldman, M.P., 99
Fell, H., 143
Field, B., 81, 98
Field, B.C., 147, 149, 174
Field, M.K. 147, 149, 174
Findikakis, A., 143

Finnveden, G., 143
first best tax, 94
First Law of Thermodynamics, 21, 24
first mover advantage, 77
Fischer-Kowalski, M., 40, 53, 54
Fishbein, B., 122, 123, 125, 143, 144
fissile material, 183
fission products, 184
  dangerous, 184, 185
fission waste, 183
Fitzgerald, M.R., 70
flammable waste, 154
Fleming, R., 150, 173
Flinn, M.W., 48, 53
flue gas cleaning, 133
fly ash, 130, 134, 135
Focht, W., 62, 69, 70
Folke, C., 14, 34
Folmer, H., 32, 100
Fourth Law of Thermodynamics, 22
Franke, M., 99
free trade rules, 111
free-riding, 4
Freudenberg, N., 146, 168, 174
furans, 136, 166

gamma rays, 184
Gandy, M., 119, 129, 143
garbage,
  archaeology, 51
  cans, 119
  grinders, 119
Garkovich, L., 151, 174
gasification, 132
GATT, 111
Geiser, K., 143
Gelb, C., 143
Georgescu-Roegen, N., 20-22, 34, 36
Gerking, S., 32
Gerlagh, R., 144
Germany and waste, 50, 51
Gertles, M.S., 99
Gill, D.A., 152, 174, 175
Glasbergen, P., 82, 98
Goddard, H., 120, 123, 143
Goklany, I.M., 172, 174
Goldfarb, W., 175
Goldschmidt, B., 180, 194
Golueke, C., 143
Gould, K.A., 147, 148, 175
Gowdy, J., 10, 34-36

Grace, R., 78, 98
Graedel, T., 34, 35
Granzin, K.L., 64, 70
Gray, 186
Green, A.E., 99
Green, D., 60, 71
greenhouse impact,
  and municipal waste treatment, 136
Greenpeace, 157, 174
Greider, T., 151, 174
Griffin, G., 174
Groundwater Directive, 111
Grünbühel, C., 54
Guagnano, G.A., 66, 71
guano, 49

Haberl, H., 40, 53, 54
half-life of radioactive material, 181
Hall, A.R., 53
Hallman, W.K., 150, 174
Hamada, R., 162, 163, 174
Hamlin, C., 48, 49, 53
Hanley, S.B., 42, 53
Hannigan, J.A., 151, 174
Harre, R., 71
Harrington, M.J., 71
Hartenstein, H.-U., 130, 132, 133,
  143
Harveson, P.M., 175
Haslett, D.E., 191, 194
Haukohl, J., 144
hay-bote, 102
hazardous material,
  classification system, 154
hazardous substance,
  psychological responses, 150
hazardous waste, 51, 146
  concept, 148
  definition, 149
  landfills, 138
  properties, 147
  sites, 166
Heal, G.M., 33, 34, 37
Health Physics Society, 185, 194
heat recovery, 119
heavy metals, 156-58
Herrmann, B., 53
Hesketh, K.W., 182, 194
hierarchist, 46
  regulating, 52
high risk wastes, 153

Hindle, P., 99
history of waste, 7, 38-52
Hjelmar, O., 143
HM Customs and Excise, 94, 99
HM Government, 93, 99
Hopper, J.R., 64, 65, 71
Horrigan, A., 125, 143
Horvay, M., 130, 132, 133, 143
Hösel, G., 47, 53
Houghton, J. 133, 134, 143
House of Commons Environment
  Committee (HCEC), 108, 113
house-bote, 102
household waste,
  charges, 95
  difficulty of management, 118
  recycling centres, 88
Howell, D.A., 175
Huang, K., 34, 36
Huchting, F., 51, 53
human excrement,
  as fertiliser, 49
  in Asian agriculture, 42
hunter-gatherer societies,
  and waste, 39
Hutson, G.V., 187, 194

IEER, 180, 194
ignitable waste, 154
incineration, 88, 130-37
  carbon dioxide, 135
  combined heat and power, 132
  economics, 132-34
  environmental impacts, 134-36
  euphoria, 50
  examples, 136, 137
  fluidised bed technology, 131, 132
  gasification and pyrolysis, 132
  history, 130
  moving grate technology, 131
  technological lock-in, 97
incinerators,
  environmentally friendly, 119
  first, 119
  heat recovery, 119
  inflexibility, 92
individualist, 46
  economising, 52
industrial,
  ecology, 35
  metabolism, 16

production,
  joint production, 13
  thermodynamic structure, 25
information,
  deficit model, 59
  expert monopolies, 59
  failure, 73
Ingram, V., 82, 99
Inhaber, H., 61, 71
instruments,
  command and control, 81
  economic incentive, 81
  market based, 81
  other, 81, 82
integrated solid waste management,
  121
  strategy, 96
intensive
  quantities, 22
  variables, 16
intergenerational equity, 101
intermediate risk wastes, 153
International Energy Agency (IEA),
  132, 143
intrinsic motivations, 63, 64
iron making,
  chemistry, 26, 27
irradiation waste, 183
irreversible processes, 16, 17
isolated thermodynamic system, 16
isotope, 180
  definition, 181

Jacques, P., 143
Jaffe, A.B., 80, 99
Jain, R.K., 170, 174
Jaritz, G., 41, 53
Jarrett, H., 33
Jeapes, A.P., 190, 194
Johannessen, L., 143
Johnson, B.L., 146, 174
joint production, 24
  industrial production, 13
  desired goods and waste, 22-30
joint products,
  undesired, 3
Jöst, F., 34

Kåberger, T., 21, 34
Kalof, L., 68, 71
Keeler, A., 141, 144

Keene, D., 47, 53
Keller, R., 48, 49, 53
Kelly, E.J., 194
Kennedy, D.D., 168, 174
Kenward, H.K., 53
kerbside recycling, 65
Khalil, E.L., 21, 34
Kido, T., 175
King, W., 41, 53
Kneese, A.V., 21, 33, 34
Knox, K., 143
Kodamanchaly, J.S., 175
Koko, Nigeria, 152
Koutsantonakis, Y., 143
Krausmann, F., 54
Kreith, F., 143, 144
Kressel, S., 70
Kubasek, N.K., 170, 174
Kuchenbuch, L., 40, 53
Kumar, V., 144
Kümmel, R., 30, 34, 36

labelling schemes, 125
LaGrega, M.D., 147, 149, 153, 155,
  174
Landau, L.D., 34, 36
Landfill Directive, 109, 111
Landfill Tax Credit Scheme, 84, 87,
  94
landfilling, 137-39
  capacity crisis, 120
  creation of order, 44
  economics, 141
  environmental impact, 139-41
  gas, 139, 140
  hazardous waste, 138
  illegal, 137
  leachate, 139
  municipal waste, 138
  sanitary, 138
  tax, 80
Landis Gabel, H., 32, 100
language and waste, 66, 67
Lave, L.B., 146, 174
Law of Conservation of Mass, 17, 21
Law of Guoy and Stodola, 20
Lawler, J.J., 62, 69, 70
Laws of Thermodynamics, 13, 17-20
Lawton, J., 143
Le Goff, P., 33
leachate, 139

lead, 160, 161
  occupational exposure, 161
  toxicity, 161
  uses, 161
Leckie, J., 143
legislative compliance, 86
Leibenstein, H., 80, 99
Lenssen, N., 194
Levine, A.G., 149, 150, 152, 166,
  167, 174
Lichtveld, M.Y., 146, 174
Liernur system,
  waste collection, 49
life cycle assessment, 74, 88
  impact assessment, 74
  inventory analysis, 74
lifestyle and waste, 51
Lifshitz, E.E., 34, 36
Lindell, M., 60, 71
Lindemann, C., 50, 53
Litmanan, T., 174
Llabrés, P., 143
Lober, D., 60, 61, 71, 122, 123, 143
local waste management, 87
Love Canal, New York, 148, 149,
  152, 164, 166, 167, 172
  cleanup, 167
Lovins, A.B.,100
Lovins, L.H., 100
low risk wastes, 153
Lowenthal, M.D., 188, 194
Lozada, G.A., 21, 33, 34, 36
LULU (Locally Undesirable Land
  Use), 60
Lutins, A.H., 179, 194
LUWA-bottoms, 106

Macé, S., 143
Macrory, R., 143
macrostates, 18, 19
Mainieri, T., 71
Makofske, W.J., 148, 174
Malone, E., 72
Månsson, B., 21, 34
Manstetten, R., 34
Margai, F.L., 64, 65, 71
market based instruments, 81
market failure, 73
  waste, 13
Martinás, K., 30, 33
Marxen, U., 144

mass balance, 26
mass incineration, 91, 92
Mata-Alvarez, J., 143, 144
materials balance principle, 17, 21
Materials Recovery Facility, 127
Mauskopf, S.H., 53
Mayer Parry Recycling Limited, case,
  105
Mayumi, K., 35, 36
McDougall, F., 88, 99
McGinn, A.P., 155, 164, 175
McKeown, B., 71, 72
Melosi, M.V., 40, 50, 53, 54
mercury, 162, 163
  bioaccumulation, 162
  uses, 162
metal waste production, 156
methylmecury poisoning, 163
miasmatic theory of pollution, 47
microstates, 18, 19
midnight dumping, 150, 168
Mikkelsen, E.K., 147, 149, 152, 168,
  173
Miller, E.W, 167, 175
Miller, G.L., 14, 35
Miller, G.T. Jr., 149, 175
Miller, R.M., 167, 175
Minamata Bay, Japan, 152, 162, 163
Misra, R.R., 176
modernity, 147
Moran, M., 33
Morris, D.R., 35
Morris, G., 33
Morris, J., 143
Motavali, J., 125, 143
motivations,
  extrinsic, 64, 65
  intrinsic, 63, 64
motives in recycling, 63
MOX, 190
Moyers, B., 157, 175
Mulder, J.M., 34
Muller, P., 164
multicriteria evaluation, 75
municipal solid waste, 78
  concept, 117, 118
municipal waste, 9, 117-42
  economics of incineration, 132-34
  historical background, 119-21
  landfills, 138
  nature, 118-22

municipal waste management,
  integrated approach, 120
  options, 122-41
municipal waste treatment,
  greenhouse impact, 136
Murphy, C., 51, 54

NAFTA, 111
Nebel, B.J., 149, 156, 164, 175
Netting, R.M., 42, 54
NIABY (Not In Anyone's Back
  Yard), 60
Nicolaï, I., 10, 34
Nielsen, J.M., 64, 65, 71
Niemes, H., 34
NIMBY (Not In My Back Yard), 51,
  58-60, 120, 152, 157,
Nogawa, K., 175
non-Persistent Organic Pollutants,
  163
Norgaard, R.B., 21, 35
North Norfolk District Council
  (NNDC), 99
Nriagu, J.O., 156, 175
nuclear decay, 181
  health risk, 181
nuclear fission, 182
nuclear fuel cycle, 178-80
nuclear power,
  discourses, 193
  economics, 191
nuclear power plants, 182, 183
nuclear reactors,
  physics, 180-83
  waste from, 183
nuclear transmutation, 189
nuclear waste, 9, 178-95
  classification, 187, 188
  dangers, 183-85
  definition, 178
  depositories, 189
  disposal in space, 189
  disposal options, 185-91
  high level, 188-90
  intermediate level, 188, 189
  intermediate storage, 191
  low level, 188
  similarity to toxic waste, 191
  storage options, 185-91
  transportation, 191
  very low level, 188

O'Connor, J., 147, 148, 173, 175
O'Hare, M., 71
O'Leary, P., 137, 138, 144, 145
Oates, W.E., 80, 98, 99
oil spills, 5
Okeke, C.U., 61, 71
Okuda, S.M., 71
Olsen, J.E., 64, 70
OPEC oil embargo, 102
open thermodynamic system, 16
order, 43
organic compounds, 163-66
  toxic synthetic, 165
  toxicity, 164
  types, 163
Organisation of Economic
  Co-operation and Development
  (OECD), 80, 81, 99, 103, 104, 110,
  111, 113
organochlorines, 164
organohalogens, 164
Ormond, Th., 52, 54
Osame, M., 162, 163, 174
Oskamp, S., 64, 65, 71
Owens, S., 59, 60, 71

Packaging Waste Directive, 111, 112
Paik, I,, 33
Palmer, K., 99
Pam, L., 190, 194
Parfitt, J., 144
Payer, P., 43, 54
PCB, 153
Pearce. D.W., 76, 99
perceptions of fairness, 61
Perrings, C., 22, 30, 35
Persistent Organic Pollutants, 163
pesticides, 147
Peters, M.D., 83, 99
Peterson, S.R., 99
Pfister, Ch., 51, 54
Phillips, P., 142, 144
Phillips, P.S., 83, 84, 99
Piasecki, B.W., 175
Picou, J.S., 150, 152, 174, 175
Pigovian taxes, 8, 13
Pigovian school, 76
Pipatti, R., 136, 144, 145
Plater, Z.J.B., 170, 175
plough-bote, 102
plutonium, 17, 182

social attitudes towards, 193
plutonium economy, 194
political economy, 76
pollution abatement systems, 133
pollution control tecnology,
  industry, 80
polution, and waste, 5
polychlorinated biphenyls, 166
Poon, C.S., 64, 70
Pope, C., 174
Porter, M.E., 77, 80, 87, 99
Portney, K.E., 61, 71
Portney, P.R., 99
Powell, J.C., 74, 75, 81, 94, 95, 98,
  99, 127, 129, 143-45
Powell, P.T., 77, 99
precautionary principle, 172
Prigogine, I., 19, 35
private sphere environmentalism, 62
Probert, S., 143
process design change, 86
process modification, 79, 80
processes,
  irreversible, 16
  reversible, 16
product redesign, 79, 80
production,
  and economic systems, 14, 15
  thermodynamic view, 22
Proops, J., 10, 33, 34, 68, 70, 191,
  194
public bad, 4
public health crisis, 153
public participation,
  in recycling schemes, 93
PVC, 51, 166
pyrolysis, 132

Q methodology, 68, 69
Qin, B., 175
Quandt, S.A., 153, 173
Queensborough Rolling Mill, case,
  107

radioactive waste,
  joint product, 179
radioactivity,
  measurement, 185-87
  natural decay, 178
Raines, B., 175
Rand, T., 132-34, 144

Rathje, W., 51, 54
Rayner, S., 60, 72
reactive waste, 154
Read, A., 120, 121, 144
Read, A.D., 99
reckless activities, 152
reclamation industry, 78
recycled material,
  versus primary material inputs, 79
recycling, 125-30
  barriers, 65
  bring systems, 127
  centres, 74
  economics, 128, 129
  environmental impacts, 129, 130
  facilitators, 65
  flows, 78
  kerbside systems, 65, 127
  mechanics, 126
  motives, 63, 64
  organic waste, 126
  primary, 125
  public participation, 93
  secondary, 125
  terminology, 125
Redclift, M., 66, 67, 71
reduction,
  economic systems, 14, 15
Reeve, D., 143
refuse derived fuel (RDF), 88, 91, 92
regulating hierarchist, 52
Reid, D., 48, 54
Reif, F., 35
Reith, R., 41, 54
Renkow, M., 141, 144
reversible processes, 16, 17
Rhodes, R., 182, 194
Rice, D., 161, 175
Richardson, B.E., 175
Richardson, S., 188, 194
Ricklefs, R.E., 14, 35
risk,
  communication, 59
  perception, 59
  society, 147
Robinson, G., 144
Roentgen, 186
Rome, waste management, 40
Rose, A., 32
Rossman, T.G., 158, 159, 176
Rothschild, E., 143

Royal Commission on Environmental
   Pollution, 113
rubbish,
   pits, 47
   theory, 44
Rubin, A., 144
Ruppel, W., 20, 34
rural waste problem, 41
Rüsen, J., 53
Rush, R., 70
Russell, C.S., 77, 81, 99
Ruth, M., 22, 23, 35

Sagoff, M., 4
   citizen, 4
   consumer, 4
Saigo, B.W., 149, 173
Salamon, P., 33
sanitary landfills, 138
Savage, G., 143
Savoilainen, I., 136, 144, 145
Schiller, J., 33
Schmalensee, R., 80, 99
Schnaiberg, A., 147, 148, 175
Schultz, P.W., 64, 71
Schüssler, U., 34, 36
Schwartz, S.H., 71, 72
Second Law of Thermodynamics, 2,
   18, 25
Sehker, M., 144
Select Committee on the
   Environment, Transport and
   Regional Affairs (SCETRA), 95, 99
Sellafield, UK, 179
Setterberg, F., 146, 175
Seveso, Italy, 152
Shavelson, L., 146, 175
Sherwood, D.L., 71
Shortland, M., 59, 60, 70
Sieglerschmidt, J., 54
Sievert, 186
Silbergeld, E., 161, 175
Silberston, A., 143
Silverman, G.S., 170, 174
Simonis, U., 16, 33
Singer, J.E., 173
Slovic, P., 60, 71
small and medium industries (SMEs),
   83-87
Smith, A.M., 162, 163, 175
Smith, E.W., 162, 163, 175

Smith, J., 71
social construction, 151
   factors for, 151
social cost, 73
social cost-benefit analysis, 75
social metabolism, 40, 52
Sorin, M.V., 33
source reduction, 122-25
   economics, 123
   environmental impact, 124
   examples, 124, 125
Spash, C., 21, 35
Stainton Rogers, R., 68, 69, 71, 72
stakeholders involvement, 121
statistical mechanics, 18
Stavins, R.N., 99
Stegmann, R., 143
Stephan, G., 34
Stephenson, W., 71, 72
Stern, P.C., 62, 66, 71, 72
Steward, F.R., 35
Strignitz, M., 53
subjectivity, 68
Superfund, 172
sustainability,
   normative issue, 32
   thermodynamics, 13
   waste, 39
sustainable development, 101, 102
Swan, O., 84, 98
Swanson, D.C., 71
synthetic fibres, 147
synthetic material waste, 51
system,
   mixed-up, 19
   orderly, 19
Szargut, J., 20, 26, 27, 35, 36

Tammemagi, H., 149, 154, 155, 166,
   175
Tarr, J.A., 40, 53, 54
Tchobanoglous, G., 137, 138, 144,
   145
technological lock-in,
   of incineration, 97
Tedeschi, R., 70
tertiarisation of the economy, 41
theory of pollution, miasmatic, 47
thermodynamic efficiency, 26, 27
   of production, 25
thermodynamic equilibrium, 16

thermodynamic properties of waste, 30
thermodynamic system,
  closed, 16
  isolated, 16
  open, 16
thermodynamic theory of waste, 2, 3, 7
thermodynamically inefficient production, 27
thermodynamics, 16-22
  ecological economics, 21, 22
  economic metabolism, 14
  engineering, 28
  environmental economics, 21, 22
  finite time/finite size, 28-30
  First Law, 17, 21, 24
  Fourth Law, 22
  industrial production, 25
  laws of, 13, 17-20
  Second Law, 2, 18, 25
    economic relevance, 18
    generalisation, 19, 20
  sustainability, 13
  sustainable economic metabolism, 30-32
  uranium enrichment, 29-30
  waste, 13-37
Thogersen, J., 63, 65, 72
Thomas, D., 71, 72
Thomas, J.K., 153, 164, 175
Thompson, M., 44-46, 51, 54, 60, 72
Thornton, J., 146-48, 164, 175
Tombesi, case, 105
Townsend, K.N., 21, 35
toxic chemicals monitoring, 150
toxic cycles, 147
toxic emissions, 93
toxic substances,
  Federal statutes, 170
toxic waste, 9, 146-77
  by industry, 155
  classification, 153-66
  control, 146
  curbing, 146
  definition, 149
  legal framework, 169-71
  social conflict, 151
  social problem, 151-53
toxicity,
  equivalents, 145
  of chemicals, 149
tradable permits, 13
treadmill
  of production, 148
  of toxics, 147, 148
Tsatsaronis, G., 33
Tsoukala, T.H., 153, 176
Tucker, P., 65, 72, 150, 176
Turner, J., 70
Turner, R.K., 75, 76-78, 98-100, 144

U.S. Office of Technology Assessment, 176
Union Carbide, 152
United Nations Environmental Programme (UNEP), 137, 138, 140, 141, 144, 145, 165, 176
Upton, A.C., 146, 174
uranium,
  enrichment, 179
    thermodynamics, 29, 30
  fertile, 183
  fissile, 183
  ore, 178
  mining, 179
Uranium Information Center, 189, 190, 194
urban history and waste, 41, 42
Urban, L.V., 174
US Bureau of Mines (BOM), 156, 176
US Department of Interior (DOT), 156, 176
US Environmental Protection Agency (EPA), 123, 124, 144, 148, 149, 155, 157, 159, 160, 170, 176, 177
US Office of Technology Assessment, 154

valuation,
  economic, 91
  methodologies, 75
  willingness to accept, 75
  willingness to pay, 75
van Beukering, P., 78, 100, 119, 121, 122, 144
van den Berg, M.M.D., 34
van den Bergh, J.C.J.M., 34, 35, 99
van der Kooi, H.J., 31, 34
van der Linde, C., 80, 87, 99
van Gool, W., 34

Van Langenhove, H., 34
Van Langenhove, L., 71
Van Liere, K.D., 63, 72
Vatn, A., 76, 77, 100
Vining, J., 63, 64, 72
Virtanen, Y., 110, 113
voluntary waste, 102
Von Saldern, A., 43, 54
Von Weizsacker, A., 80, 100

Waalkes, M.P., 176
Waite, A., 106, 113
Waite, R., 126-30, 144, 145
Walter, I., 98
Wandersman, A., 150, 174
Wang, Z., 158, 159, 176
Warren Spring Laboratory, 98
waste,
  attitudes, 8, 57-70
    negative. 58-60
    positive. 62-65
  audits, 125
  cardboard, 86
  concept,
    non-substantive, 105
    value, 107
  charges,
    household, 95
  classification, 146
  contested notion, 103
  cultural history, 43
  culture, 5
  damage, 102
  definition, 2, 5, 39, 149
    legal, 102-7
  discourses, 67
  disposal,
    financial compensation, 61
    incentives, 61
    trust, 61
  domestic heating, 49
  dynamics, 38
  economic history, 40-41
  economics, 3, 8, 73-98
  exchange, 86
  facilities,
    opposition to, 58
  faeces, 3
  flammable, 154
  free trade rules, 111
  Germany, 50, 51

government intervention, 6
  hazardous, 146
    definition, 149
  high risk, 153
  history, 7, 38-52
  ignitable, 154
  intermediate risk, 153
  joint production with desired goods,
    22-30
  language, 66, 67
  lifestyle, 51
  literature, 1, 2
  low risk, 153
  market failure, 13
  municipal, 9, 117-42
    historical background, 119-21
    nature, 118-22
  municipal solid,
    concept, 117, 118
  National Socialist policies, 50
  nuclear reactors, 183
  nuclear, 9, 178-95
    dangers, 183-85
    definition, 178
  pollution, 5
  reactive, 154
  social order, 5
  social theory, 6
  stickiness, 44
  sustainability, 39
  synthetic materials, 51
  thermodynamics, 2, 3, 7, 13-37
    properties, 30
    theory, 3
  toxic, 9, 146-77
    definition, 149
  unavoidable, 23-25
  urban history, 41-42
  voluntary, 102
  water vapour, 4
  ways of dealing with, 45
Waste Framework Directive, 112
waste heat, 4
waste hierarchy, 73
  conceptual framework, 109
waste law, 8, 101-12
  historical development, 101, 102
waste management futures, 93-98
waste management hierarchy, 8, 101,
  108-12, 117,
  and the law, 111-12

critique, 110
evolution, 108-10
problems of implementation, 122
versus integrated approach, 121, 122
waste management strategy,
integrated, 96
waste management,
evaluation, 74-76
history of, 47-52
local, 87
Norfolk, 87, 88
waste minimisation,
voluntary initiative, 83
waste paper,
problems of recycling, 110
waste policy, 6
waste reduction, 63
waste-pits, 39
water vapour as waste, 4
water closet, 49
Waymer, M., 70
Weber, W., 54
Weisz, H., 40, 47, 53, 54
Westlake, K., 137, 138, 140, 144
White, P., 99

Whiting, K., 131-33, 144
Wilkinson, D., 107, 113
Williams, P., 130, 144
Williamson, A.G., 21, 35
Wilson, P.D., 179, 180, 194, 195
Windscale fire, 179
Winiwarter, V., 41, 49, 53, 54
Woburn, Massachusetts, 148, 149,
166, 168, 171, 172
types of pollutants, 168
World Resources Institute (WRI),
161, 176
Wright, R.T., 149, 156, 164, 175

xenobiotics, 148
x-inefficiency, 80

Young, J.T., 21, 35
Yucca Mountain, USA, 190
Yucca Mountain Project, 190, 195

Zaglara, V., 143
Zastrow, C., 151, 176
Zemansky, M.W., 35, 36